ISBN: 978129026419

Published by:
HardPress Publishing
8345 NW 66TH ST #2561
MIAMI FL 33166-2626

Email: info@hardpress.net
Web: http://www.hardpress.net

Macmillan's Science Monographs

STUDIES IN WATER SUPPLY

MACMILLAN AND CO., Limited
LONDON . BOMBAY . CALCUTTA
MELBOURNE

THE MACMILLAN COMPANY
NEW YORK . BOSTON . CHICAGO
DALLAS . SAN FRANCISCO

THE MACMILLAN CO. OF CANADA, Ltd
TORONTO

STUDIES IN
WATER SUPPLY

BY

A. C. HOUSTON, D.Sc., M.B., C.M.

Director of Water Examination, Metropolitan Water Board

MACMILLAN AND CO., LIMITED
ST. MARTIN'S STREET, LONDON
1913

COPYRIGHT

RICHARD CLAY AND SONS, LIMITED,
BRUNSWICK STREET, STAMFORD STREET, S.E., AND
BUNGAY, SUFFOLK.

PREFACE

For several years past I have been urged to write a text-book on Water Supply, but I have been unable to find the time to devote to a task that seemed so formidable. When, however, the Editor of the series in which this volume appears, was good enough to ask me to write, not a text-book, but a *monograph* dealing with my own personal experiences and investigations, I felt the case was different. It was also pointed out to me that this did not involve an exhaustive review of other men's work, but only gathering together in one volume an epitome of my own researches, which are necessarily scattered through a considerable number of reports and papers.

London possesses the largest water works undertaking in the world; and the Metropolitan Water Board, by instituting an elaborate system of water examination, by providing facilities for carrying out many important researches, and generally by looking at the whole subject of water supply from an imperial point of view, has shown itself fully alive to its serious responsibilities. The investigations which have been carried out are now public property, but in endeavouring to bring into one volume the results of my experience gained under such favourable auspices I incidentally pay a tribute to the pioneer work and wise counsels of the Metropolitan Water Board.

I am much indebted to Mr. H. F. Fermor for making the drawings illustrating this monograph, to Dr. A. Norman for the microphotographs of Algæ, to Mr. J. I. Goodlet for compiling the index, and assisting in other ways, and to Dr. D. G. Sutherland, Mr. A. E. Jury, and several of my other assistants for their invaluable help.

My special and grateful thanks are also due to Prof. R. A. Gregory, the accomplished Editor of this series of monographs. His advice and experience have been of inestimable value to me.

. I desire to dedicate this monograph to my Staff, as a small token of my deep appreciation of their willing help and loyal co-operation during the eight years I have had the honour of serving the Metropolitan Water Board as Director of Water Examination.

A. C. HOUSTON.

September, 1913.

CONTENTS

CHAPTER I
SOURCES OF WATER SUPPLY

	PAGE
Upland gathering grounds—underground sources of supply—rivers—health of London—Rivers Thames and Lee considered as sources of water supply	1

CHAPTER II
RESEARCHES TENDING TO JUSTIFY RIVERS AS SOURCES OF WATER SUPPLY

The streptococcus test—tests for pathogenic bacteria—results of the examination of *raw* river water for the typhoid bacillus and Gärtner's bacillus—results of search for the typhoid bacillus in crude sewage—general observations 27

CHAPTER III
THE QUESTION OF ABSTRACTION

Variations in the Thames colour results during a period of six years—effect of different methods of abstraction on colour results—number of days during a period of six years that the colour results were 100 and over, and over 200—epidemiological considerations—deterioration of water as supplied to consumers during the winter months of the year 39

CHAPTER IV
SUPPLEMENTARY PROCESSES OF WATER PURIFICATION

York mechanical gravity filters—Chester's proposed pressure filters—small pre-storage settlement reservoirs—advantages of passing raw river water through small reservoirs antecedent to storage in large reservoirs—New River results—Sunbury results—advantage of using coagulants, antecedent to the storage of raw river water in large reservoirs—Sunbury results—Puech-Chabal system of pre-filters 51

LIST OF ILLUSTRATIONS

FIG.		PAGE
1.	Rivers Thames and Lee. Chemical Results for the years 1906–1911	8
2.	River Thames. Ammoniacal and Albuminoid Nitrogen Results for the seventy-two months ended December 31st, 1911	9
3.	River Lee. Ammoniacal and Albuminoid Nitrogen Results for the seventy-two months ended December 31st, 1911	10
4.	River Thames. Permanganate and Turbidity Results for the seventy-two months ended December 31st, 1911	11
5.	River Lee. Permanganate and Turbidity Results for the seventy-two months ended December 31st, 1911	12
6.	River Thames. Colour Results for the seventy-two months ended December 31st, 1911	13
7.	River Lee. Colour Results for the seventy-two months ended December 31st, 1911	14
8.	Rivers Thames and Lee. Bacteriological Results for the years 1906–1911	17
9–11.	River Thames. Bacteriological Results for the seventy-two months, fifty-three months Agar and Bile-salt-Agar Tests, ended December 31st, 1911	19, 20, 21
12–14.	River Lee. Bacteriological Results for the seventy-two months, fifty-three months Agar and Bile-salt-Agar Tests, ended December 31st, 1911	23, 24, 25
15–17.	Diagrams illustrating certain points as regards abstraction of river water for waterworks purposes	41, 43, 45
18.	All London waters. B. coli Results for the sixty months ended December 31st, 1911	49
19.	Diagram illustrating the advantages of Simple Sedimentation	55
20–22.	Diagrams illustrating the beneficial effects of Storage	97, 98, 99
23, 24.	Diagrams illustrating the Typhoid Fever death rates in certain American cities	*Facing pages* 122 and 123
25.	Diagram illustrating the annual death rate among children from Diarrhœal diseases	129

LIST OF ILLUSTRATIONS

FIG.
26. Typhoid Fever death rates in certain European and American cities
27. Reproduction of a label of a sample bottle
28. Illustration of a page in a label book
29. Sample collection box
30. Rack as set up for the examination of a sample of water
31. Apparatus for keeping melted Agar tubes at a uniform temperature of 45° C.
32. Rack as set up for the examination of a sample of water and the alterations at each stage of the process of examination
33. An illustration of the author's method of making sub-cultural tests for B. coli
34. Classification of B. coli
35. B. coli test. Raw waters (Thames, Lee and New River)
36. B. coli test. London waters
37. Diagram illustrating the delicacy of the method for isolating the Cholera Vibrio from water
38–43. Illustrations of some Algal growths (Asterionella, Oscillaria, Tabellaria, Dinobryon) 195, 196,

STUDIES IN WATER SUPPLY

CHAPTER I

SOURCES OF WATER SUPPLY

THERE are three main sources of water supply, namely :—

(1) *Upland Gathering Grounds.*—In most cases the

> The gelatin, agar and bile-salt-agar results are per 0·01. 0·1. and 1 c.c. respectively.

of unpolluted or sparsely populated land, and may require little or no purification before distribution.

Birmingham, Leeds, Wakefield, Edinburgh, Cardiff, Manchester, and Liverpool are examples of towns supplied with water from upland sources. Fifty-three samples of water collected from taps in these towns were found to contain *B. coli* (*lactose + indol +*) in only four cases, even when as much as 100 cubic centimetres of water were submitted to such cultural tests as will afterwards be described.

(2) *Underground Sources of Supply.*—Shallow wells are presumably quite safe, or highly dangerous, according to their environment.

Deep wells are usually satisfactory sources of supply, especially if the boring has been carried through an

B

LIST OF ILLUSTRATIONS

FIG.		PAGE
26.	Typhoid Fever death rates in certain European and American cities	133
27.	Reproduction of a label of a sample bottle	139
28.	Illustration of a page in a label book	139
29.	Sample collection box	141
30.	Rack as set up for the examination of a sample of water	152
31.	Apparatus for keeping melted Agar tubes at a uniform temperature of 45° C.	153
32.	Rack as set up for the examination of a sample of water and the alterations at each stage of the process of examination	155
33.	An illustration of the author's method of making subcultural tests for B. coli	163
34.	Classification of B. coli	165
35.	B. coli test. Raw waters (Thames, Lee and New River)	167
36.	B. coli test. London waters	169
37.	Diagram illustrating the delicacy of the method for isolating the Cholera Vibrio from water	177
38–43.	Illustrations of some Algal growths (Asterionella, Oscillaria, Tabellaria, Dinobryon)	195, 196, 197

STUDIES IN WATER SUPPLY

CHAPTER I

SOURCES OF WATER SUPPLY

THERE are three main sources of water supply, namely:—

(1) *Upland Gathering Grounds.*—In most cases the water is stored either naturally in lakes or lochs or artificially by damming across the outlet from a valley. Such waters are commonly derived from the drainage of unpolluted or sparsely populated land, and may require little or no purification before distribution.

Birmingham, Leeds, Wakefield, Edinburgh, Cardiff, Manchester, and Liverpool are examples of towns supplied with water from upland sources. Fifty-three samples of water collected from taps in these towns were found to contain *B. coli* (*lactose* + *indol* +) in only four cases, even when as much as 100 cubic centimetres of water were submitted to such cultural tests as will afterwards be described.

(2) *Underground Sources of Supply.*—Shallow wells are presumably quite safe, or highly dangerous, according to their environment.

Deep wells are usually satisfactory sources of supply, especially if the boring has been carried through an impermeable bed, before reaching the water-bearing strata.

The Kent deep well waters are good examples of very pure well water. In a period of seven consecutive years, out of 1565 samples examined, only 5·7 per cent. were found to contain B. coli ($lactose + indol +$), even when as much as 100 cubic centimetres of water were tested.

Springs are often very pure, but here again everything depends on their geological source and local surroundings.

(3) *Rivers.*—Increase of population and of trade, and the progressive growth of towns in the neighbourhood of rivers, have resulted in this source of supply being regarded with some disfavour, and, when a choice exists, frequently abandoned in favour of those previously mentioned.

There can be no question that rivers are liable in a special way to contaminating influences; and long before they reach the sea, nearly all rivers are quite unfit for domestic use in their unpurified state. Nevertheless, London, the largest and most important city in the world, derives the great bulk of its supply from the Thames and Lee,[1] both of which rivers drain populous areas and are admittedly sewage-polluted.

Despite this fact, the general health of the Metropolis has for long been a source of pride to Londoners, and almost of wonder to the world. This is true, not only as regards sickness and death from all causes, but also as regards the incidence of those diseases which are liable to be water-borne.

In support of this statement, the following quotations may be made from the Registrar-General's Annual Summary for Births, Deaths, and Causes of Deaths in England and Wales for 1905, 1906, 1907, 1908, 1909, 1910 and 1911 :—

---

[1] About 60 per cent. from the Thames and about 20 per cent. from the Lee.

SOURCES OF WATER SUPPLY

1905. *Enteric fever* accounted (in London)[1] for 234 deaths, and pyrexia (of uncertain origin) for 3. Thus to the continued fevers in the aggregate (referred to in the returns as "fever") 237 deaths are attributed. The 234 deaths from enteric fever were equal to a rate of 0·05 per 1,000, or 0·07 less than the decennial average rate. The highest death rates from enteric fever were 0·09 in Finsbury and 0·12 in Hackney. (Page xviii.)

1906. *Enteric fever* (in London) caused 260 deaths, and pyrexia (of uncertain origin) 4, while no death during the year was referred to typhus. Thus to the continued fevers in the aggregate (referred to in the returns as "fever") 264 deaths were attributed. The 260 deaths from enteric fever were equal to a rate of 0·06 per 1,000, or 0·05 less than the decennial average rate. The highest death rates from enteric fever were 0·11 in Bethnal Green and 0·14 in Finsbury. (Page xxix.)

In the year 1907 enteric fever caused 194 deaths and pyrexia (of uncertain origin) 4, while no deaths were referred to typhus. Thus to the continued fevers in the aggregate (referred to in the returns as "fever") 198 deaths were attributed. The 194 deaths from enteric fever were equal to a rate of 0·04 per 1,000, or 0·03 less than the average in the preceding five years. The highest death rates from enteric fever were 0·07 in Borough of Stepney, 0·09 in Hackney, and 0·10 in the City of London. (Page xxxiii.)

In the year 1908 enteric fever caused 225 deaths, and pyrexia (of uncertain origin) 2, while no deaths were referred to typhus.

Thus to the continued fevers in the aggregate (designated "fever" in the returns) 227 deaths were attributed. The 225 deaths from enteric fever were equal to a rate of 0·05 per 1,000 as compared with 0·06, the average rate in the preceding five years.

The highest death rates from enteric fever were 0·09 in Holborn, in Shoreditch, and in Bermondsey, 0·10 in Bethnal Green, and 0·12 in Finsbury. (Page xl.)

In the year 1909 the deaths from enteric fever of persons belonging to London numbered 146, and those from pyrexia (of uncertain origin) 2, while no deaths were referred to typhus. Thus to the continued fevers in the aggregate (designated "fever" in the returns) 148 deaths were attributed. The 146 deaths from enteric fever were equal to a rate of 0·03 per 1,000 as compared with 0·05, the average rate in the preceding five years. In St. Marylebone and Lewisham the death rate from enteric fever was only 0·01 per 1,000. The highest death rates were 0·05 in Hampstead, Shoreditch, and Deptford, 0·06 in the City of London, and 0·08 in Poplar. (Pages xxxi–xxxii.)

Enteric fever.—In the year 1910 the deaths from enteric fever of persons belonging to London numbered 196, and those from pyrexia (of uncertain origin) 4, while no deaths were referred to typhus.

Thus to the continued fevers in the aggregate 200 deaths were attributed. The 196 deaths from enteric fever were equal to a rate of 0·04 per 1,000, which is 0·01 per 1,000 below the average rate in the preceding five years. In Fulham and in Woolwich, the death rate from enteric fever was only 0·01

---

[1] London as dealt with by the Registrar-General is not co-terminous with "Water London."

per 1,000. The highest death rates were 0·07 in Shoreditch, 0·08 in Poplar, 0·09 in Holborn, 0·12 in the City of London, and 0·14 in Bethnal Green. (Pages xxxi–xxxii.)

Enteric fever.—In the year 1911 the deaths from enteric fever of persons belonging to London numbered 144, corresponding to a rate of 0·03 per 1,000, which is 0·01 per 1,000 below the average rate in the preceding five years. No death from enteric fever belonged to Chelsea, to the City of London or to Woolwich, and in Shoreditch the death rate from enteric fever was only 0·01 per 1,000. The highest death rates were 0·05 in Fulham, 0·06 in Hammersmith and in Holborn, and 0·09 in Finsbury and in Poplar. (Page xxv.)

It thus becomes a matter of supreme interest to inquire minutely into the quality of the sources of London's Water Supply, the methods actually in operation for purifying the water, and those in process of being adopted, together with those which are likely to receive consideration in the immediate future. Such a survey ought to throw useful light on the general question of water purification and the best means to be adopted to render waters, initially of doubtful purity, "safe" for domestic use.

The Rivers Thames and Lee[1] as Sources of Water Supply.

The chief arguments against the use of these rivers as sources of water supply are based on: (1) Physical, topographical, and epidemiological grounds. (2) The results of chemical and bacteriological analyses.

As regards (1), against the known fact that many pollutions of undesirable sort exist on these watersheds must be set the circumstance that most of the contaminating matters do not reach the rivers concerned without first undergoing some form of natural or artificial purification process.

In regard to the second point, which will chiefly be

---

[1] The New River is really the Upper Lee water mixed with about 50 per cent. of deep well water.

SOURCES OF WATER SUPPLY

dealt with here, a great amount of work has been carried out since 1905 at the Laboratories of the Metropolitan Water Board.

Chemical Results.—Table I. shows the chief average chemical results of the Rivers Thames and Lee for the aggregate of six years 1906–1911, and also for each separate year. Tables II. and III., pp. 6, 7, show the average results for each month during the six year period, 1906–1911.

The accompanying diagrams, Figs. 1–7, serve to illustrate the facts set forth in the tables.

TABLE I.—CHEMICAL RESULTS (PARTS PER 100,000, UNLESS OTHERWISE STATED).

	Year.	Ammoniacal Nitrogen.	Albuminoid Nitrogen.	Oxidised Nitrogen.	Chlorine.	Oxygen absorbed from permanganate, 3hrs. at 80°F (At room temp. during 1906.)	Turbidity, in terms of saccharated carbonate of iron.‡	Colour, mm. brown, 2 ft. tube.§	Total hardness.	Permanent hardness.
River Thames.	1906	0·0073	0·0159	0·22	1·68	0·1615	2·90	56	22·77	*
	1907	0·0069	0·0165	0·24	1·74	0·2158	3·29	72	22·39	5·67†
	1908	0·0063	0·0134	0·27	1·70	0·1734	2·30	63	23·88	6·26
	1909	0·0072	0·0159	0·23	1·75	0·2198	3·05	67	23·46	6·60
	1910	0·0071	0·0173	0·24	1·69	0·2363	·3·56	82	23·28	6·06
	1911	0·0081	0·0150	0·25	1·78	0·1752	2·49	61	22·44	5·44
	Averages 1906–11	0·0072	0·0157	0·24	1·72	0·2039 (1907-11)	2·93	67	23·05	6·09 (1908–11)
River Lee.	1906	0·0124	0·0170	0·26	2·05	0·1621	3·02	54	21·97	*
	1907	0·0116	0·0157	0·27	2·02	0·1762	3·17	63	25·51	6·87†
	1908	0·0109	0·0146	0·29	2·04	0·1833	3·77	69	27·85	7·44
	1909	0·0123	0·0172	0·27	2·18	0·2172	3·49	68	27·69	7·89
	1910	0·0121	0·0175	0·26	2·03	0·2252	4·07	90	26·69	6·96
	1911	0·0114	0·0151	0·29	2·14	0·1879	3·07	71	25·68	6·76
	Averages 1906–11	0·0118	0·0162	0·27	2·08	0·1977 (1907-11)	3·43	69	26·42	7·27 (1908–11)

* Not estimated during 1906.
† July to December only.
‡ Anthony's turbidimeter was used. Definite mixtures of saccharated carbonate of iron (B.P.) were made, and the results read off on the scale. Plotted out these gave a curve and figures for all intermediate readings. The method is fully described in the last edition of Thresh's treatise on "The Examination of Waters and Water Supplies," pp. 277-279.
§ Burgess's apparatus was used; see *Analyst*, Vol. XXVII., No. 319, October, 1902.

TABLE II.—AVERAGE RESULTS OF THE CHEMICAL EXAMINATION OF THE RAW THAMES RIVER WATER FOR EACH MONTH OF THE SIX-YEAR PERIOD, 1906–1911.

Parts per 100,000 unless otherwise stated.

Year.	Month.	Ammoniacal nitrogen.	Albuminoid nitrogen.	Oxidised nitrogen.	Chlorine.	Oxygen absorbed from permanganate; 3 hours at 80° F. *	Turbidity in terms of saccharated carbonate of iron	Colour, mm, brown, 2 ft. tube.	Total hardness.	Permanent hardness.
1906	January	0·0092	0·0228	0·27	1·76	0·2788	9·57	153	23·51	—
	February	0·0100	0·0149	0·29	1·65	0·1740	3·97	88	23·78	—
	March	0·0051	0·0133	0·28	1·65	0·1397	1·68	50	24·82	—
	April	0·0023	0·0123	0·24	1·54	0·0918	1·03	29	25·46	—
	May	0·0036	0·0148	0·21	1·56	0·1199	1·55	29	21·93	—
	June	0·0067	0·0182	0·20	1·58	0·1477	2·77	30	22·83	—
	July	0·0072	0·0200	0·14	1·66	0·1734	3·12	37	21·40	—
	August	0·0066	0·0159	0·15	1·71	0·1407	2·14	34	20·68	—
	September	0·0057	0·0129	0·16	1·73	0·1139	1·11	31	19·87	—
	October	0·0068	0·0114	0·20	1·78	0·1184	0·69	34	20·94	—
	November	0·0121	0·0190	0·27	1·81	0·2685	4·33	89	22·85	—
	December	0·0137	0·0149	0·31	1·76	0·1607	2·54	60	25·51	—
1907	January	0·0138	0·0146	0·37	1·71	0·2365	3·85	80	24·21	—
	February	0·0161	0·0147	0·37	1·74	0·1771	2·97	74	24·87	—
	March	0·0035	0·0123	0·31	1·78	0·1292	0·55	44	23·65	—
	April	0·0074	0·0179	0·23	1·76	0·2314	2·88	74	22·10	—
	May	0·0053	0·0165	0·22	1·79	0·2057	1·09	54	22·12	—
	June	0·0041	0·0189	0·22	1·70	0·1998	1·65	45	22·15	—
	July	0·0033	0·0227	0·19	1·69	0·1762	2·86	45	18·90	5·30
	August	0·0029	0·0140	0·18	1·73	0·1504	0·95	39	22·04	5·41
	September	0·0023	0·0114	0·18	1·74	0·1128	0·23	34	21·54	5·37
	October	0·0080	0·0142	5·17	1·82	0·2197	1·79	56	20·17	5·92
	November	0·0082	0·0177	0·23	1·71	0·3132	6·19	113	25·20	7·05
	December	0·0078	0·0237	0·21	1·65	0·4756	16·83	239	22·47	7·65
1908	January	0·0150	0·0147	0·33	1·72	0·2355	4·71	77	25·02	7·67
	February	0·0095	0·0102	0·35	1·69	0·1313	1·28	53	27·70	7·90
	March	0·0073	0·0171	0·29	1·76	0·2545	5·18	104	25·12	7·23
	April	0·0047	0·0176	0·27	1·67	0·2491	1·64	109	24·40	7·11
	May	0·0034	0·0167	0·24	1·57	0·2698	1·97	93	23·95	7·10
	June	0·0031	0·0141	0·26	1·58	0·1365	2·09	43	22·98	5·76
	July	0·0038	0·0129	0·23	1·55	0·1223	1·59	39	22·47	4·90
	August	0·0030	0·0123	0·19	1·63	0·1104	0·78	38	21·94	4·90
	September	0·0034	0·0120	0·22	1·71	0·1305	1·38	41	22·52	5·20
	October	0·0069	0·0115	0·25	1·78	0·1397	1·82	51	23·25	5·52
	November	0·0065	0·0102	0·27	1·85	0·1254	1·41	40	23·40	5·52
	December	0·0095	0·0116	0·28	1·89	0·1758	3·58	69	24·57	6·27
1909	January	0·0141	0·0111	0·31	1·87	0·1676	2·77	63	24·50	6·82
	February	0·0086	0·0087	0·31	1·77	0·1020	1·52	45	25·32	6·72
	March	0·0124	0·0186	0·28	1·85	0·2699	4·94	112	23·28	7·30
	April	0·0046	0·0161	0·24	1·73	0·1858	2·90	67	24·25	6·97
	May	0·0031	0·0161	0·19	1·71	0·1386	1·66	37	22·17	5·92
	June	0·0074	0·0180	0·20	1·72	0·2070	2·17	49	22·76	5·96
	July	0·0027	0·0162	0·19	1·65	0·1936	1·68	45	22·47	6·22
	August	0·0046	0·0136	0·15	1·73	0·1506	1·43	39	22·28	5·74
	September	0·0035	0·0123	0·20	1·82	0·1391	1·40	39	22·05	5·67
	October	0·0059	0·0237	0·22	1·80	0·4242	5·21	89	24·47	6·62
	November	0·0087	0·0132	0·27	1·67	0·2277	3·11	67	24·90	7·20
	December	0·0111	0·0230	0·25	1·73	0·4259	8·21	151	23·20	8·12
1910	January	0·0101	0·0143	0·28	1·63	0·2424	4·52	91	24·32	6·52
	February	0·0104	0·0205	0·27	1·71	0·3641	8·22	161	23·47	6·37
	March	0·0067	0·0134	0·30	1·60	0·1910	3·34	81	24·32	6·57
	April	0·0026	0·0120	0·28	1·59	0·1352	1·50	44	23·45	5·65
	May	0·0031	0·0167	0·24	1·57	0·1489	1·51	49	23·84	5·62
	June	0·0054	0·0238	0·20	1·59	0·3031	2·98	72	23·80	6·20
	July	0·0038	0·0155	0·21	1·63	0·1756	1·61	44	22·13	4·95
	August	0·0038	0·0147	0·21	1·71	0·1357	1·28	38	21·82	4·92
	September	0·0036	0·0139	0·22	1·77	0·1173	1·10	40	22·40	4·82
	October	0·0068	0·0137	0·25	1·83	0·1611	1·59	47	23·25	5·50
	November	0·0144	0·0225	0·24	1·87	0·3249	5·61	105	23·14	6·74
	December	0·0109	0·0266	0·23	1·68	0·5253	10·11	214	23·17	7·37
1911	January	0·0141	0·0143	0·33	1·63	0·1852	2·88	78	25·82	6·34
	February	0·0109	0·0108	0·33	1·62	0·1140	1·35	43	24·70	5·52
	March	0·0083	0·0169	0·27	1·73	0·2495	3·74	101	25·25	6·60
	April	0·0059	0·0148	0·28	1·70	0·1630	2·04	57	24·27	5·65
	May	0·0044	0·0159	0·24	1·71	0·1586	1·61	40	22·64	5·18
	June	0·0049	0·0212	0·21	1·69	0·1737	2·46	43	23·47	5·45
	July	0·0044	0·0164	0·15	1·72	0·1379	1·42	37	21·28	4·62
	August	0·0053	0·0152	0·15	1·78	0·1390	1·19	36	20·40	4·15
	September	0·0037	0·0113	0·18	1·80	0·1080	0·90	35	19·55	3·90
	October	0·0091	0·0102	0·25	1·82	0·1143	1·34	43	20·74	4·36
	November	0·0132	0·0139	0·28	2·07	0·1999	2·91	81	20·80	6·65
	December	0·0119	0·0227	0·34	2·04	0·3999	9·36	150	23·15	7·12

* During 1906 this test was carried out at room temperature.

TABLE III.—AVERAGE RESULTS OF THE CHEMICAL EXAMINATION OF THE RAW LEE RIVER WATER FOR EACH MONTH OF THE SIX YEAR PERIOD, 1906–1911.

Parts per 100,000 unless otherwise stated.

Year.	Month.	Ammoniacal nitrogen.	Albuminoid nitrogen.	Oxidised nitrogen.	Chlorine.	Oxygen absorbed from permanganate, 3 hours at 80° F. *	Turbidity in terms of saccharated carbonate of iron.	Colour, mm. brown, 2 ft. tube.	Total hardness.	Permanent hardness.
1906	January ..	0·0216	0·0248	0·37	2·18	0·2920	11·74	153	27·77	—
	February	0·0197	0·0172	0·39	2·07	0·1851	4·97	99	28·79	—
	March	0·0088	0·0133	0·33	2·04	0·1128	1·35	40	28·68	—
	April	0·0038	0·0170	0·27	1·91	0·1024	1·46	30	26·99	—
	May	0·0053	0·0160	0·20	1·85	0·1087	1·33	26	23·93	—
	June	0·0062	0·0163	0·18	1·89	0·1253	1·15	27	23·56	—
	July	0·0099	0·0170	0·16	2·01	0·1645	1·11	34	22·32	—
	August ..	0·0086	0·0153	0·12	2·12	0·1342	0·99	32	20·35	—
	September	0·0108	0·0146	0·16	2·26	0·1209	0·80	29	19·95	—
	October ..	0·0120	0·0135	0·22	2·17	0·1270	1·07	31	23·76	—
	November	0·0215	0·0201	0·38	2·11	0·2637	5·59	75	27·55	—
	December	0·0210	0·0187	0·39	1·99	0·2075	4·69	73	28·30	—
1907	January ..	0·0238	0·0176	0·41	1·85	0·2467	5·82	78	27·70	—
	February	0·0200	0·0157	0·40	1·88	0·1910	5·20	77	29·82	—
	March	0·0070	0·0135	0·33	1·91	0·1195	0·91	41	28·38	—
	April	0·0096	0·0174	0·26	2·00	0·1599	1·72	53	26·52	—
	May	0·0093	0·0215	0·24	1·90	0·2198	2·46	61	25·50	—
	June	0·0082	0·0191	0·23	1·88	0·1680	1·58	40	24·02	—
	July	0·0082	0·0145	0·20	1·89	0·1318	0·69	38	22·26	5·10
	August ..	0·0056	0·0123	0·17	2·07	0·1115	0·21	93	22·02	6·14
	September	0·0049	0·0111	0·15	2·15	0·1029	0·16	32	22·72	5·93
	October ..	0·0095	0·0116	0·19	2·24	0·1279	0·88	38	23·40	6·40
	November	0·0141	0·0138	0·28	2·34	0·1881	4·03	77	25·82	6·70
	December	0·0214	0·0223	0·34	2·17	0·3886	17·34	218	28·62	9·37
1908	January ..	0·0226	0·0169	0·37	2·13	0·2742	10·82	85	30·02	8·85
	February	0·0148	0·0136	0·35	2·11	0·1752	4·64	69	32·43	8·50
	March	0·0121	0·0135	0·35	2·16	0·2694	9·15	128	30·05	9·43
	April	0·0087	0·0189	0·30	2·00	0·2765	3·24	123	27·69	8·47
	May	0·0097	0·0202	0·29	1·99	0·2637	3·63	106	27·75	8·85
	June	0·0060	0·0185	0·21	1·80	0·1591	2·29	44	24·32	5·90
	July	0·0094	0·0129	0·22	1·87	0·1550	1·80	45	24·95	6·20
	August ..	0·0061	0·0110	0·19	1·97	0·1156	0·90	38	25·10	6·28
	September	0·0064	0·0108	0·22	2·02	0·1179	1·52	42	25·55	6·22
	October ..	0·0081	0·0116	0·27	2·05	0·1200	·1·66	41	27·60	6·25
	November	0·0101	0·0106	0·33	2·13	0·1203	1·30	38	29·40	6·48
	December	0·0172	0·0130	0·37	2·25	0·1838	3·62	74	30·75	7·37
1909	January ..	0·0157	0·0116	0·35	2·23	0·1501	2·41	57	31·50	9·15
	February	0·0135	0·0097	0·36	2·19	0·1133	1·91	50	30·52	9·02
	March	0·0183	0·0191	0·37	2·28	0·2679	5·71	115	28·46	9·58
	April	0·0079	0·0206	0·23	2·17	0·1891	2·81	55	27·02	7·97
	May	0·0051	0·0183	0·19	2·13	0·1563	1·83	42	25·50	6·65
	June	0·0122	0·0169	0·22	2·08	0·1780	1·15	46	26·38	7·22
	July	0·0057	0·0168	0·19	2·11	0·1948	1·12	47	25·80	7·10
	August ..	0·0046	0·0156	0·17	2·18	0·1744	1·09	42	24·92	6·26
	September	0·0040	0·0134	0·23	2·23	0·1261	1·10	35	24·90	6·80
	October ..	0·0087	0·0217	0·26	2·29	0·3332	6·95	86	27·02	7·27
	November	0·0276	0·0167	0·31	2·14	0·2472	3·78	77	30·80	8·24
	December	0·0238	0·0275	0·31	2·12	0·4868	12·84	171	29·50	9·50
1910	January ..	0·0229	0·0176	0·32	2·18	0·2713	5·47	105	29·82	8·16
	February	0·0207	0·0259	0·34	2·19	0·4049	12·21	187	27·00	8·90
	March	0·0157	0·0173	0·32	2·08	0·2234	4·65	103	29·02	7·92
	April	0·0079	0·0138	0·29	1·89	0·1549	2·32	55	27·22	7·00
	May	0·0102	0·0169	0·24	1·92	0·1721	1·84	55	27·36	6·62
	June	0·0085	0·0169	0·20	1·85	0·1690	1·82	56	25·45	5·97
	July	0·0067	0·0146	0·20	1·92	0·1736	1·00	47	25·43	5·48
	August ..	0·0047	0·0121	0·19	1·95	0·1091	0·70	35	24·67	5·57
	September	0·0043	0·0122	0·22	2·02	0·1111	0·77	36	25·62	5·70
	October ..	0·0079	0·0134	0·26	2·02	0·1178	1·10	41	26·32	5·10
	November	0·0180	0·0208	0·27	2·16	0·2985	6·66	133	25·02	7·57
	December	0·0205	0·0301	0·32	2·14	0·5211	11·46	231	26·52	9·70
1911	January ..	0·0222	0·0153	0·35	2·10	0·2262	4·65	97	30·00	8·96
	February	0·0158	0·0108	0·35	1·99	0·1332	2·78	61	29·45	7·67
	March	0·0141	0·0184	0·28	2·17	0·2732	5·43	116	28·92	8·92
	April	0·0069	0·0160	0·30	2·06	0·1786	2·46	63	26·75	6·80
	May	0·0075	0·0234	0·27	2·03	0·2281	3·95	54	25·86	6·24
	June	0·0076	0·0168	0·25	1·91	0·1517	1·55	40	25·67	5·47
	July	0·0055	0·0151	0·20	1·98	0·1295	0·79	37	22·96	4·98
	August ..	0·0066	0·0126	0·16	2·07	0·1194	0·80	37	21·52	5·15
	September	0·0053	0·0104	0·25	2·15	0·1031	0·97	39	20·90	4·25
	October ..	0·0096	0·0110	0·26	2·18	0·1389	0·09	59	24·08	4·88
	November	0·0163	0·0128	0·38	2·47	0·2061	0·64	83	27·62	8·20
	December	0·0188	0·0192	0·47	2·53	0·3888	0·47	182	24·37	10·70

* During 1906, this test was carried out at room temperature.

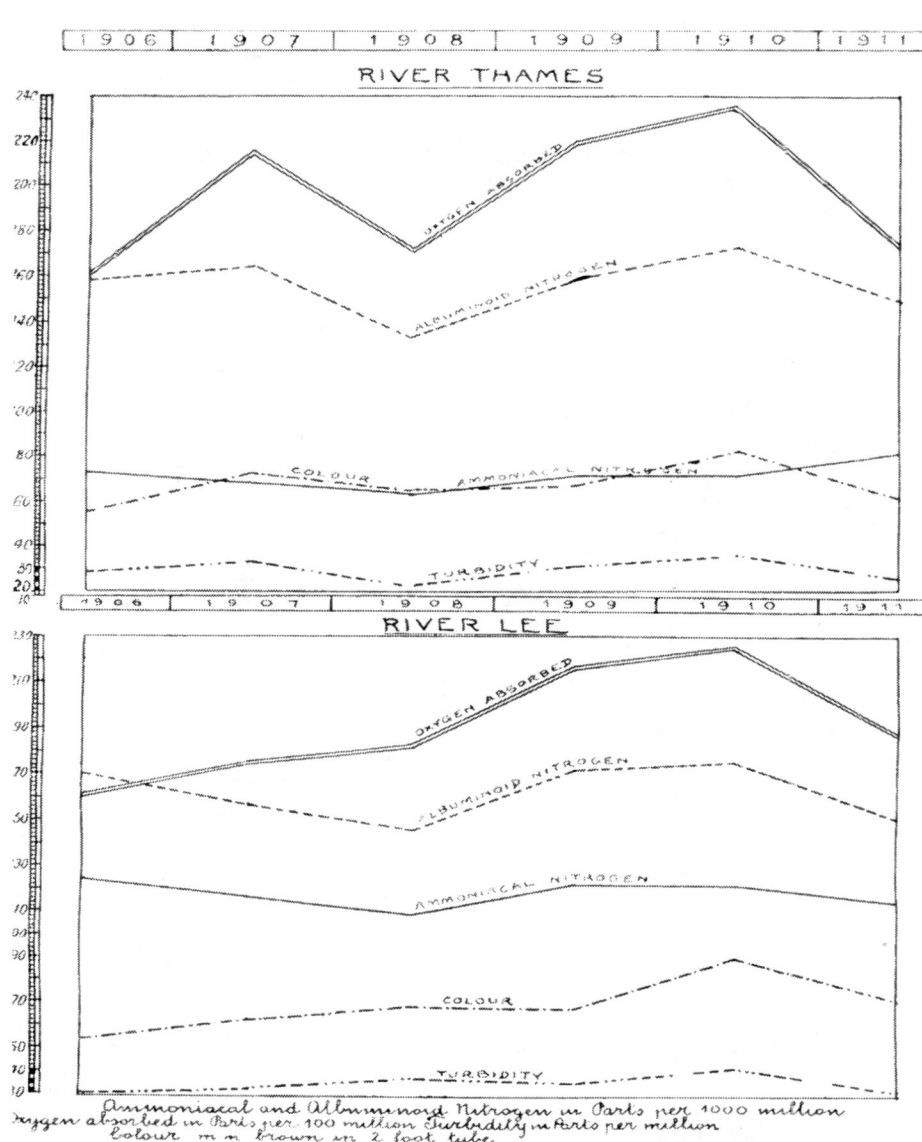

Fig. 1

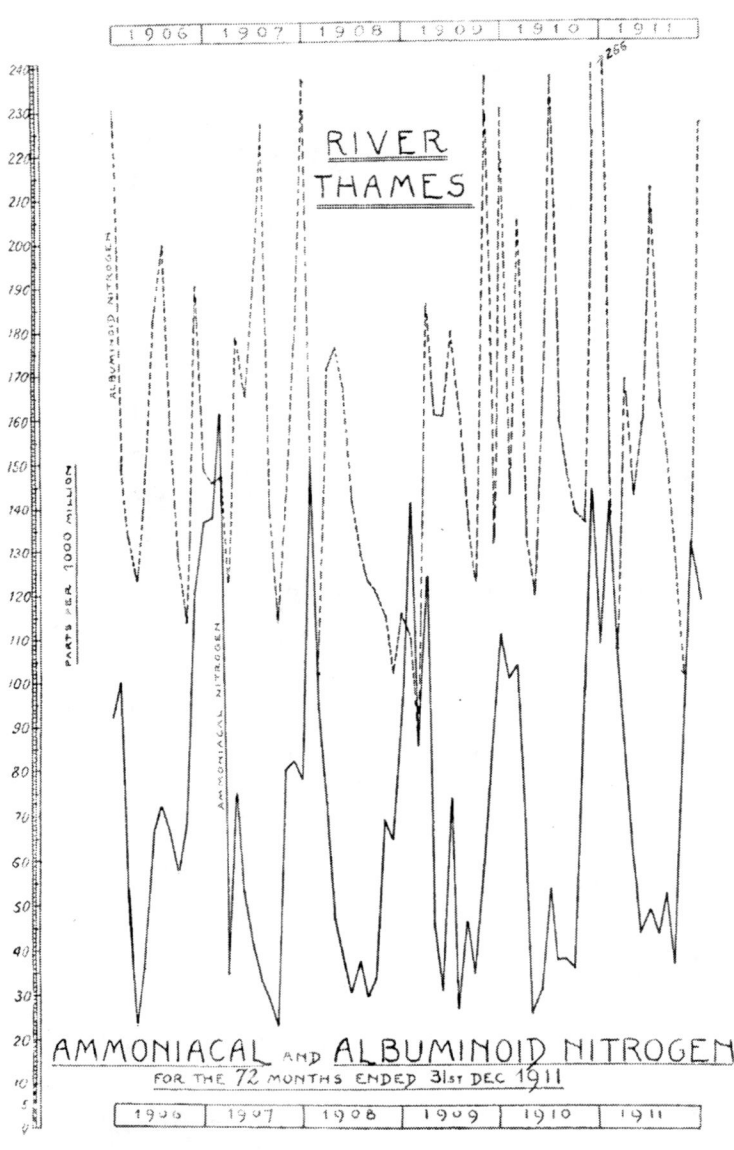

Fig. 2.

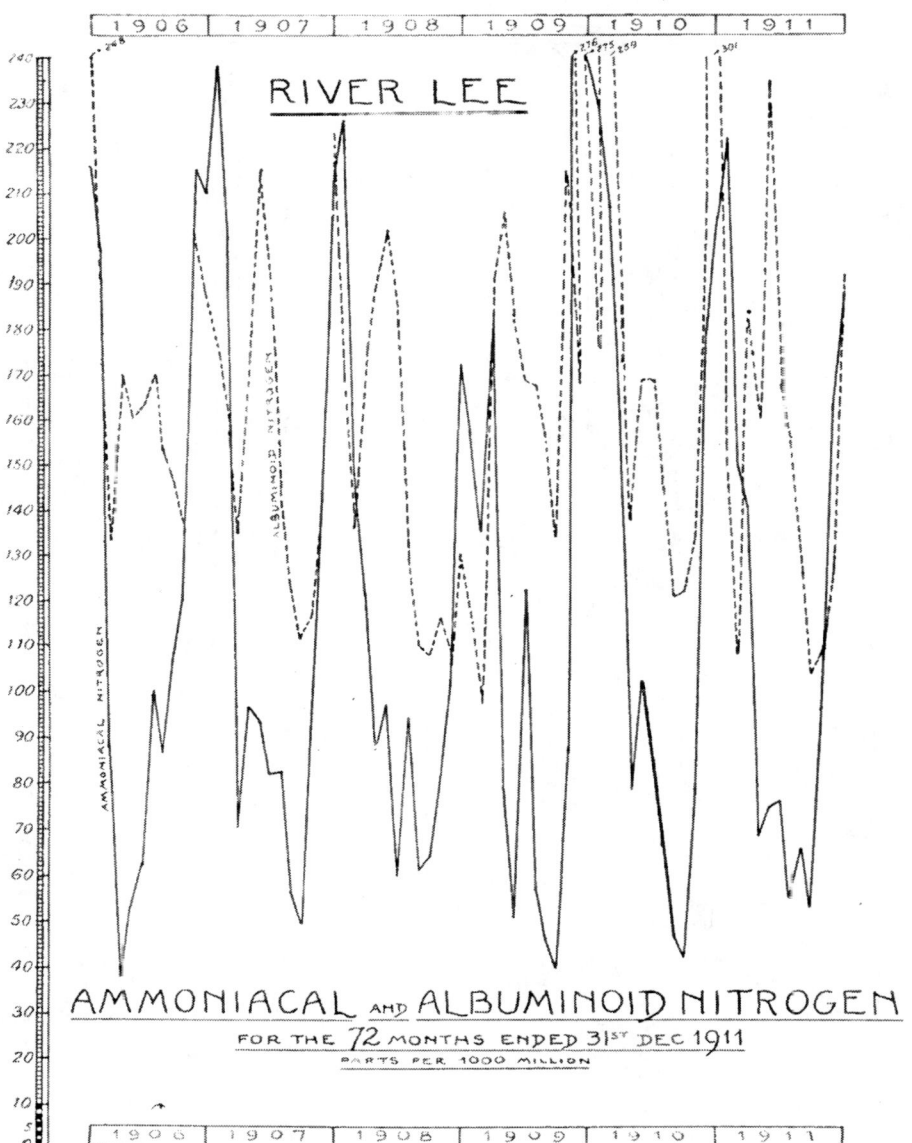

Fig. 3.

SOURCES OF WATER SUPPLY

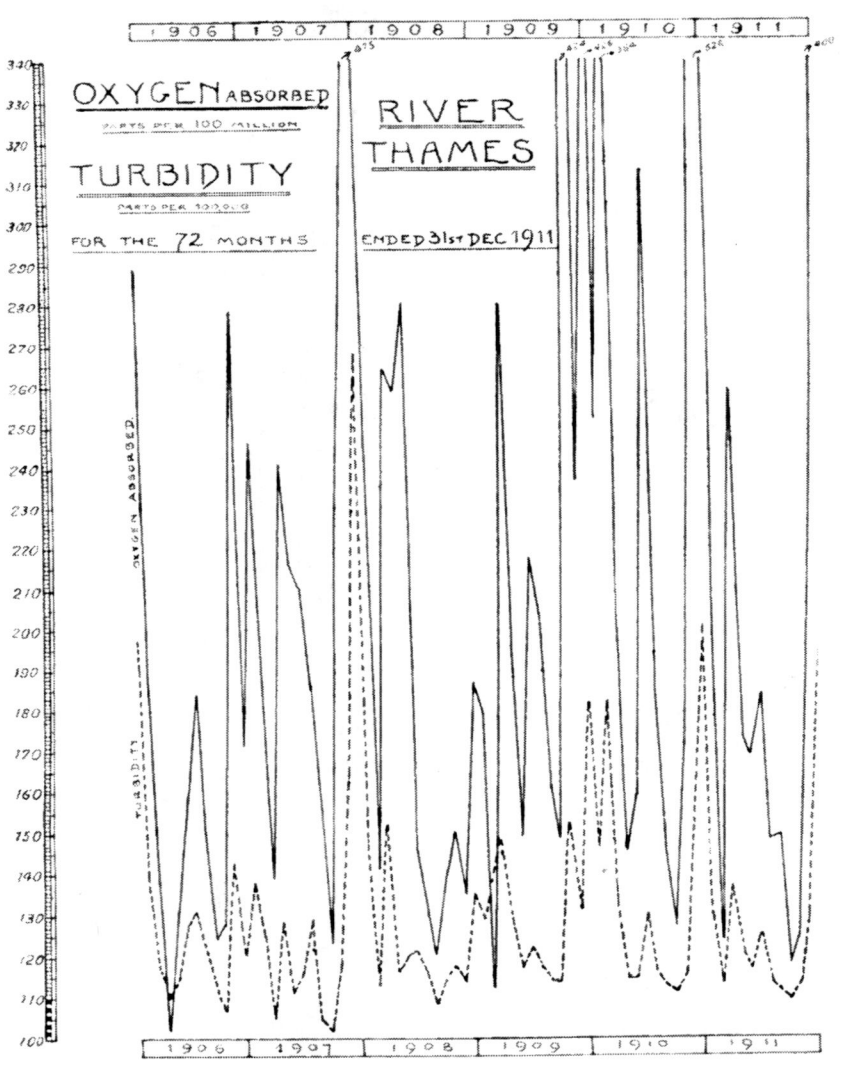

Fig. 4.

12 STUDIES IN WATER SUPPLY CHAP.

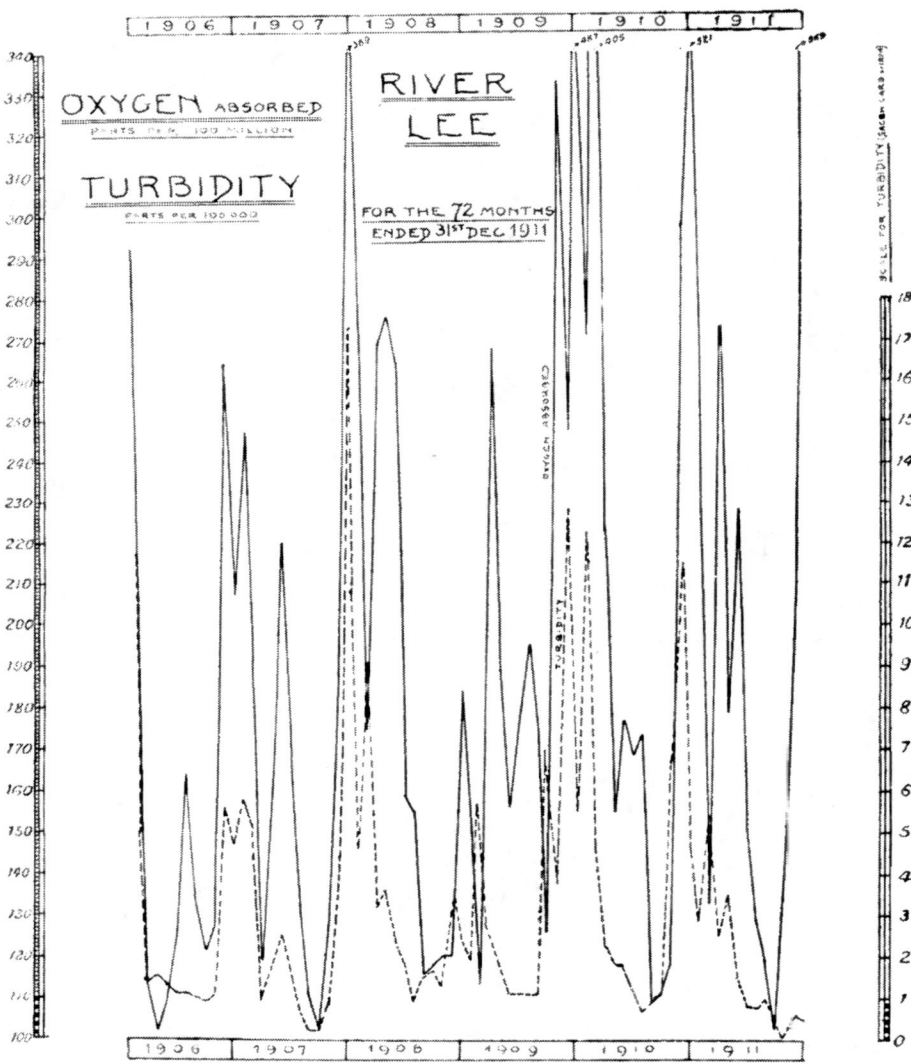

Fig. 5.

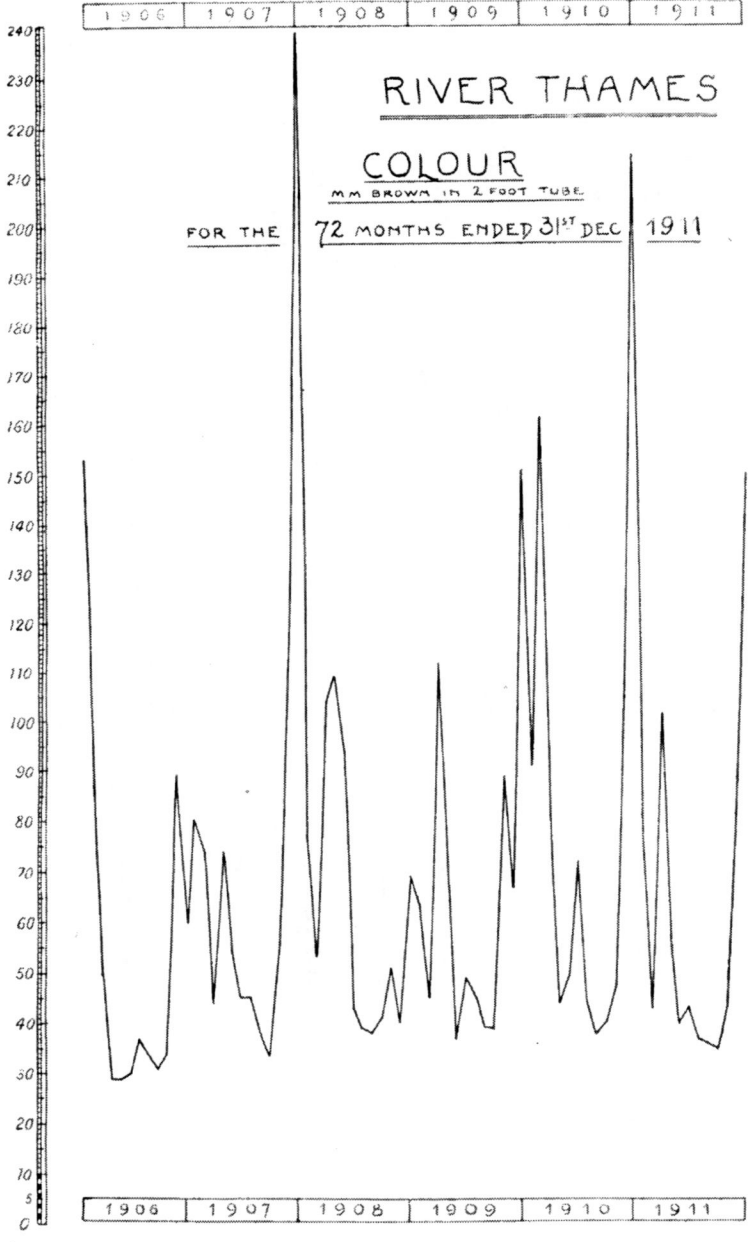

Fig. 6.

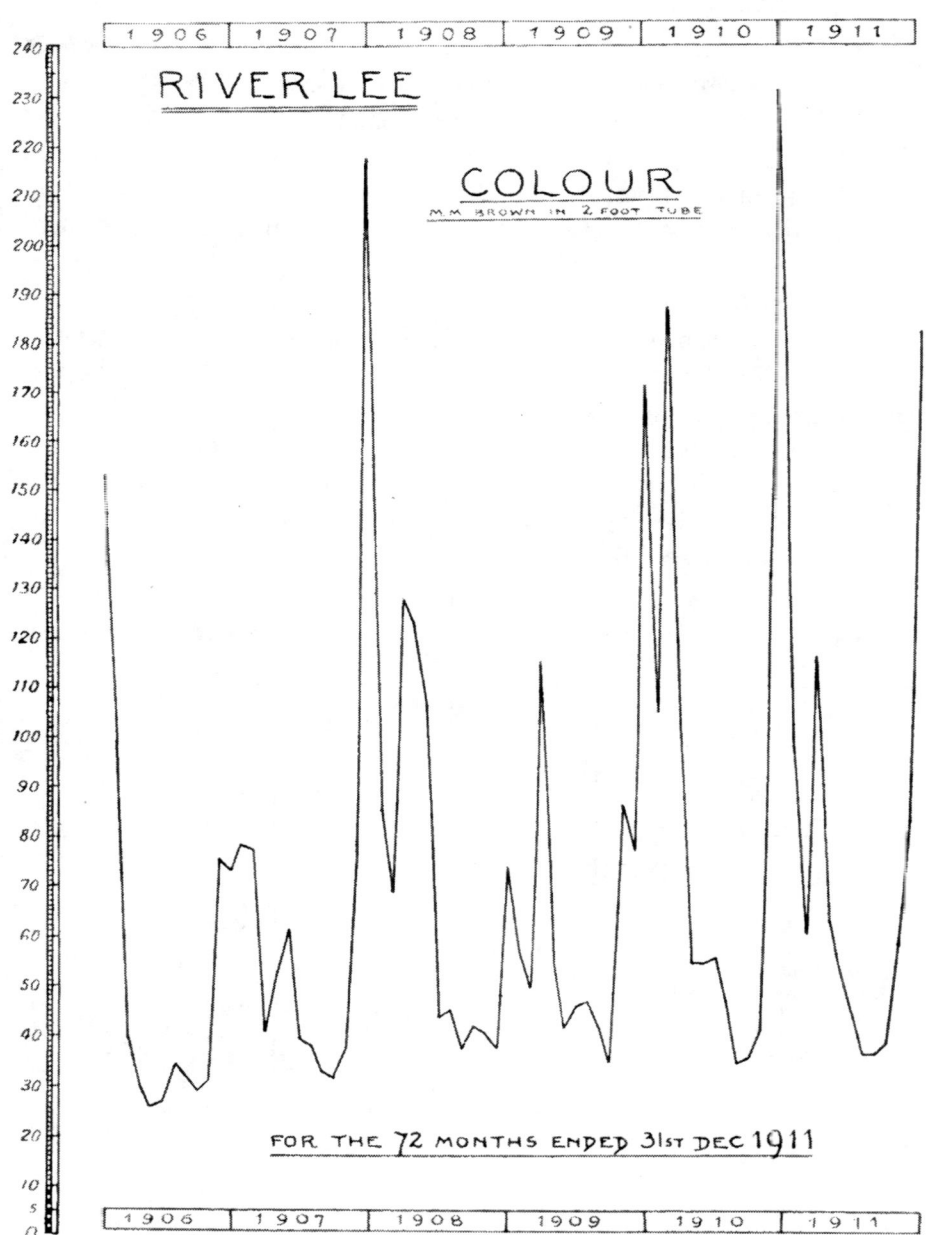

Fig. 7.

SOURCES OF WATER SUPPLY

Standards are of variable significance, but if, for purposes of illustration, it be considered that a water ought to be objected to if it yields respectively 0·01 and 0·1 part per 100,000 of albuminoid nitrogen and oxygen absorbed from permanganate, it is obvious that, judged by these standards, the Rivers Thames and Lee are necessarily unfit for domestic use without previous purification.

Bacteriological Results.—Tables IV.–VI., pp. 15, 16, show the average bacteriological results of the Rivers Thames and Lee for the six years 1906–1911 combined, and for each separate year as a whole. Tables VII. and VIII., pp. 18, 22, show the average bacteriological results for each month during the six-year period 1906–1911.

The accompanying diagrams (Figs. 8–14) serve to illustrate the facts set forth in the tables.

TABLE IV.—BACTERIOLOGICAL RESULTS. RIVER THAMES *Raw* WATER AT HAMPTON.

Year.	Average Number of Microbes per c.c.			Negative 100 c.c. %	B. coli Test (typical B. coli). (Percentage results.)							Aggregate of Cols. 7–11
	Gelatin at 20–22°C 3 days.	Agar at 37°C.	Bile-salt Agar at 37°C.		+ 100 c.c. %	+ 10 c.c. %	+ 1 c.c. %	+ 0·1 c.c. %	+ 0·01 c.c. %	+ 0·001 c.c. %	+ 0·0001 c.c. %	
Cols.	1	2	3	4	5	6	7	8	9	10	11	12
1906	1207	—	—	3.9	10·4	19·5	29·5	27·9	8·7	—	—	66·1
1907	2365	—	—	—	1·6	15 3	35·2	39·3	8·5	—	—	83 0
1908	3251	272	37	—	2·0	10·4	39·9	36·7	10·1	0·8	—	87·5
1909	3900	504	62	0·5	0·5	6·7	33·2	49·2	9·8	—	—	92·2
1910	7377	333	21	0·4	2·9	11·5	34·3	40·9	9·9	—	—	85·1
1911	7982	313	32	—	0·4	11·6	36·9	39·0	11·2	0·8	—	87·9
1906–11	4310	368	42	0·8	3·1	12·8	34·9	38·4	9·7	0·2	—	83·2

* Agar and Bile salt-agar results, counted after two days during 1908 and 1909.
,, ,, ,, ,, ,, ,, 20–24 hours ,, 1910 and 1911.

TABLE V.—BACTERIOLOGICAL RESULTS. RIVER LEE *RAW* WATER AT PONDERS END.

Year.	Average Number of Microbes per c.c.			B. coli Test (typical B. coli). (Percentage results.)								Aggregate of Cols 7-11
	Gelatin at 20-22°C 3 days.	*Agar at 37°C.	Bile-salt Agar at 37°C.	Negative 100 c.c. %	+ 100 c.c. %	+ 10 c.c. %	+ 1 c.c. %	+ 0.1 c.c. %	+ 0.01 c.c. %	+ 0.001 c.c. %	+ 0.0001 c.c. %	
Cols.	1	2	3	4	5	6	7	8	9	10	11	12
1906	3709	—	—	3·2	1·2	13·1	35·7	38·9	7·5	0·4	—	82·5
1907	7362	—	—	0·4	0·8	8·9	46·1	34·8	7·7	1·2	—	89·3
1908	8144	432	45	—	0·8	4·8	36·7	39·9	13·7	2·8	1·2	94·3
1909	16318	849	84	—	—	5·7	32·1	40·4	14·5	6·2	0·0	94·2
1910	35125	468	20	0·8	2·1	7·8	36·4	36·4	11·5	4·5	0·4	89·2
1911	11757	512	52	—	0·8	12·4	40·2	38·6	7·5	0·4	—	86·7
1906–11	13581	591	55	0·8	0·9	8·9	38·1	38·1	10·2	2·4	0·3	89·2

1909 average R. Lee, Col. 1, excludes two samples containing 1,120,000, and 1,240,000 microbes per c.c. respectively.
1909, B. Coli test:—also 0·5% in 0·00001 c.c. and 0·5% in 0·000001 c.c.
1906–11, B. Coli test :— ,, 0·07% ,, ,, ,, 0·07% ,, ,,
1910 average R. Lee, Col. 1, excludes two samples containing 1,300,000 and 1,430,000 microbes per c.c. respectively.

TABLE VI.— B. ENTERITIDIS SPOROGENES TEST.

Year. (Jan.–Dec.)	*Raw* Thames Water. %					*Raw* Lee Water. %				
	10 c.c. −	10 c.c. +	1 c.c. +	·1 c.c. +	·01 c.c. +	10 c.c. −	10 c.c. +	1 c.c. +	·1 c.c. +	·01 c.c. +
Average, 1906...	57·9	37·7	3·9	0·4	—	64·7	30·1	4·7	0·4	—
,, 1907...	62·9	27·5	8·4	1·1	—	62·9	30·5	5·9	0·6	—
,, 1908..	71·6	26·4	1·8	—	—	54·7	35·8	9·4	—	—
,, 1909...	69·2	26·9	3·8	—	—	67·2	26·9	5·8	—	—
,, 1910...	51·9	42·3	5·8	—	—	55·8	36·5	7·7	—	—
,, 1911...	65·4	32·7	1·9	—	—	67·3	30·8	0·0	1·9	—
,, 1906–11	61·4	33·1	4·9	0·5	—	63·0	31·0	5·4	0·5	—

SOURCES OF WATER SUPPLY

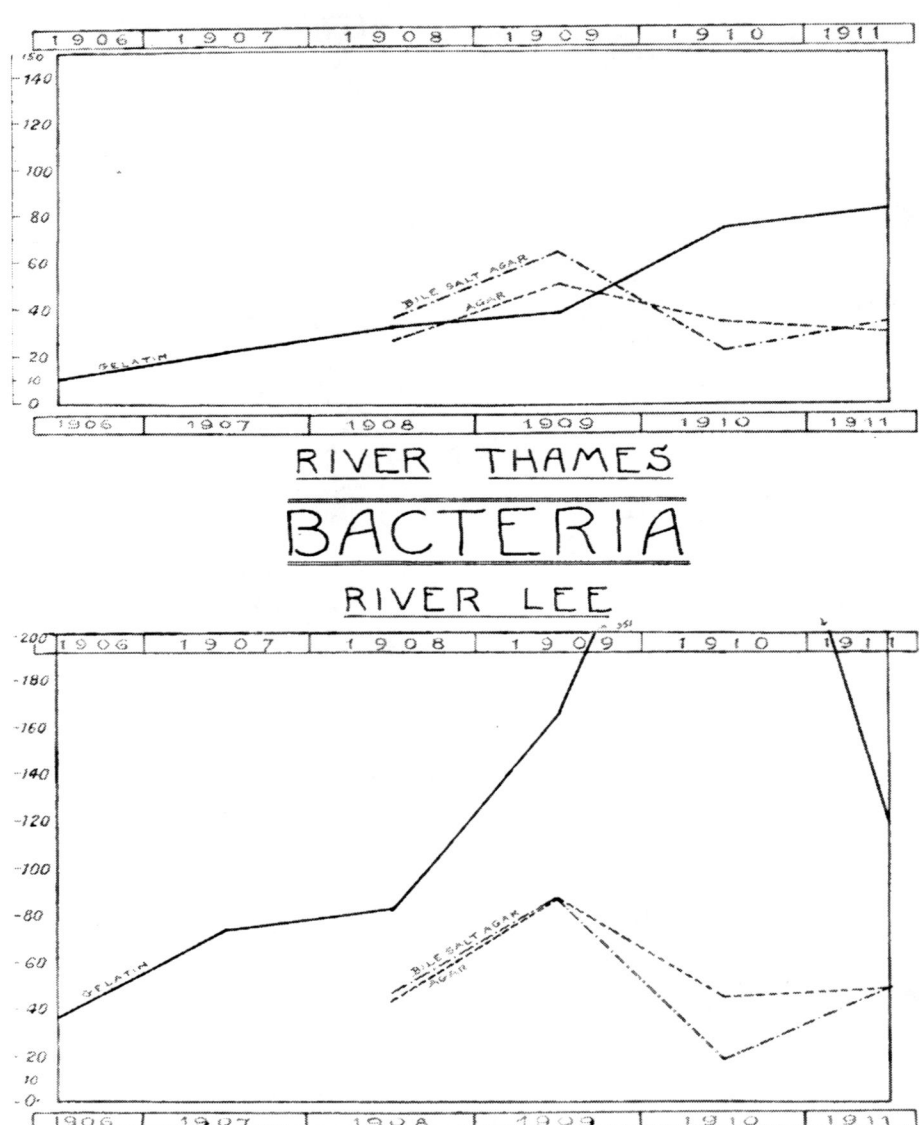

RIVER THAMES

BACTERIA

RIVER LEE

Fig. 8.

TABLE VII.—BACTERIOLOGICAL RESULTS. RIVER THAMES *Raw* WATER AT HAMPTON.

		Average Number of Microbes per c.c.			B. coli test (Typical B. coli) (Percentage results.)								
	Cols.	Gelatin at 20-22° C. 3 days.	Agar at 37° C.*	Bile-salt Agar at 37° C.*	Negative 100 c.c. %	+ 100 c.c. %	+ 10 c.c. %	+ 1 c.c. %	+ 0·1 c.c. %	+ 0·01 c.c. %	+ 0·001 c.c. %	+ 0·0001 c.c. %	Aggregate of Cols. 7-11
		1	2	3	4	5	6	7	8	9	10	11	12
1906	Jan.	2075	—	—	—	—	4·5	22·7	59·1	13·6	—	—	95·4
	Feb.	1679	—	—	—	—	5·0	30·0	45·0	20·0	—	—	95·0
	Mar.	1161	—	—	—	—	13·6	36·4	36·4	13·6	—	—	86·4
	April	277	—	—	—	21·1	31·6	31·6	15·7	—	—	—	47·3
	May	1064	—	—	8·7	13·0	34·7	26·1	17·4	—	—	—	43·5
	June	382	—	—	5·0	20·0	35·0	40·0	—	—	—	—	40·0
	July	952	—	—	9·1	22·7	22·7	40·9	0·0	4·5	—	—	45·4
	Aug.	727	—	—	13·6	27·3	27·3	22·6	9·1	—	—	—	31·7
	Sept.	450	—	—	10·5	15·8	52·6	15·8	5·2	—	—	—	21·0
	Oct.	439	—	—	—	4·3	8·7	60·9	21·7	4·3	—	—	86·9
	Nov.	2580	—	—	—	—	—	13·6	54·5	31·8	—	—	99·9
	Dec.	2943	—	—	—	—	—	5·9	76·5	17·6	—	—	100·0
1907	Jan.	5246	—	—	—	—	—	13·6	68·2	18·2	—	—	100·0
	Feb.	3625	—	—	—	—	—	40·9	50·0	10·0	—	—	100·0
	Mar.	1590	—	—	—	—	10·5	42·1	47·4	—	—	—	89·5
	April	1803	—	—	—	—	19·0	38·1	38·1	4·7	—	—	80·9
	May	961	—	—	—	—	9·5	47·6	28·5	14·3	—	—	90·4
	June	1366	—	—	—	—	30·0	35·0	35·0	—	—	—	70·0
	July	493	—	—	—	4·3	30·4	52·2	13·0	—	—	—	65·2
	Aug.	436	170	67	—	10·0	15·0	45·0	25·0	5·0	—	—	75·0
	Sept.	575	101	26	—	4·7	42·9	28·6	19·0	4·7	—	—	52·3
	Oct.	1658	317	63	—	—	13·0	39·1	43·5	4·3	—	—	86·9
	Nov.	4902	338	51	—	—	9·5	33·3	42·8	14·3	—	—	90·4
	Dec.	6710	578	72	—	—	—	—	68·7	31·2	—	—	99·9
1908	Jan.	13454	352	62	—	—	—	9·1	72·7	18·2	—	—	100·0
	Feb.	3627	146	20	—	—	—	50·0	45·0	5·0	—	—	100·0
	Mar.	2646	311	24	—	—	9·1	50·0	31·8	4·5	4·5	—	90·3
	April	6177	242	19	—	5·2	0·0	47·4	31·6	15·8	—	—	94·3
	May	2185	254	28	—	—	14·3	42·8	38·1	4·7	—	—	85·6
	June	1767	160	31	—	—	30·0	15·0	50·0	5·0	—	—	70·0
	July	1107	232	38	—	—	18·2	59·1	18·2	4·5	—	—	81·3
	Aug.	1127	268	63	—	—	15·0	60·0	25·0	—	—	—	85·0
	Sept.	1327	98	9	—	9·1	18·2	45·4	13·6	13·6	—	—	72·5
	Oct.	1853	493	66	—	4·5	9·1	40·9	31·8	13·6	—	—	86·3
	Nov.	1187	242	45	—	4·7	9·5	33·3	38·2	14·3	—	—	85·3
	Dec.	2188	321	28	—	—	—	23·5	47·1	23·5	5·9	—	100·0
1909	Jan.	2233	606	51	—	—	—	21·4	64·3	14·3	—	—	100·0
	Feb.	1107	291	22	—	—	—	56·2	43·7	—	—	—	99·9
	Mar.	8072	470	43	—	—	—	27·8	55·5	16·6	—	—	99·9
	April	2026	289	32	—	—	21·4	21·4	57·1	—	—	—	78·5
	May	913	118	9	—	7·1	35·7	50·0	7·1	—	—	—	57·1
	June	1012	424	66	—	—	11·7	29·4	58·8	—	—	—	88·2
	July	1320	310	40	—	—	6·2	62·5	25·0	6·2	—	—	93·7
	Aug.	2000	330	52	—	—	12·5	50·0	31·2	6·2	—	—	87·4
	Sept.	1073	322	38	—	—	—	44·4	50·0	5·5	—	—	99·9
	Oct.	5290	780	105	—	—	—	29·4	58·8	11·7	—	—	99·9
	Nov.	2963	724	90	—	—	—	5·9	70·6	23·5	—	—	100·0
	Dec.	19794	1235	173	6·2	0·0	0·0	—	62·5	31·2	—	—	93·7
1910	Jan.	9845	490	47	—	—	—	20·0	65·0	15·0	—	—	100·0
	Feb.	12640	294	14	—	—	—	5·0	75·0	20·0	—	—	100·0
	Mar.	6326	209	7	—	—	—	15·8	57·9	26·3	—	—	100·0
	April	3109	139	2	—	4·7	4·7	66·7	19·0	4·7	—	—	90·4
	May	1522	94	1	—	6·2	43·7	37·5	12·5	—	—	—	50·0
	June	2721	400	20	—	13·6	4·5	31·8	50·0	—	—	—	81·8
	July	2589	208	14	—	—	—	47·4	36·8	15·8	—	—	100·0
	Aug.	2702	600	25	—	4·5	22·8	59·0	13·7	—	—	—	72·7
	Sept.	3035	111	7	4·5	4·5	40·9	36·4	13·6	—	—	—	50·0
	Oct.	3736	165	11	—	—	19·0	42·8	33·3	4·7	—	—	80·9
	Nov.	17982	522	59	—	—	4·5	27·3	54·6	13·6	—	—	95·5
	Dec.	22939	760	42	—	—	—	16·6	61·1	22·2	—	—	99·9
1911	Jan.	10438	340	36	—	—	4·8	9·5	57·1	23·8	4·8	—	95·2
	Feb.	8035	350	9	—	—	—	30·0	50·0	20·0	—	—	100·0
	Mar.	9300	415	12	—	—	—	21·7	56·5	21·7	—	—	99·9
	April	5569	511	29	—	6·2	6·2	56·3	25·0	6·2	—	—	87·5
	May	2516	286	19	—	—	22·7	45·4	27·3	4·6	—	—	77·3
	June	5426	149	38	—	—	25·0	75·0	—	—	—	—	75·0
	July	5247	239	45	—	—	33·3	42·8	14·3	9·5	—	—	66·6
	Aug.	17524	202	37	—	—	9·5	42·8	38·1	9·5	—	—	90·4
	Sept.	3053	238	37	—	—	33·3	28·6	33·3	4·7	—	—	66·6
	Oct.	4499	213	37	—	—	4·6	45·4	40·9	9·1	—	—	95·4
	Nov.	7409	479	42	—	—	—	31·8	54·5	9·1	4·5	—	99·9
	Dec.	18219	377	46	—	—	—	25·0	62·5	12·5	—	—	100·0

* Agar results counted after two days from August, 1907, to December, 1909. During 1910 and 1911, after 20–24 hours. Samples collected at Sunbury during January–November, 1906.

CH. I SOURCES OF WATER SUPPLY 19

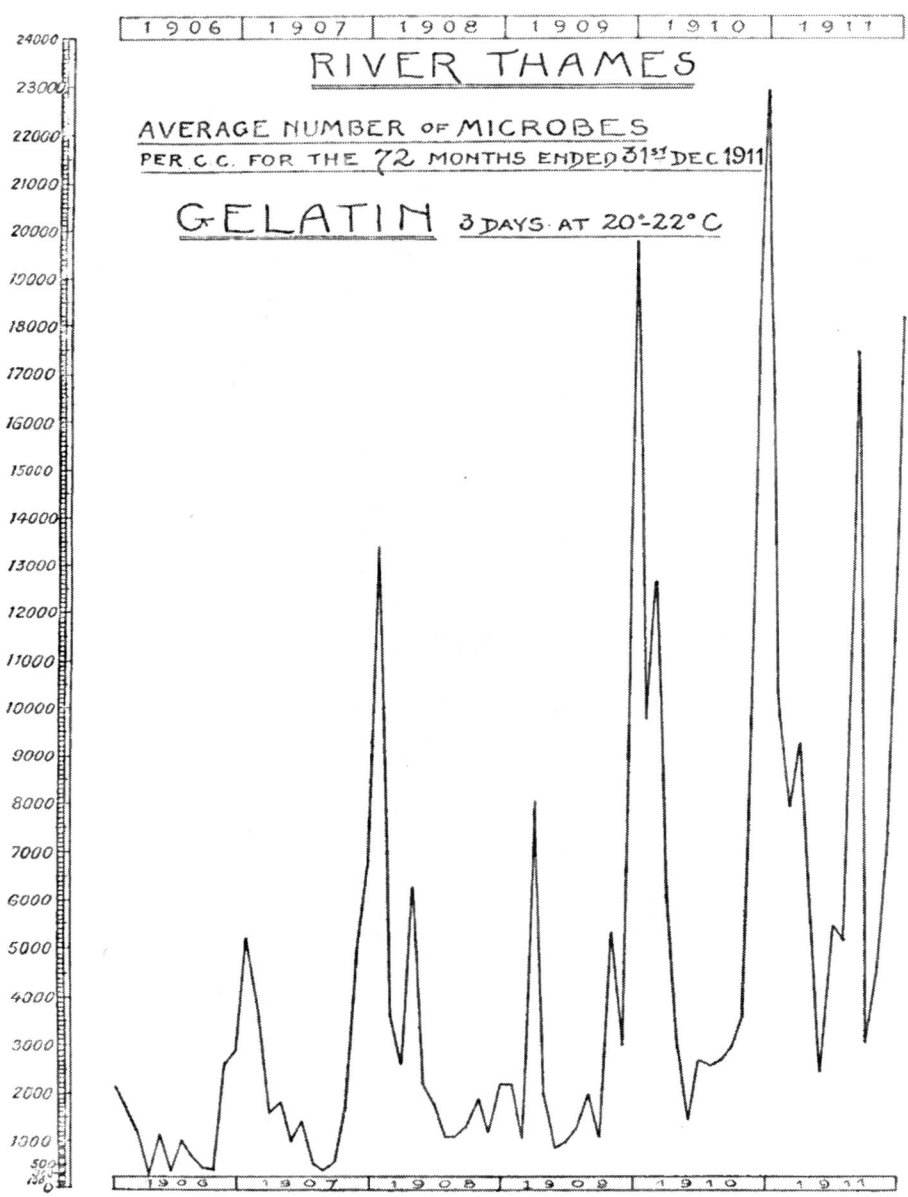

Fig. 9.

20 STUDIES IN WATER SUPPLY CHAP.

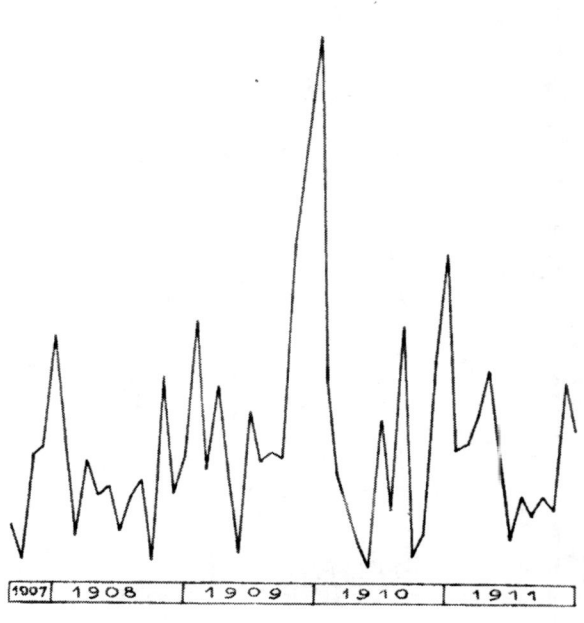

Fig. 10.

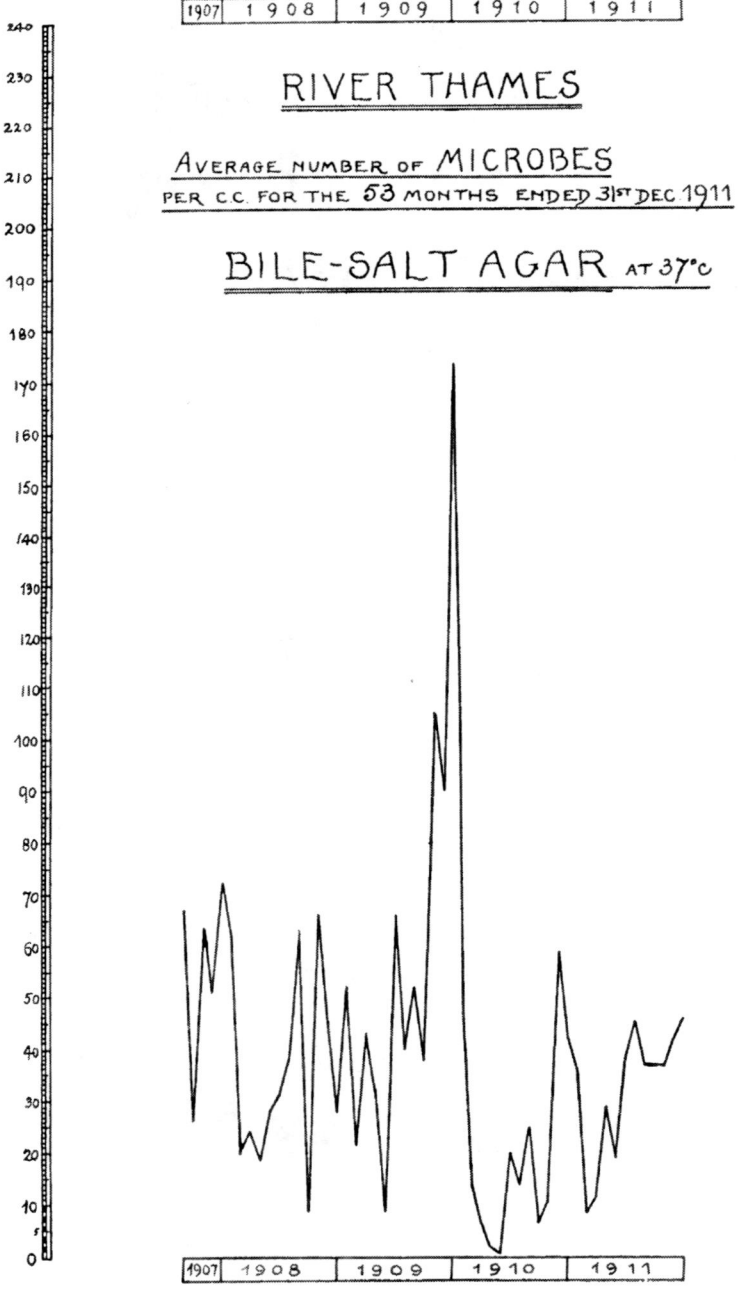

Fig. 11.

TABLE VIII.—BACTERIOLOGICAL RESULTS. RIVER LEE *RAW* WATER AT PONDERS END.

		Average Number of Microbes per c.c.			B. coli test (typical B. coli). (Percentage results.)								
		Gelatin at 20-22° C 3 days.	Agar at 37° C.	Bile-salt Agar at 37° C.	Negative % 100 c.c.	+ 100 c.c. %	+ 10 c.c. %	+ 1 c.c. %	+ 0·1 c.c. %	+ 0·01 c.c. %	+ 0·001 c.c. %	+ 0·0001 c.c. %	Aggregate of Cols. 7–11
	Cols.	1	2	3	4	5	6	7	8	9	10	11	12
1906	Jan.	5192	—	—	—	—	4·5	13·6	72·8	9·1	—	—	95·5
	Feb.	3083	—	—	—	—	5·0	30·0	60·0	5·0	—	—	95·0
	March	1308	—	—	—	—	4·5	54·5	36·4	4·5	—	—	95·4
	April	471	—	—	—	—	31·6	42·1	26·3	—	—	—	68·4
	May	1350	—	—	4·3	0·0	21·7	43·5	30·4	—	—	—	73·9
	June	598	—	—	—	—	20·0	55·0	15·0	10·0	—	—	80·0
	July	1190	—	—	9·1	0·0	31·8	31·8	22·7	4·5	—	—	59·0
	Aug.	1986	—	—	18·2	4·5	13·6	45·4	18·2	—	—	—	63·6
	Sept.	1499	—	—	5·0	5·0	15·0	40·0	25·0	10·0	—	—	75·0
	Oct.	2397	—	—	—	4·3	4·3	43·5	30·4	17·4	—	—	91·3
	Nov.	9986	—	—	—	—	—	9·1	72·7	13·6	4·5	—	99·9
	Dec.	17792	—	—	—	—	5·9	17·6	58·8	17·6	—	—	94·0
1907	Jan.	28986	—	—	—	—	—	31·8	54·5	13·6	—	—	99·9
	Feb.	19115	—	—	—	5·0	—	30·0	50·0	15·0	—	—	95·0
	March	3001	—	—	—	—	10·5	63·1	21·1	5·2	—	—	89·4
	April	1861	—	—	—	—	—	61·9	33·3	4·7	—	—	99·9
	May	1594	—	—	—	—	19·0	33·3	33·3	14·3	—	—	80·9
	June	1095	—	—	—	—	20·0	45·0	35·0	—	—	—	80·0
	July	854	—	—	—	—	17·4	52·1	30·4	—	—	—	82·5
	Aug.	812	351	43	5·0	5·0	15·0	50·0	25·0	—	—	—	75·0
	Sept.	1453	400	56	—	—	4·7	71·5	14·3	4·7	4·7	—	95·2
	Oct.	2593	430	49	—	—	17·4	52·2	30·4	—	—	—	82·6
	Nov.	15614	373	25	—	—	—	42·8	38·1	14·3	4·7	—	99·9
	Dec.	11725	595	45	—	—	—	12·5	56·2	25·0	6·2	—	99·9
1908	Jan.	22452	515	26	—	—	—	27·3	59·1	9·1	4·5	—	100·0
	Feb.	14070	162	14	—	—	5·0	35·0	40·0	15·0	0·0	5·0	95·0
	March	7204	347	34	—	—	—	36·3	45·4	13·6	4·5	—	99·8
	April	8999	291	16	—	—	—	36·8	52·6	10·5	—	—	99·9
	May	4638	407	18	—	—	9·5	47·6	33·3	4·7	0·0	4·7	90·3
	June	2333	205	34	—	—	10·0	60·0	25·0	5·0	—	—	90·0
	July	6032	509	76	—	4·5	0·0	18·2	45·4	27·2	4·5	—	95·3
	Aug.	4895	891	223	—	—	10·0	40·0	35·0	10·0	0·0	5·0	90·0
	Sept.	4682	257	36	—	—	4·5	40·9	31·8	13·6	9·1	—	95·4
	Oct.	3780	597	42	—	—	4·5	40·9	31·8	22·7	—	—	95·4
	Nov.	1706	287	36	—	4·7	4·7	38·1	38·1	14·3	—	—	90·5
	Dec.	18589	867	46	—	—	11·7	17·6	41·2	17·6	11·7	—	88·1
1909	Jan.	3361	299	19	—	—	—	21·4	64·3	14·3	—	—	100·0
	Feb.	6280	294	25	—	—	—	31·2	43·7	18·7	6·2	—	99·8
	March	38469	1228	73	—	—	5·5	16·6	33·3	27·8	16·6	—	94·3
	April	2071	174	22	—	—	7·1	28·5	64·3	—	—	—	92·8
	May	1735	205	10	—	—	21·4	50·0	28·5	—	—	—	78·5
	June	1759	372	39	—	—	23·5	41·2	23·5	11·7	—	—	76·4
	July	3565	312	50	—	—	6·2	25·0	21·2	31·2	6·2	—	93·6
	Aug.	4852	642	91	—	—	—	50·0	31·2	12·5	6·2	—	99·9
	Sept.	1679	465	69	—	—	—	61·1	27·7	11·1	—	—	99·9
	Oct.	17033	2276	215	—	—	5·9	29·4	29·4	17·6	5·9	0·0	94·1
	Nov.	22954	1115	115	—	—	—	17·6	47·1	17·6	17·6	—	99·9
	Dec.	105750	2539	250	—	—	—	12·5	68·7	6·2	12·5	—	99·9
1910	Jan.	73878	544	31	—	—	—	15·0	30·0	40·0	15·0	—	100·0
	Feb.	166131	420	20	—	—	—	20·0	65·0	0·0	10·0	5·0	100·0
	March	72697	188	5	—	5·3	15·8	31·5	31·5	5·3	10·5	—	78·8
	April	10676	389	7	—	4·7	9·5	57·1	23·8	4·7	—	—	85·6
	May	2317	139	2	12·5	0·0	12·5	50·0	25·0	—	—	—	75·0
	June	1672	345	15	—	4·5	9·1	36·4	40·9	9·1	—	—	86·4
	July	4258	752	38	—	—	15·8	36·8	31·6	15·8	—	—	84·2
	Aug.	2886	275	39	—	—	4·5	50·0	36·4	4·5	4·5	—	95·4
	Sept.	4248	310	16	—	9·1	13·6	45·4	31·8	—	—	—	77·2
	Oct.	3735	255	13	—	—	9·5	52·4	38·1	—	—	—	90·5
	Nov.	42677	1228	24	—	—	4·5	36·4	27·3	31·8	—	—	95·5
	Dec.	52322	942	28	—	—	—	—	55·5	27·8	16·6	—	99·9
1911	Jan.	12619	360	15	—	—	9·5	19·0	47·6	23·8	—	—	90·4
	Feb.	11490	152	5	—	—	15·0	35·0	40·0	5·0	5·0	—	85·0
	March	24648	670	23	—	—	—	56·5	30·4	13·0	—	—	99·9
	April	6100	376	15	—	—	12·5	56·3	31·2	—	—	—	87·5
	May	13950	871	55	—	—	9·1	59·1	18·2	13·6	—	—	90·9
	June	5912	867	48	—	—	25·0	56·2	18·7	—	—	—	74·9
	July	5855	406	95	—	—	28·6	42·8	28·6	—	—	—	71·4
	Aug.	4476	315	41	—	4·8	23·8	23·8	47·6	—	—	—	71·4
	Sept.	3647	555	86	—	—	4·7	28·6	61·9	4·7	—	—	95·2
	Oct.	13454	492	59	—	—	13·6	31·8	50·0	4·6	—	—	86·4
	Nov.	9754	405	72	—	—	9·1	50·0	36·3	4·5	—	—	90·8
	Dec.	28906	1157	111	—	6·2	0·0	25·0	50·0	18·7	—	—	93·7

Oct., 1909, B. coli test :—also 5·9% in 0·00001 and 5·9% in 0·000001 c.c.
Dec., 1909, Column 1 :—Average excludes two samples containing 1,120,000 and 1,240,000 microbes per c.c. respectively.

CH. I   SOURCES OF WATER SUPPLY   23

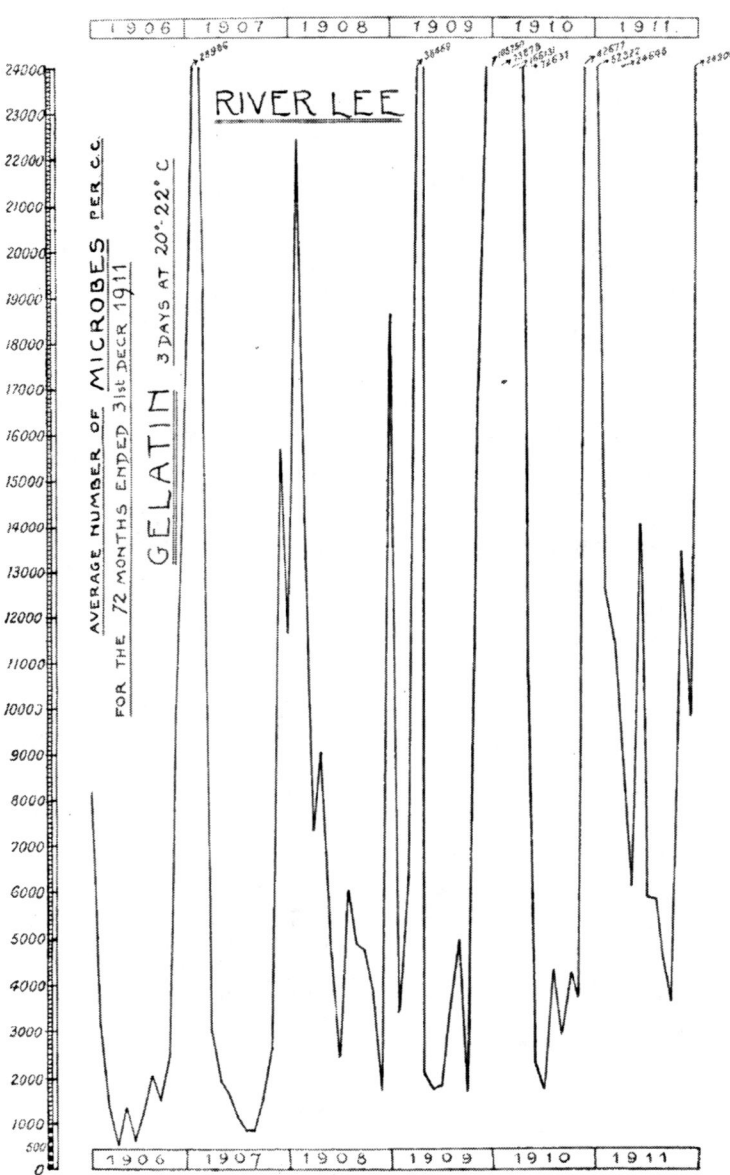

Fig. 12.

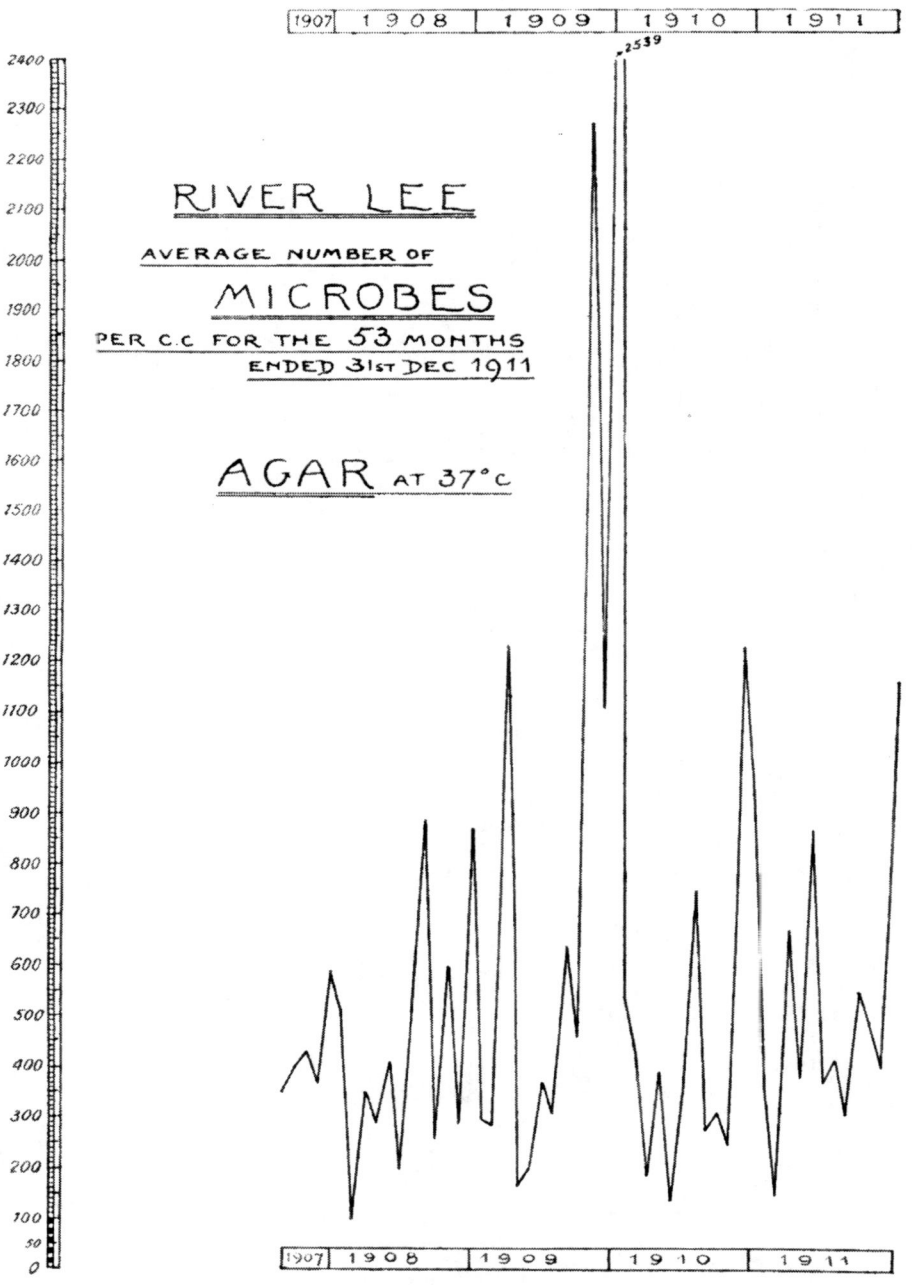

Fig. 13.

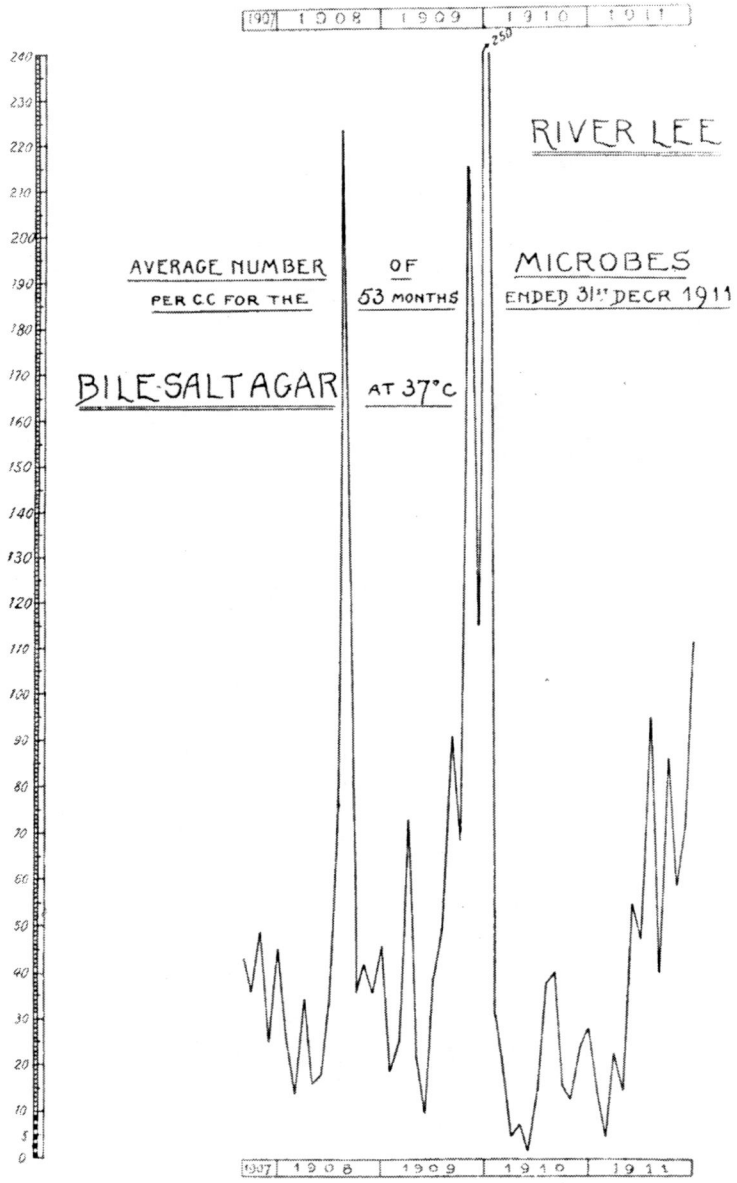

Fig. 14.

In the face of the foregoing chemical and bacteriological results, corroborating and measuring the known, or suspected, facts as regards sewage and other undesirable pollutions, no man of science could support the continued use of the Rivers Thames and Lee as sources of supply, in the absence of :—

(*a*) Further information tending to free the Rivers Thames and Lee from the full gravity of the charge of their being sewage-polluted rivers.

(*b*) Evidence that the purification processes in actual operation were uniformly efficient.

As regard (*a*), this will form the text of the next chapter, and in respect to (*b*), nearly the whole of this Monograph deals with the remarkable transformation of an impure raw river water actually into water of good quality, and not only so, but, when considered in relation to its source of origin, into a water of remarkable purity.

CHAPTER II

RESEARCHES TENDING TO JUSTIFY RIVERS AS SOURCES OF WATER SUPPLY

It will be convenient to deal in the first place with the streptococcus test and then with tests for definitely pathogenic bacteria (*e.g.* Gärtner's bacillus and the typhoid bacillus).

In 1898–9 and in subsequent years the writer reported to the Local Government Board on the significance of streptococci in water. It is of this test that primary mention may be made.

Streptococcus Test.—The chief reasons for considering the streptococcus test of value in the examination of water supplies, are :—

(1) That streptococci are superabundant in human fæces. (2) That fæcal streptococci are absent or non-discoverable in a relatively large volume of *pure* water. (3) That fæcal streptococci do not multiply in *pure* water. (4) That some fæcal streptococci are of feeble vitality and that the presence of such streptococci in a water, if they could be differentiated from their more robust companions, would seem to indicate pollution of *recent* and therefore specially dangerous sort.

It is desirable to consider the subject under three headings :—

(1) What are the results, as regards streptococci, of the

examination of a mixture representative of the fæces of a large number of individuals?

To solve this point and in corroboration and amplification of previous work, a visit was made to a sewage-works where the lumps of fæces reach the outfall in a fairly fresh, *i.e.* unbroken, condition. One hundred stabs with 100 sterile iron wires (the aggregate weight of which had previously been determined) were made into 100 lumps of fæces. The lumps of fæces had previously been consecutively fished out of the sewage by the aid of a wire gauze scoop. The contaminated wires were placed in a sterile test-tube of known weight. The tube *plus* its contents of contaminated wires was next weighed, and by a simple calculation the weight of the adhering fæcal matter ascertained. Sterile water was then added to form an emulsion of fæces and water, in such proportion as rendered 1 c.c. of the mixture equivalent to 0·1 gramme of fæces. The wires were next rotated and moved about in the liquid so as to detach and break up the fæces. One cubic centimetre of the fæcal emulsion was then added to a second tube (2) containing 9 c.c. of sterile water. 1 c.c. of (2) was then added to a third tube (3), also containing 9 c.c. of sterile water. In the same way a fourth tube (4) received 1 c.c. from tube (3), a fifth tube (5), 1 c.c. from tube (4), a sixth tube (6), 1 c.c. from tube (5), a seventh tube (7), 1 c.c. from tube (6), and so on until 10 tubes had been seeded.

The next step in searching for streptococci, was to take 0·1 c.c. from each of the various dilutions and spread it over a series of previously prepared Drigalski and Conradi [1]

---

[1] Composition of Drigalski and Conradi's medium :—Agar, 3%; nutrose and peptone, each 1%; sodium chloride, 0·5%; lactose, 1·5%; 1 c.c. of 0·1% solution of crystal violet (Höchst); 13 c.c. of litmus solution (Kübel and Tiemann); 0·2 c.c. of a 10% solution of sodium carbonate in excess of amount required to render medium slightly alkaline. Beef broth (1 lb. beef per litre of water), 100 c.c.

plates by means of a sterile glass spreader working always from the lesser to the greater amount of fæces.

After incubation at 37° C., the minute colonies developing on the plates were next subcultured into a lactose medium (lemco 1%, peptone 1%, sodium carbonate 0·1%, lactose 0·5%, tap water tinted with litmus solution up to 100).

Only those tubes showing acidity, after two days' incubation at 37° C., were examined microscopically, and 100 of those yielding satisfactory morphological evidence were studied further, with results as follows :—

One streptococcus was isolated from one ten-millionth of a gramme of the fæces.

Twenty-seven streptococci were isolated from one-millionth of a gramme.

Seventy-two streptococci were isolated from one hundred-thousandth of a gramme.

None of the streptococci reduced nitrates to nitrites [1]— at all events to any appreciable extent. Nor, of course, did they produce any gas in the media given below.

The "types" of streptococci may be classified as follows :—

la = acid in a *la*ctose medium.[2]
ma = acid in a *ma*nnite medium.
mi = clot in a *mi*lk medium.[3]
ra = acid in a *ra*ffinose medium.
sac = acid in a *sac*charose medium.
sal = acid in a *sal*icin medium.

[1] The nitrate broth was of the following composition :—Beef broth 10% (1 lb. of beef per litre), potassium nitrate 0·1%, tap water up to 100. In testing for nitrites, a solution of 0·5 gramme of metaphenylenediamine in 100 c.c. of a 1% solution of hydrochloric acid is used.

[2] The lactose, mannite, raffinose, saccharose and salicin media contained 1% of the respective fermentable substances, together with lemco 1%, peptone 1%, sodium carbonate 0·1%, and tap water tinted with litmus solution up to 100.

[3] The milk medium was ordinary sterilised milk.

The combinations were as under :—

lamirasal	49
lamirasacsal	44
lamamirasacsal	4
lamirasac	1
lamira	2
Total	100

Avoiding technicalities, the main point is that streptococci were found in great abundance in the fæcal mixture representative of the fæces of a large number of individuals.

(2) What are the results as regards streptococci, of the examination of multiple samples of *raw* river water?

Drigalski and Conradi plates were inoculated with 1 c.c. amounts of the raw Thames, Lee and New River waters, and all the minute colonies were subcultured and made the subject of attentive study. The summarised results were as follows :—

1908 (764 + 896 + 248) subcultures were made from 1 c.c. amounts of 156 (52 + 52 + 52) samples of *raw* river water (Thames, Lee and New River). Twenty-eight (13 + 13 + 2) of these samples contained streptococci (lactose +), and the total number of streptococci isolated was 71 (19 + 50 + 2).

It should be noted, however, that in three instances (Thames 2 samples, Lee 1 sample), the 1 c.c. plates were so crowded that it was necessary to make the subcultures from 0·1 c.c. plates. In these three samples one streptococcus was isolated from 0·1 c.c. (= 10 per c.c.) of one of the Thames samples, and none from 0·1 c.c. (= less than 10 per c.c.) of the other sample.

Two streptococci were isolated from 0·1 c.c. (= 20 per c.c.) of the Lee sample. It may therefore be desirable to amend the 71 figure by adding to it, either $10 + 0 + 20 = 30$, or $10 + 10 + 20 = 40$. If we adopt the latter figure, then $71 + 40 = 111$ streptococci. It is of interest to compare this figure with the aggregate number of bacteria (gelatine and agar) in the raw waters, and also the aggregate number of microbes growing in bile-salt agar (chiefly B. coli and excremental bacteria).

The *aggregate* number of bacteria and streptococci in 156 c.c. of water derived in equal amounts from 156 comparable samples of *raw* river water (Thames, Lee and New River) collected at weekly intervals during the year 1909 was as follows:—

A.	B.	C.	D.
		Number of Bacteria.	
Number of Streptococci.	Bile-salt-agar at 37°C.	Agar at 37°C.	Gelatine at 20–22°C.
111	6,650	59,645	2,199,190

The ratio figure is 1 streptococcus to 59 under *B.*, 537 under *C.*, and 19,812 under *D.*

(3) What are the results, as regards streptococci, of the examination of raw river water (*a*) in its normal condition and (*b*) after being purposely inoculated artificially with minute traces of human fæces (one part of fæces in one million parts of water)?

Ten samples of raw Thames water were examined, and 400 subcultures were made under (*a*) non-infected conditions, and a like number under (*b*) infected conditions.

In the former case 36, and in the latter 204 streptococci were isolated, the preponderance under infected conditions being 168. The results would have been *relatively* still more striking had it not been for the fact that the particular samples of *raw* water used in the experiments happened to be exceptionally impure.

The following points may be noted specially in connection with these investigations:—

(1) The superabundance of streptococci in human fæces.

(2) The relative difficulty of isolating any streptococci of a comparable sort from *raw* river water as exemplified by the Thames, Lee and New River.

(3) The ease with which streptococci can be isolated from raw river water, artificially inoculated with human fæces in the proportion of one part of fæces in 1,000,000 parts of water.

As a corollary it surely follows that the wholesale condemnation of raw river water, comparable with the Thames, Lee and New River, does not seem urgently warrantable as the result of the application of the streptococcus test.

The writer has made many experiments on the vitality of streptococci in water, and has found that whereas some streptococci die very speedily, others persist for a long time, and he has so far been unable *satisfactorily* to associate this variability as regards vitality, with differences in the biological characters of the streptococci.

Tests for pathogenic bacteria.—The value of the streptococcus and B. coli tests, rests primarily on the assumption that these bacteria are present in abundance in human fæces, and, relatively speaking, absent from substances not exposed to excremental pollution. Hence their numerical estimation in water, is an indirect gauge of the degree of probability of their being accompanied, habitually or occasionally, by other microbes of truly pathogenic import.

Until comparatively recently the search for pathogenic microbes in water was regarded as almost labour lost, for the reason that the practical difficulties attending their isolation were so great that failure to isolate them afforded no satisfactory indication of their real absence. Of late years, however, improvements in technique and methods have altered the whole complexion of affairs, and it is now possible, although still a difficult and laborious task, to isolate the typhoid bacillus when present in only small numbers, from a water, even when that water is swarming with other bacteria. How far this statement is true may be gathered from the following account of the search for pathogenic bacteria in London's raw sources of water supply.

In the first investigation 294 experiments in eight series were made with 156 samples of raw river water during the twelve months ended July 31st, 1908. The total number of bacteria (gelatine at 20–22°C.) in the 29,400 c.c. examined was in the aggregate 135,687,500. Owing to the temperature of incubation, the composition of the media employed, and the fact of their appearing on the particular plate cultures, as *coloured* colonies, the great majority of these bacteria were excluded from consideration. The actual number subcultured and subsequently more minutely studied was 7,329. Not one of them proved to be the typhoid bacillus. Later the inquiry was extended so as to include the search for Gärtner's bacillus, and it differed from the previous research in a most important particular.

Each sample of raw river water examined was divided into two equal portions of 500 c.c. (A and B). The A sample was inoculated with a very small number of typhoid bacilli and Gärtner's bacilli, separately determined by Agar plate cultures in the usual manner. The B sample was not so infected, and was, therefore, normal raw river water. A and B were then examined in a strictly comparable manner.

The object of this procedure was to show that the search for pathogenic bacteria in raw river water is not, as has been suggested, as hopeless as looking for a needle in a haystack. On the contrary, the results, on the average, showed that in the case of the A sample (artificially infected) the test was delicate to the extent of isolating the typhoid bacillus and Gärtner bacillus, when only 1 was present per about 7 c.c. of water in the first case, and per about 18 c.c. of water in the second case.

It follows that failure to isolate these same microbes from the B samples (non-infected) under comparable conditions of experiment, although a *negative* result, acquired a *positive* significance.

Twenty-four experiments were carried out altogether, and the results are summarised in Table IX. :—

TABLE IX.

Total number of Colonies Sub-cultured.	Typhoid part of Experiment.				Gärtner part of Experiment.			
	Average number of *artificially* added Typhoid bacilli per c.c. of the *raw* river water.		Average number of Typhoid bacilli recovered from :—		Average number of *artificially* added Gärtner bacilli per c.c. of the *raw* river water.		Average number of Gärtner bacilli recovered from :—	
	Infected Sample A.	Non-infected Sample B.	Infected Sample A.	Non-infected Sample B.	Infected Sample A.	Non-infected Sample B.	Infected Sample A.	Non-infected Sample B.
5451	2·242	None	14·54 $\frac{14·54}{2·242}$ = 1 to 6·485	None (? 1 out of 5,451 sub-cultures)	0·686	None	12·417 $\frac{12·417}{0·686}$ = 1 to 18·10	None (? 1 out of 5,451 sub-cultures)

One typhoid-like microbe and one Gärtner-like microbe were isolated; excepting these two, none of the 5,451 microbes studied, bore any reasonable resemblance either to the typhoid bacillus or Gärtner's bacillus. Practically the experiments showed that the typhoid bacillus cannot be uniformly present in 7 c.c. nor Gärtner's bacillus in 18 c.c. of *raw river water*. In a still later investigation exactly the same methods were adopted, 35 additional experiments having been carried out.

The results are summarised in Table X. (p. 35).

One typhoid-like microbe[1] was isolated; with this

---

[1] This microbe was motile, multi-flagellated, and fulfilled all the ordinary tests for the typhoid bacillus. It was agglutinated with an anti-typhoid serum in practically the same dilutions as a stock laboratory culture of B. typhosus. It was, however, decidedly less virulent to rodents, than is usual with strains of typhoid bacilli isolated from cases of typhoid fever.

exception, none of the 7,991 microbes studied bore any reasonable resemblance either to the typhoid bacillus or Gärtner's bacillus.

In this series of experiments the average number of typhoid bacilli added to the A (infected) samples was 0·653 per c.c. of river water, and the average number recovered was 11·6, so that, by inference, it may be concluded that the test was delicate to the extent of detecting

TABLE X.

Total number of Colonies Sub-cultured.	Typhoid part of Experiment.				Gärtner part of Experiment.			
	Average number of *artificially* added Typhoid bacilli per c.c. of the *raw* river water.		Average number of Typhoid bacilli recovered from :—		Average number of *artificially* added Gärtner bacilli per c.c. of the *raw* river water.		Average number of Gärtner bacilli recovered from :—	
	Infected Sample A.	Non-infected Sample B.	Infected Sample A.	Non-infected Sample B.	Infected Sample A.	Non-infected Sample B.	Infected Sample A.	Non-infected Sample B.
7991	0·653	None.	11·6 11·6 / 0·653 = 1 to 17·7	None (? 1 out of 7,991 sub-cultures)	0·633	None	7·86 7·86 / 0·633 = 1 to 12·4	None

1 typhoid bacillus per 17·7 c.c. of river water. The average number of Gärtner's bacilli added was 0·633, and the average number recovered was 7·86, so that, by inference, it may be concluded that the test was delicate to the extent of detecting 1 Gärtner's bacillus per 12·4 c.c. of river water. Practically, therefore, the experiments showed that the typhoid bacillus cannot be uniformly present in 17·7 c.c. or the Gärtner's bacillus in 12·4 c.c. of river water.[1]

---

[1] The above results represent the practical, but not the absolute, limits of delicacy of the method. For instance, when the quality of the river water was good, more than 500 c.c. could have been centrifugalised; when it was bad, more primary plates could have been used. In either case the number of subcultures could have been increased. On the other hand, the work involved in "picking off" 250 colonies from the plates, as was done in these experiments, is so considerable, that it would scarcely be practicable, greatly to increase this number of subcultures.

Taking all the foregoing researches together, the study of $7,329 + 5,451 + 7,991 = 20,771$ specially selected colonies derived from $156 + 24 + 35 = 215$ separate, raw river water samples, has resulted in the discovery of only two typhoid-like microbes. One Gärtner-like microbe was found; the number of separate samples examined having been $24 + 35 = 59$, and the number of colonies studied $5,451 + 7,991 = 13,442$.

It may perhaps be objected that the bacilli experimentally added were "cultivated" specimens (*i.e.*, grown on artificial media in the laboratory), and that similar results would not have been obtained if "uncultivated" bacilli (as present in the urine of a typhoid "carrier") had been used. This objection, however, falls to the ground; for special experiments were subsequently made, in which the urine of a typhoid "carrier" case was added experimentally to river water, and the typhoid bacillus was successfully isolated from the mixture.

In one experiment, 1 part of typhoid urine was added to 50 million parts of Thames river water, the typhoid bacillus being present in the proportion of 152 per litre of water. Yet the typhoid bacillus was recovered without difficulty from the artificially infected water.

The writer's latest experiments have been with sewage, and it has been found that with samples, *artificially infected*, it is possible to isolate the typhoid bacillus when present in the proportion of one typhoid bacillus per 0.001 c.c. of sewage. No typhoid bacilli having been found in *duplicate non-infected* samples, the conclusion is surely legitimate that the typhoid bacillus cannot be present in sewage, in the proportion of one per 0.001 c.c., though it may of course be present in larger quantities of sewage. Now, it is easy to show by separate bacterial tests (*e.g.*, the bile-salt agar test) that the river Thames, on the average, is about 20,000 times less impure than sewage, and hence inferentially may it not be safely concluded that there are usually *no* typhoid bacilli in 20 c.c. of Thames river water?

This is a novel, if indirect, method of gauging the quality, in relation to water-borne disease, of any river water. For instance, the number of bacteria per c.c. of the river water may be estimated by means of the bile-salt agar test, and the figure obtained used to divide the number of bacteria (bile-salt agar) in 0·001 c.c. of sewage. The product gives the number of c.c. of river water which, on the basis of the writer's experiments, cannot be expected to contain the typhoid bacillus.

The conclusions which may be drawn from the foregoing observations seem to be:—

(1) A watershed may be exposed to manifold pollutions, all more or less objectionable.

(2) The river draining the watershed may be impure as judged by the ordinary chemical and bacteriological tests.

(3) The river water may nevertheless be shown to contain none or scarcely any of the microbes of water-borne disease, when tested by methods of proven value.

Epidemiologists have for long marvelled at the comparative, and oft-times long continued, immunity from typhoid fever, enjoyed by towns drinking sand-filtered water, from a polluted river source. The explanation usually forthcoming is the perfection of the filtration process, but may not the true explanation really be that the river water is never primarily so thoroughly noxious that it does not subsequently become relatively innocuous, 98 per cent. of its total bacteria having been removed by sand-filtration?

These views, although tending to free rivers from the full share of blame hitherto attached to them, are not inconsistent with the writer's continued and continual advocacy of a source of supply, wherever possible, of the greatest initial purity.

Having now learnt a little of the inherent and adventitious quality of river water, as illustrated by the Thames and Lee, it seems next desirable to consider the purification processes which seem absolutely necessary or at least desirable, before such a water is rendered reasonably safe for domestic use.

CHAPTER III

THE QUESTION OF ABSTRACTION

The Question of Abstraction.—In the case of upland gravitation schemes of supply, storm water courses are frequently provided so that when a flood occurs the worst water is prevented from entering the reservoirs, and flows instead along the water-courses on one or both sides of the reservoirs and so escapes down the valley. Even with a pumping scheme, assuming adequate storage capacity, a great deal can be done to safeguard the purity of the supply by closing the "intakes" during the worst period of each flood.

It seems to be insufficiently realised that there is no *necessary* or absolute parallelism between the flow of a river and its current quality. At the commencement of a flood the results, as regards quality, are apt to be disproportionately bad, but the quality of the water may improve more quickly than the rate of subsidence of the flood. Further, the first autumn or early winter flood may produce a much worse water than floods occurring after the bed of the river has been well scoured.

It follows that, given adequate storage accommodation, it is unnecessary and most undesirable to leave the intakes open during the worst period of a flood should there be a prospect of an oversufficiency of water still available for abstraction of far better quality at a not much later period.

Of course, in the case of many water-works, owing to deficiency in storage accommodation and to there not always being sufficient water available in the river, it is impossible to place the abstraction question on a strictly scientific basis. Nevertheless, although it may be practically impossible for these and other reasons to approach the ideal as regards abstraction, it is always well to aim at as high a standard as is reasonably practicable.

In illustration of different methods of abstraction, the River Thames colour-results for the 72 months ended December 31st, 1911, have been chosen as an example. The consumption of water has been taken arbitrarily as 100 million gallons a month, and questions of insufficiency of water due to drought have been ignored.

In the first diagram (Fig. 15, p. 41) it is assumed that there is no storage and that therefore the water must be abstracted uniformly at the rate of 100 million gallons per month. The remarkable fluctuations in the colour [1] are apparent, varying indeed from a maximum of 239 in December, 1907, to a minimum of 29 in April and May, 1906, the average for the whole period being 67·4.

In such a case, not only would the average colour of the water to be dealt with by the filters be fairly distinct, but during certain months the colour would be so marked (even after filtration) that the water on delivery would be appreciably brown in colour.

In the next two diagrams (Figs. 16–17) a large reserve of storage has been assumed, but the matter has been considered independently of the known effect of storage in reducing colour, and also of the circumstance, that it may really be better to store a worse water for a longer period than a better water for a shorter period.

---

[1] The colour results have been chosen for purposes of illustration, as this is a matter which appeals at once to the sense of sight, and is commonly, although erroneously, used by the consumer as a gauge of probable quality. Burgess's apparatus was used in determining the colour of the water.

III THE QUESTION OF ABSTRACTION 41

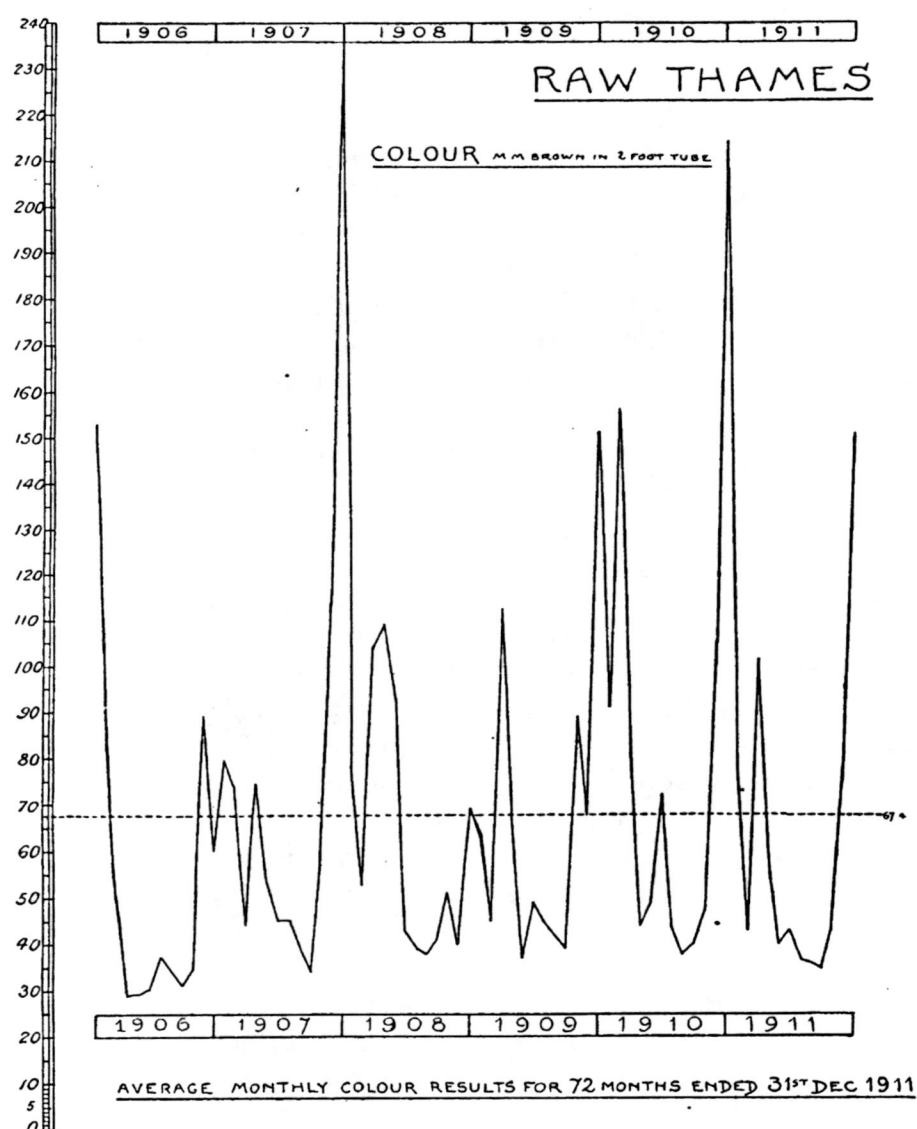

Fig. 15.

Average monthly colour results (colour × volume abstracted ÷ 100) for the 72 months ended December 31, 1911.
Abstraction uniform at the rate of 100 million gallons per month.
No storage.
Average colour result for the whole period, 67·4.
Here the abstraction is constant and the colour variable.

In the second diagram (Fig. 16, p. 43) the abstraction has been varied in proportion to the colour, the net result being that the colour has been kept constant at 52·6 (colour × volume abstracted ÷ 100) and the abstraction varied from as much as 181·67 million gallons in April and May, 1906, to as little as 22·04 in December, 1907. To attain this end an immense reserve of water would be necessary, and it has been calculated, that starting with storage reservoirs capable of holding 611 million gallons, and containing 250 million gallons to begin with, the amount of water in store at the end of the period would be the same, namely 250 million gallons. In October, 1906, the reservoirs would have been full and in April, 1911, they would have contained 133·91 million gallons. Here, apart from the effect of storage in reducing colour, the actual colour of the water abstracted would have remained constant at 52·3.

In the next diagram (Fig. 17, p. 45) the storage has been taken as 343·7 million gallons and whenever the reservoirs became depleted and the water coincidently better than the average, the opportunity has been taken to fill them on the following basis:—A water with a colour of 29 has been taken as the best water ever likely to be obtainable and in order to arrive at the permissible volume of water for filling the reservoirs, the storage capacity has been multiplied by 29 and the answer divided by the current colour. Thus with a colour of 29, 343·7 million gallons could be taken, or as much as was needed to fill the reservoirs. But with a colour of 57, only 174·87 could be taken. In cases, however, when the river water was worse than the average (67·4), the abstraction figure has been proportional to the impurity, the balance of water required for filtration purposes being borrowed from the storage reservoirs. For example, with a colour of 74, 71·19 million gallons would be abstracted, but with a colour of 150 only 35·12.

THE QUESTION OF ABSTRACTION

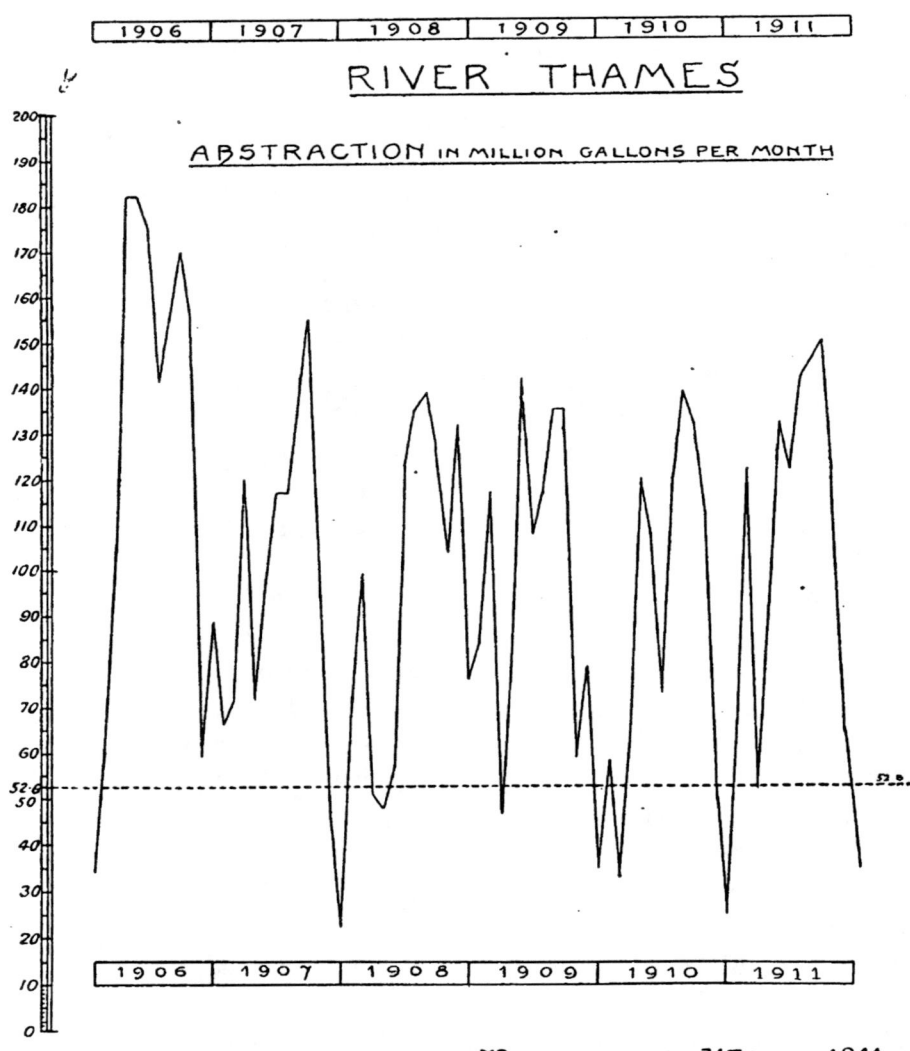

Fig. 16.

Average monthly abstraction figures in million gallons for the 72 months ended December 31, 1911, the average for the whole period being at the rate of 100 million gallons per month.
Colour constant at 52·6 (colour × volume abstracted ÷ 100).
Here the colour is constant and the abstraction variable.
Storage, 610·79 million gallons.

It will be seen (*see* Fig. 17) that this leads to an average colour of 46 (colour × volume abstracted ÷ 100); the reservoirs would be full during 34 out of the 72 months, the smallest amount being 27·90 (about 8½ days' supply) in May, 1908, and the volume left in store at the close of the period being 244 million gallons. Of course, in the case of London it would be impossible to abstract on the lines here suggested (merely for illustrative purposes), as the volume of water required is about 244 million gallons[1] per day, whereas in the foregoing example the consumption has been taken at only 100 million gallons per month; and at the very times when it would be desirable to fill up the reservoirs owing to the purity of the river there may be no water available for abstraction purposes. Nevertheless, there can be no question that, without risking a shortage of water, knowledge of the current quality of river water, on the average and the probable variations from that average, from time to time should assist in determining the abstraction of water to the best advantage from the point of view of purity.

On the other hand, it must be remembered that water is now known really to improve so much under storage, that it might be contended to be better to keep the reservoirs full even when the river water was of unsatisfactory quality, and so utilise storage to its fullest extent, rather than close the intakes and deplete the reservoirs with consequent curtailment of the number of days the water should be stored after the flood had subsided and river water was again admitted into the reservoirs.

Although we know the *average* reduction of colour effected during storage for certain known periods, it is obviously difficult, if not impossible, to say for each individual sample of river water what its condition will be after it has traversed a reservoir.

---

[1] A certain proportion (about 20%) of this, however, is of non-river water origin.

III THE QUESTION OF ABSTRACTION 45

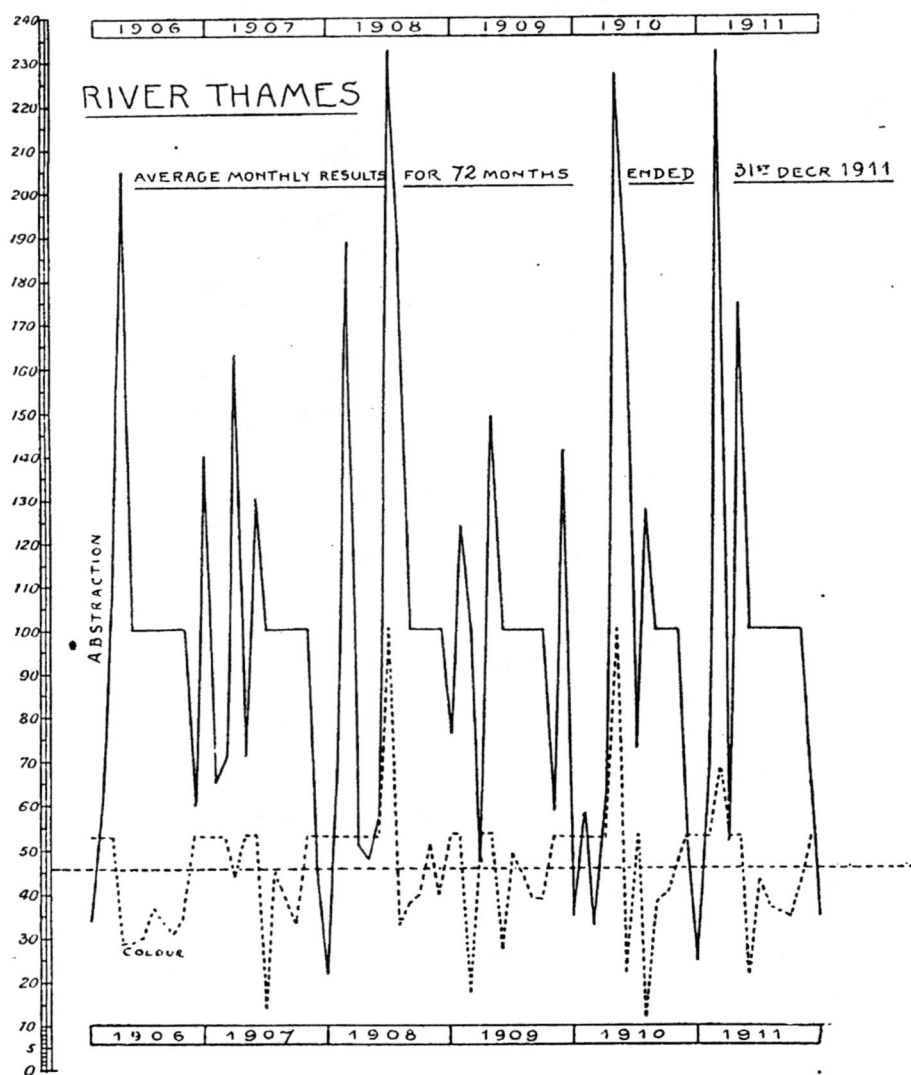

Fig. 17.

——————— = average monthly abstraction figures in million gallons for the 72 months ended December 31, 1911, the average for the whole period being at the rate of 100 million gallons per month.

- - - - - - - - - = average monthly colour results (colour × volume abstracted ÷ 100).

Here both the colour and abstraction vary (see text), the average for the former being 46 and for the latter at the rate of 100 million gallons per month.

Storage, 343·7 million gallons.

On comparing the best and worst *raw* river water results with the best and worst *stored* water results, although the percentage reduction in the two sets of cases is not widely dissimilar, the actual results are markedly different. For example, during the 12 months ended July, 1908, the best and worst river Thames colour results were 31 and 384 respectively. The comparable figures (*i.e.* best and worst) for the same water after storage in the Chelsea reservoirs were 18 and 200.

Judging from the writer's general experience of storage it would probably be safe to conclude, at all events, that the worst samples of river water may still be so highly coloured even *after* storage that it is a matter of great æsthetic importance always to aim at excluding from supply as much flood water as is reasonably practicable.

The matter, indeed, should be judged, *not* by the *percentage* improvement in the two cases, but by the *actual* state of the water after storage, corresponding on the one hand to flood, and on the other to non-flood, conditions of the river water.

It is of interest to note (Table XI.) the number of days when the colour of the River Thames was 200 or over and 100 or over [1] during the six years 1906–1911.

TABLE XI.—RIVER THAMES. COLOUR RESULTS. NUMBER OF DAYS THE COLOUR WAS 100 AND OVER AND OVER 200.

	Number of days the colour was	
	100 and over.	200 and over.
1906	38	10
1907	55	20
1908	49	11
1909	61	6
1910	85	24
1911	56	5
Average (appro.)	57	13

[1] Samples are not collected on Saturdays, Sundays or certain holidays. To overcome this difficulty, the figure for the blank days has been arrived at by taking the average of the preceding and succeeding samples actually examined.

The average colour (all results included) for the foregoing period (1906–1911) was 65·75, but if we exclude all samples yielding 100 (or over) and 200 (or over) the amended results become 48 and 59 respectively. It is evident from the table that even in the worst year only 24 days' storage would be required to enable the intakes to be closed whenever the colour results were 200 or over, even if the unsatisfactory results occurred in sequence. On the other hand, to close the intakes, when the colour results were 100 or over would have called for 85 days' storage in the worst year, 38 in the best year, and 57 in an average year.

It is impossible to lay down a fixed method of abstraction to suit all cases, but, for purposes of illustration, the months might be selected, during which the *filtered* water was noticeably free from colour, and the average colour of the *raw* water taken for the same period, using the latter figure as some sort of guide as to what volume should be abstracted during the rest of the year in order to obtain the best possible final results.

It will be said by the epidemiologist that colour is only of secondary importance, and that the behaviour of the microbes of water-borne disease in water of varying degrees of impurity is the essential factor for judging the question of abstraction.

There is much truth in this contention, but the physical quality of water is not only intrinsically of importance, but is the only means the public have of judging the quality of a water supply.

The writer's experience has been that there is not a very wide difference between the death-rate of pathogenic bacteria artificially added to river water of varying degrees of impurity. These microbes, however, are more likely to be present in river water during floods than under more normal conditions and so it seems prudent to exclude either partially or wholly, such flood water from storage reservoirs.

It must also be remembered that it is easier (for technical reasons) to isolate artificially-added pathogenic bacteria from a pure water, than from an impure water, although the difference in the two cases tends to disappear with the lapse of time.

It follows, therefore, that a negative result in the former case is apt to have a greater significance than in the latter; and perhaps the critic might even go so far as to suggest that, in the case of very impure waters, the failure subsequently to isolate artificially-added pathogenic bacteria was sometimes due, not to their real extinction, but to the technical difficulties involved in their isolation under these circumstances.

On the whole, however, the writer is convinced that artificially-added typhoid bacilli die fairly rapidly in stored water even when such water was of great initial impurity, but this view is not inconsistent with belief in the desirability of avoiding impure flood water for storage purposes.

If one might predicate from the actual quality of water as delivered to London consumers, using the B. coli test as an indicator, there can be no doubt that during the winter flood months of the year, the results tend to deteriorate to a considerable extent. This is illustrated in Fig. 18, and the writer is of opinion that the observed results are largely due to the inclusion of flood water in the storage reservoirs.

In conclusion, it must be remembered that many water works unfortunately depend almost solely on heavy floods to replenish their depleted reservoirs, and in such cases it is obvious that questions of quality must be subordinated to questions of quantity.

There remain, however, it is to be feared, not a few instances of waterworks, which might improve the quality

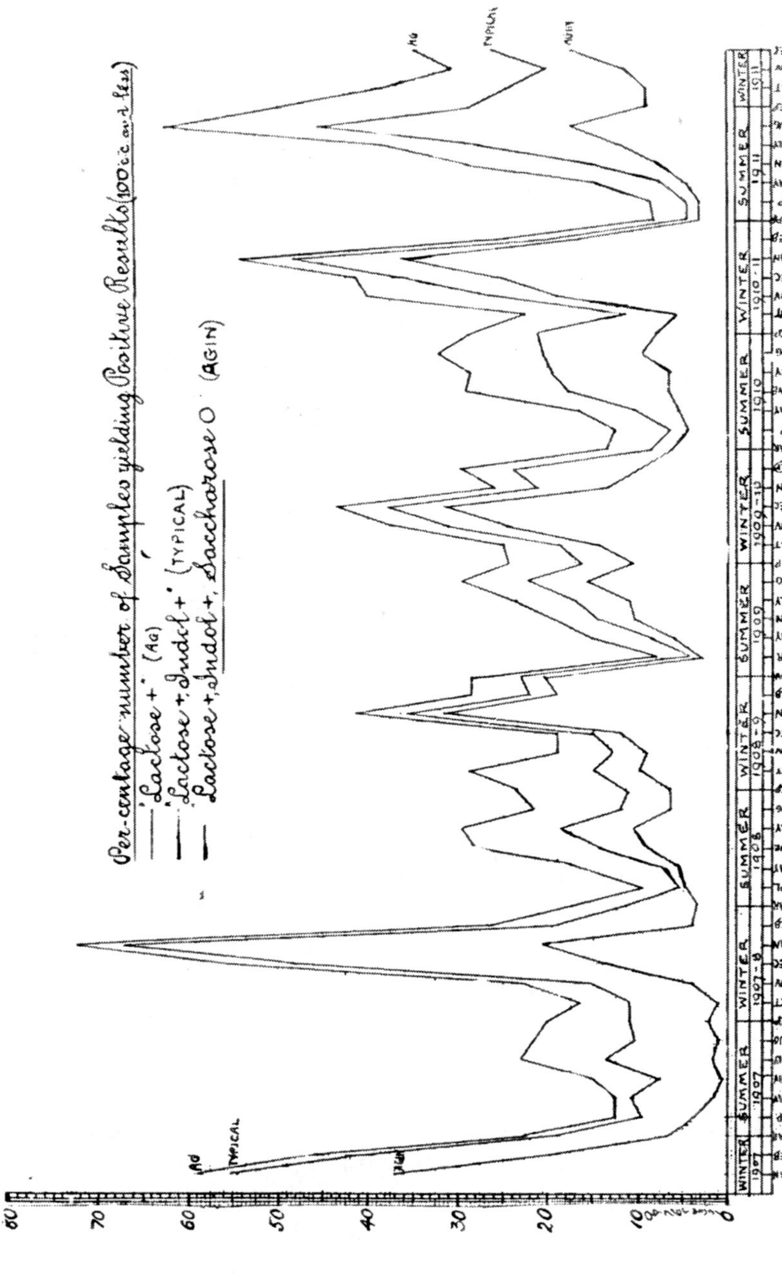

III THE QUESTION OF ABSTRACTION 49

Fig. 18.—*B. coli Test. All London Waters. Sixty Months, ended December 31st, 1911. 35,325 Samples.*

of their supply by an applied study of this important question of abstraction.

In some cases where storage is absent or inadequate it is impossible to avoid the use of flood water, and in these circumstances some supplementary process of purification ought to be interposed between the river and the storage reservoirs (if of insufficient size) or the river and the filter beds where no storage exists, or alternatively, between the reservoirs and the filter beds.[1]

---

[1] Reference may be made to the writer's Third Research Report on Storage, Metropolitan Water Board.

CHAPTER IV

SUPPLEMENTARY PROCESSES OF WATER PURIFICATION.

THE so-called mechanical or pressure filters worked either with or without a coagulant may be used with great advantage. This, for example, is the preliminary process carried on at York (River Ouse) where, for various reasons, it was decided to select this system in preference to storage reservoirs.

According to the published returns, excellent results were obtained[1] and the writer has had sufficient experience of pressure filters to have faith in this method of treatment. Frequent tests of the efficiency of the York mechanical gravity filters during a period of three years (without the use of a coagulant) showed the following satisfactory reduction in the number of bacteria.

		Reduction of bacteria per cent.	
No. 1 filter	... ...	86·4	
,, 2 ,,	... ...	86·9	
,, 3 ,,	... ...	86·2	Average
,, 4 ,,	... ...	87·0	86·27
,, 5 ,,	... ...	86·5	
,, 6 ,,	... ...	85·9	
,, 7 ,,	... ...	85·1	

Quite recently Chester has decided not only to construct storage reservoirs, but also to interpose pressure filters between the River Dee and these reservoirs.

[1] Presidential Address to Association of Water Engineers, 1910 "Mechanical Gravity Filters," by W. H. Humphreys, C.E., York.

Alternatively, small pre-storage settlement reservoirs may be placed between the river and the large storage reservoir proper and they may be worked with or without a coagulant.

The advantages of passing raw river water through small reservoirs antecedent to storage in large reservoirs is seen by the results of the following experiments carried out in connection with the New River and East London (Sunbury) supplies :—

New River :—At the Hornsey Works there is a small storage reservoir having a capacity of about seven million gallons. During the period under observation about eleven million gallons were passing daily through this reservoir, the nominal storage thus being only fifteen to sixteen hours.

The average results may be summarised as follows :—

TABLE XII.
EXPERIMENT 1.—HORNSEY (NEW RIVER) EXPERIMENTS.
March 10th to April 25th ; May 2nd to May 24th ; and May 29th to June 10th, 1910.

Description of the Sample.	Average number of Bacteria per c.c. (Agar at 37° C.)	Parts per 100,000.				Colour (mm. brown 2-ft. tube).
		Ammoniacal Nitrogen.	Albuminoid Nitrogen.	Oxy. abs. fr.permanganate.	Turbidity.	
Inlet (New River) water to Hornsey Reservoir. (Samples : 47 chemical and 52 bacteriological)	92·2	0·0030	0·0093	0·0750	1·33	34
Outlet water from Hornsey Reservoir. (Samples : 47 chemical and 52 bacteriological)	56·0	0·0024	0·0089	0·0708	1·04	33
Percentage Improvement	39·2	20·0	4·3	5·6	21·8	2·9

It is apparent that the continuous flow of the New River water through a reservoir, holding even less than a day's supply, produced a considerable improvement in the quality of the water, especially as judged by the reduction in the number of bacteria, and by the ammoniacal nitrogen and turbidity tests.

PROCESSES OF WATER PURIFICATION

TABLE XIII.
EXPERIMENT 2.—HORNSEY (NEW RIVER) EXPERIMENTS.
October 13th to December 2nd, 1910.

Description of the Sample.	Average number of Bacteria per c.c. (Agar at 37° C.)	Parts per 100,000.				Colour (mm. brown 2-ft. tube).
		Ammoniacal Nitrogen.	Albuminoid Nitrogen.	Oxy. abs. fr. permanganate.	Turbidity.	
Inlet (New River), Hornsey Reservoir. (Samples: 37 chemical and 37 bacteriological)	188	0·0038	0·0068	0·0718	2·17	47
Outlet water from Hornsey Reservoir. (Samples: 37 chemical and 37 bacteriological)	108	0·0036	0·0062	0·0631	1·55	39
Percentage Improvement	42·5	5·26	8·82	12·12	28·57	17·02

East London (Thames) Supply:—Here the reservoir has a capacity of only five million gallons. During the period covered by the experiments, about eight million gallons were passed daily through it, the nominal storage thus being only about fifteen hours.

TABLE XIV.
EXPERIMENT 3.—SUNBURY (THAMES) EXPERIMENTS.

Bacteriological:—March 22nd to April 15th; and April 27th to May 10th, 1910.
Chemical:—April 7th to April 15th; and April 27th to May 10th, 1910.

Description of Sample.	Average number of Bacteria per c.c. (Agar at 37° C.)	Parts per 100,000.				Colour (mm. brown 2-ft. tube).
		Ammoniacal Nitrogen.	Albuminoid Nitrogen.	Oxy. abs. fr. permanganate.	Turbidity.	
Inlet (Thames) water to Sunbury Reservoir. (Samples: 18 chemical and 27 bacteriological)	155	0·0026	0·0130	0·1304	1·54	43
Outlet water from Sunbury Reservoir. (Samples: 18 chemical and 27 bacteriological)	111	0·0021	0·0126	0·1246	1·42	41
Percentage Improvement	28·4	19·2	3·08	4·45	7·8	4·65

The improved condition of the Thames water even after only a few hours' continuous flow settlement is well shown by the foregoing results, especially as regards number of bacteria and amount of ammoniacal nitrogen.

The results given in experiments 1, 2, and 3, are illustrated in Fig. 19 (p. 55).

The advantages of using coagulants, antecedent to the storage of raw river water in large reservoirs may now be considered.

Apart from the questions of cost and of altering the mineral composition of a water, practically any desired result can be attained by the use of certain coagulants, e.g. alumino-ferric, as the following experiment shows :—

TABLE XV.

ALUMINO-FERRIC.

16 parts per 100,000 parts.   16 lbs. per 10,000 gallons.   6d. per 10,000 gallons.
Average of three experiments.   Quiescent settlement.

Sample.	Bacteria per c.c. (Agar 37° C.)	Percentage Improvement.	Colour m.m. brown 2 ft. tube.	Percentage Improvement.	Permanganate, 3 hrs. at 80° F. parts per 100,000.	Percentage Improvement.	Turbidity (saccharated carb. of Iron) Parts per 100,000.	Percentage Improvement.
Raw Thames water before treatment...	1390	—	217	—	0·4395	—	8·9	—
Raw Thames water after treatment...	40	97·1	31	85·7	0·1103	74·9	0·75	91·6

It is to be noted that not only are the results excellent on the basis of percentage improvement but also that the actual state of the " treated " water was remarkably good.

Next, dealing with more practical doses of coagulant, the following results are of interest :—

Raw Thames water was passed through the East London Waterworks Reservoir at Sunbury at the rate of about eight million gallons per day. (Nominally about 15 hours' storage.)   March 22nd to May 10th.
From May 23rd to June 28th (both inclusive) *raw* Thames water was passed through the reservoir at a slower rate, viz., about 5½ million gallons per day (about 21·8 hours' storage).

PROCESSES OF WATER PURIFICATION

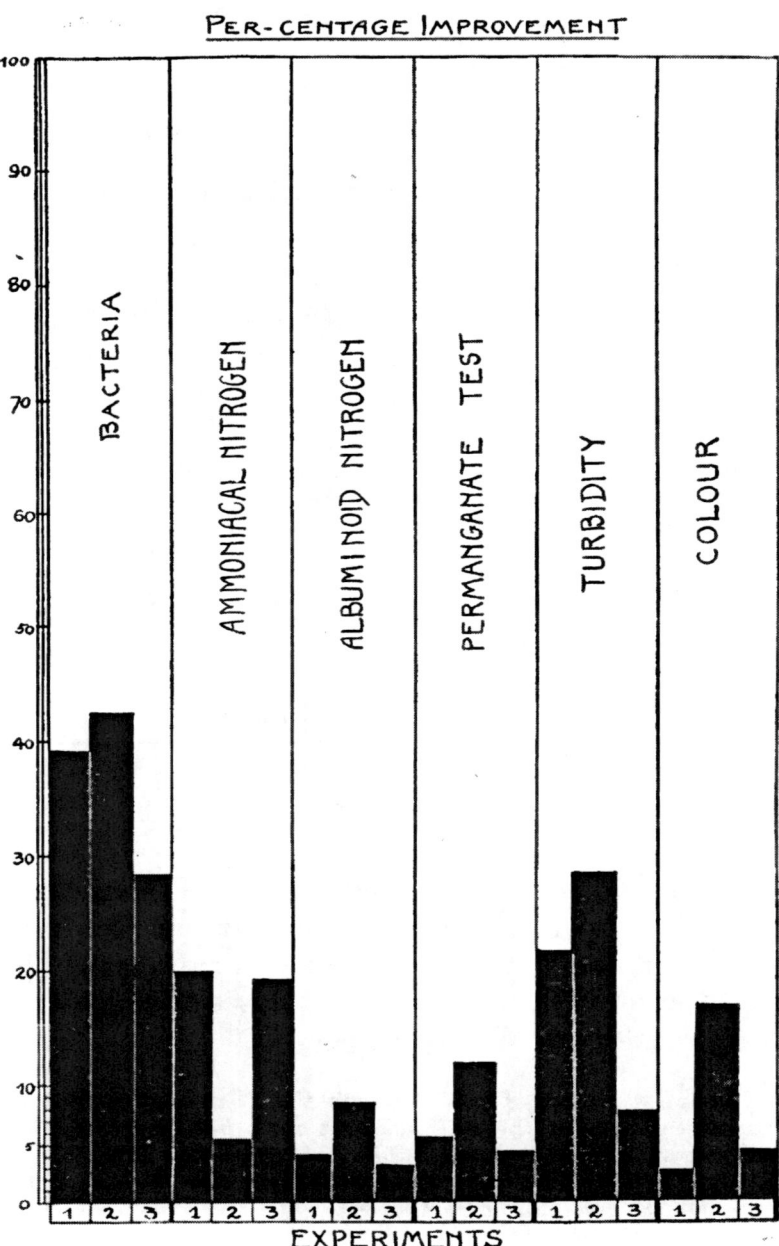

Fig. 19

PERIOD 1.—From March 22nd to April 15th, 1910 (both inclusive), no precipitant was used.

PERIOD 2.—From April 16th to April 26th, 1910 (both inclusive), alumino-ferric[1] was used in the proportion of about 3 parts of alumino-ferric to 100,000 parts of water (3 lbs. to 10,000 gallons).

PERIOD 3.—From April 27th to May 10th, 1910 (both inclusive), no precipitant was used.

PERIOD 4.—From May 23rd to May 27th, 1910 (both inclusive), no precipitant was used.

PERIOD 5.—From May 30th to June 14th, 1910 (both inclusive), alumino-ferric was used in the following proportions :—

May 30th to June 5th, about 2 parts per 100,000.
June 6th to June 8th, about 2·4 parts per 100,000.
June 9th to June 14th, about 2·85 parts per 100,000.

That is, about two or three lbs. of alumino-ferric were added to every 10,000 gallons of water.

PERIOD 6.—From June 15th to June 28th (both inclusive), the amount of alumino-ferric was raised to about 5·7 (or roughly double) parts per 100,000 (5·7 lbs. per 10,000 gallons of water).

During the first period when no precipitant was used the number of bacteria was reduced by *simple sedimentation* from an average of 178 to 129 (27·6 per cent.).

During the second period, when alumino-ferric was used (about three parts per 100,000), the percentage reduction was 63·6 (162 reduced to 59 bacteria per c.c.).

During the third period, when the precipitant was no longer in use, the percentage reduction fell to 31 (117 reduced to 81 bacteria per c.c.).

During the fourth period, when the rate of flow was reduced[2] and still no precipitant was used, the percentage reduction was 21·8 per cent. (78 reduced to 61 bacteria per c.c.).

During the fifth period, when alumino-ferric was again used (about two—three parts per 100,000), the percentage reduction was 49·8 (395 reduced to 198 bacteria per c.c.).

During the sixth period, when the dose of precipitant was doubled, the percentage reduction was 70·1 (678 reduced to 203 bacteria per c.c.).

The results are shown in Table XVI. (p. 57).

---

[1] This is really a commercial form of sulphate of alumina, containing some iron. The sample used in these experiments contained 15·99 per cent. Al_2O_3 (including the iron).

[2] For some unexplained reason the results were less good, instead of being better, with the reduced rate of flow.

PROCESSES OF WATER PURIFICATION

TABLE XVI.

EAST LONDON (SUNBURY) BACTERIOLOGICAL RESULTS.

Period and Description of Samples.	Average number of Bacteria per c.c. Agar at 37° C.	Percentage Reduction.
PERIOD 1.—No coagulant. Inlet Water.—17 samples Outlet Water.—17 samples	178 129	— 27·6
PERIOD 2.—Coagulant 3 parts to 100,000 parts of water. Inlet Water.—7 samples Outlet Water.—7 samples	162 59	— 63·6
PERIOD 3.—No coagulant. Inlet Water.—10 samples Outlet Water.—10 samples	117 81	— 31
PERIOD 4.—No coagulant. Inlet Water.—5 samples Outlet Water.—5 samples	78 61	— 21·8
PERIOD 5.—From 2 to 2·85 parts coagulant to 100,000 parts of water. Inlet Water.—16 samples Outlet Water.—16 samples	395 198	— 49·8
PERIOD 6.—5·7 parts coagulant to 100,000 parts of water. Inlet Water.—14 samples Outlet Water.—14 samples	678 203	— 70·1

There can be no question, therefore, that, bacteriologically, there is considerable advantage to be gained by even less than twenty-four hours' continuous flow settlement, and that when alumino-ferric is added, still better results are obtained.

The actual chemical results are shown in Table XVII. (p. 58).

The percentage chemical and bacteriological improvement is shown in Table XVIII. (p. 59).

Taking the chemical and bacteriological results together, there can be no doubt that the beneficial effects observed in connection with simple continuous flow settlement could be considerably enhanced by the use of coagulants.

Unfortunately the experiments did not happen to have

been carried out during the flood months of the year. Had it been otherwise the results would in all probability have been much more striking from the point of view of percentage reduction, although doubtless it would have been necessary to increase the dose of coagulant.

TABLE XVII.

EAST LONDON (SUNBURY) CHEMICAL RESULTS.

Parts per 100,000.

Period and Description of Samples.	Ammoniacal Nitrogen.	Albuminoid Nitrogen.	Oxygen absorbed from Permanganate.	Turbidity.	Colour.
PERIOD 1.—No coagulant.					
Inlet Water.—8 samples	0·0023	0·0127	0·1173	1·64	39
Outlet Water.—8 samples	0·0020	0·0118	0·1054	1·41	37
PERIOD 2.—Coagulant 3 parts to 100,000 parts of water.					
Inlet Water.—7 samples	0·0042	0·0144	0·1580	1·96	45
Outlet Water.—7 samples	0·0033	0·0119	0·1193	1·33	36
PERIOD 3.—No coagulant.					
Inlet Water.—10 samples	0·0029	0·0131	0·1409	1·46	46
Outlet Water.—10 samples	0·0023	0·0133	0·1399	1·42	44
PERIOD 4.—No coagulant.					
Inlet Water.—5 samples	0·0055	0·0175	0·1651	1·38	48
Outlet Water.—5 samples	0·0068	0·0215	0·1608	1·48	44
PERIOD 5.—From 2 to 2·85 parts coagulant to 100,000 parts of water.					
Inlet Water.—16 samples	0·0083	0·0211	0·2315	2·80	68
Outlet Water.—16 samples	0·0071	0·0198	0·1768	1·86	55
PERIOD 6.—5·7 parts coagulant to 100,000 parts of water.					
Inlet Water.—14 samples	0·0042	0·0222	0·3662	2·77	78
Outlet Water.—14 samples	0·0058	0·0216	0·3032	1·73	64

As regards cost, the coagulant used in these experiments was alumino-ferric (15·99 per cent. of Al_2O_3, including the iron), which cost £3 12s. 6d. per ton. Bought in larger quantities, no doubt the cost would be less, say £3 10s. 0d. per ton.

In the experiments, two to six parts per 100,000 parts were used, that is, two to six lbs. per 10,000 gallons.

Each lb. of the material cost (on the basis of £3 10s. 0d. per ton) 1·5 farthings, so that the experiments cost three farthings (¾d.) to twopence halfpenny (2½d.) per 10,000 gallons of water treated.

As sand filtration is said to cost only 1d. per 10,000 gallons, the use of a coagulant as a supplementary process would thus increase the total cost of purification to a

TABLE XVIII.
PERCENTAGE REDUCTION.
Outlet as compared with *Inlet* water.

Description.	Ammoniacal Nitrogen.	Albuminoid Nitrogen.	Oxygen absorbed from permanganate.	Turbidity.	Colour.	Per cent. Reduction. No. of Bacteria (Agar at 37° C.)
PERIOD 1.—No precipitant used	13·04	7·09	10·14	14·02	5·13	27·6
PERIOD 2.—Aluminoferric used, about 3 pts. per 100,000	21·43	17·36	24·49	32·14	20·0	63·6
PERIOD 3.—No precipitant used	20·69	Increase	0·71	2·74	4·35	31
PERIOD 4.—No precipitant used	Increase	Increase	2·60	Increase	8·33	21·8
PERIOD 5.—Aluminoferric used, about 2·3 pts. per 100,000	14·46	6·16	23·63	33·57	19·12	49·8
PERIOD 6.—Aluminoferric used, nearly 6 pts. per 100,000	Increase	2·7	17·20	37·55	17·95	70·1

considerable extent. But for emergency purposes, a much higher cost than the above might be regarded as relatively unimportant. The question of dose is one of great difficulty. If too little of the coagulant is used, the beneficial effects may be practically *nil*, and therefore the process would be wasteful, or at all events, the improvement might be so slight as not to be commensurate with the cost involved. On the other hand, obviously any increase of the dose in excess of actual requirements is economically undesirable. On the whole, however, it is better to face the cost of a dose which is certain to be markedly effective, than by being too niggardly, to run the risk of spending money without effecting any very tangible result. The effective dose varies not only with the amount of suspended matter in the water, but also with its character. Less than about three parts per 100,000 (3 lbs. per 10,000 gallons) is usually ineffective with *raw* Thames water or not sufficiently effective to justify completely the expenditure involved.[1] With very bad waters a much larger dose may be required, but, apart from the question of cost, even the foulest water can be brought to almost any pitch of perfection by the use of enough of the coagulant.

The advantages of pre-storage-settlement reservoirs, especially if so arranged as to permit of the use of coagulants would thus appear to be considerable. Although recommended chiefly in conjunction with storage proper, these small reservoirs would be of real value in those cases where river water is taken directly on to the filter beds, for the reason that during floods coagulants could be judiciously used to counteract the evil effects of the use of storm water for filtration purposes.

The author has had no personal experience of the Puech-Chabal Multiple System of pre-filters, but remarkably good results appear to have been obtained by their use. The principle involved is that of rapid filtration by decantation through a series of filters consisting of materials of diminishing grade (very coarse to very fine). It is claimed that complete clarification is obtained. A strong point in favour of this system is that the whole of the material in the filters is in full action and not merely

---

[1] These remarks apply, of course, to waters about to be stored. In the case of waters about to be filtered, the dose may be considerably reduced, and yet good results obtained. Here, the coagulant and the filter particles combine to produce the best results.

the surface layers, as is solely or largely the case with most filters.

Another supplementary process of water purification recently put forward by the writer is known as the "Excess Lime Method," but it seems desirable to consider this matter under the head of sterilisation processes.

CHAPTER V

STERILISATION PROCESSES WITH SPECIAL REFERENCE TO THE "EXCESS LIME" METHOD

EARLY in 1905 the author [1] sterilised the Lincoln Water Supply (population above 50,000) by means of "Chloros." [2] The dose varied according to circumstances, but was usually 1 to 100,000 (about 1 in 1 million in terms of available chlorine).

The conditions were far from ideal, as the contaminated river water, which often contained much suspended matter and a good deal of organic matter, was run, practically speaking, directly on to the filter beds; the consequence being that larger doses of chloros were required than are found to be necessary in general cases.

The treatment was continued up to 1911, when a new supply was introduced. The best series of results occurred during a period of about ten months, when 62 *samples collected consecutively contained no typical B. coli even in 100 c.c. of water.*

As regards dose (in terms of available chlorine), the usual limits are from 1 in 1 million to 1 in 5 millions. With a water containing a good deal of organic matter, and

---

[1] In conjunction with Dr. McGowan, who controlled the chemical part of the investigation. For further information reference may be made to the Fifth Report of the Royal Commission on Sewage Disposal, Appendix IV.

[2] Chloros is an alkaline solution of sodium hypochlorite containing about 10–15% of available chlorine. Bleaching powder (about 33% available chlorine) is equally suitable.

subject to considerable fluctuations in composition, it is not always an easy task to secure uniform sterilisation and invariable absence of objectionable taste.

Well waters containing but little organic matter and of fairly constant composition lend themselves readily to treatment. The following is an example of the results that may be achieved with this class of water :—A particular well in the series of experiments is situated in the Upper Chalk. The water has to be filtered, as, apart from its constant liability to contamination, it is occasionally visibly turbid. The chloros (dose 1 in 200,000 to 1 in 400,000)[1] was mixed with the water as it flowed on to the sand filters. The average chemical analysis of the well water, before treatment, was as follows :—

	Parts per 100,000.
Ammoniacal Nitrogen	0·0003
Albuminoid ,,	0·0022
Oxidised ,,	0·23
Chlorine	1·80
Oxygen absorbed from Permanganate (3 hrs. 80°F.)	0·0134
Total Hardness	28·47
Permanent Hardness	5·97

The bacteriological results, before and after treatment, were as under :—

During a period of one year's working, 102 samples of the water both before and after treatment (collected at approximately equal intervals) were examined bacteriologically. Out of these 102 samples, 83 contained typical B. coli in 100 c.c. (or less) *before* treatment, whereas *after* treatment only 8 yielded positive results, and *for more than five consecutive months the results were uniformly negative even in* 100 c.c.

The treatment of the Lincoln water early in 1905 has been followed since about 1907 by similar forms of

---

[1] The chloros contained from 10–15% of available chlorine.

treatment in the United States, and apparently with excellent results, although occasionally difficulty has been experienced, in obtaining successful bacteriological results, without imparting a slight mawkish taste to the treated water. It also appears to have been insufficiently realised that to obtain the best results with the smallest dose, *time is required.*

The following extract from Hooker's treatise on "Chloride of Lime in Sanitation" (1913) shows that some at least of the American authorities are evidently not fully cognisant of what took place at Lincoln in 1905 :

"The use of extremely minute quantities of chloride of lime has offered a very practical and simple solution of the sanitary troubles of nearly every city water supply. The most astonishing part of all this is that the true import of these facts has only been realised within the last four years.

"As a practical process it dates from 1908, when Mr. G. A. Johnson, of New York City, was called in to remedy some serious trouble in the water purification at the Chicago Stock Yards. The filtered water of Bubbly Creek contains a large amount of sewage, and it had been purified by a process of filtration in conjunction with copper sulphate, but it was the complaint of the large stock shippers that animals drinking this filtered water made less gain in weight than when city water was supplied to them. Under pressure of a lawsuit brought by the City of Chicago against the Union Stock Yards Company, the contractors for the filter plant were, however, enabled to fulfil their guarantees by Mr. Johnson substituting chloride of lime for the copper sulphate. The treatment raised the quality of the sewage-laden water from the Creek far above that of the Chicago City water, as was shown in its low percentage of cases where B. coli were found.

	B. coli. found.
Bubbly Creek, treated	0·34% of cases.
Chicago City water	12·8% ,,

"The hypochlorite was added 7½ hours before filtration ; the addition after filtration did not give as satisfactory results. The amount of chloride of lime added was forty-five pounds per 1,000,000 gallons.

"Thus a new epoch in the annals of water purification dates from Mr. Johnson's success at Chicago."

In the United Kingdom, things have not gone altogether smoothly, there being among the public an almost invincible repugnance to the use of chemicals (except lime) in connection with water supply.

It is easy to carry conservatism too far in these matters, and more than one case could be quoted where a more tolerant attitude would have saved the ratepayers large sums of money.

There are, of course other methods of sterilising water, *e.g.*, by heat, ozone, ultra-violet rays. Sterilisation by heat is the ideal method bacteriologically, but it is too costly a process to meet with general acceptance. Ozone can be successfully employed for the destruction of the microbes of water-borne disease, but it labours under some disadvantages. The capital cost involved is serious, the working cost is considerable, and the process is not well adapted for waters containing much oxidisable and suspended matters. Sterilisation by means of ultra-violet rays has many advocates, but the feasibility of the method on a large scale has still to be demonstrated.

It is convenient here to consider the "excess lime method" of sterilisation, described by the writer in his Eighth Research Report to the Metropolitan Water Board.

The Excess Lime Method

In the ordinary lime softening process as commonly practised, quicklime or slaked lime is added to the total bulk of the water to be softened. It is always in amount purposely calculated to be rather less than is needed to combine with the bicarbonates present (*i.e.*, just short of removing the whole of the temporary hardness).

If on testing with phenolphthalein or silver nitrate solution, a pink or brown colour develops with these two tests respectively, this indicates an excess of lime, which is always to be carefully avoided. When, however, such an event happens, the dose of lime has either to be reduced at once or carbonic acid pumped into the water, so as to combine with the excess of free lime.

Apart from the fact that any excess of lime re-hardens the water, it is not desirable to give the consumer lime-water to drink. In short, in practice, a purely *chemical* standard being kept in view, the utmost care has, wittingly or unwittingly, been exercised so to arrange the process as to prevent any *true bactericidal* action taking place, by accurately treating the whole of the water to be softened with *less* than the amount of lime required to combine with the bicarbonates, so as to form an insoluble and bacteriologically inert carbonate of lime.

In the method now under consideration, part of the water is purposely *overdosed* with lime so as to bring about a known *bactericidal* effect, and then, after a suitable interval this is mixed with enough "untreated," *i.e.*, unlimed, water to combine with the excess of lime. Anticipating what follows, it may be convenient at this stage to give an example :

(1) 15 lbs. of quicklime costing 1·5 pence (1½d.) added to 7,500 gallons of raw River Thames water (1 in 5,000) would suffice to kill the B. coli present in the water within 5–24 hours. The liquid, being decidedly alkaline, must next be neutralised.

(2) *Not less* that 2,500 gallons of *adequately* stored water (*i.e.*, a bacteriologically "safe" water)[1] must subsequently be added for neutralisation purposes.

(3) The resulting mixture (10,000 gallons) antecedent to final filtration would be epidemiologically safe, and its initial hardness would be reduced about 65 per cent.

(4) Of course, *any larger* proportion than 25 per cent. of stored water could be used, the only difference being that the mixture of lime-treated and stored water would be "softened" to a correspondingly less extent.

(5) The only essential points to remember are that 1 part of quicklime is needed to over-combine with the bicarbonates and to sterilise 5,000 parts of River Thames

---

[1] For evidence of this, *see* Chapter VI.

raw water, and that a sufficiency of stored water must be added subsequently to neutralise the excess of lime.

Dose of Lime.—As regards the dose of lime required for sterilisation purposes, this depends primarily on the degree of temporary hardness of the water, the degree of its impurity, and the duration of contact.

Table XIX shows the dose necessary to sterilise Loch Katrine water, notoriously known to be an exceedingly "soft" and pure water. So as artificially to render it most impure, bacteriologically, 1 per cent. of crude sewage was *purposely* added to the water before lime treatment.

TABLE XIX.—STERILISATION OF LOCH KATRINE WATER.

L. Katrine water (+1 per cent. sewage) CaO.			+ = B. coli alive ; − = B. coli dead.		
			Duration of contact.		
			1 hour.	5 hours.	24 hours.
1 A	1 in	5,000	− 10 and 1 c.c.	− 10 and 1 c.c.	− 100, 10 and 1 c.c.
1 B	,,	,,	,,	,,	,,
2 A	1 in	10,000	+10 and 1 c.c.	,,	,,
2 B	,,	,,	,,	,,	,,
3 A	1 in	20,000	,,	+10 −1 c.c.	,,
3 B	,,	,,	,,	− 10 and 1 c.c.	,,
4 A	1 in	40,000	,,	+10 and 1 c.c.	,,
4 B	,,	,,	,,	,,	,,
5 A	1 in	80,000	,,	,,	+100 and 10 −1 c.c.
5 B	,,	,,	,,	,,	,,
6 A	1 in	160,000	,,	,,	+100, 10 and 1 c.c.
6 B	,,	,,	,,	,,	,,

It will be seen that a dose of from 1 to 10,000 to 1 to 20,000 was effective in 5 hours, and a dose of 1 to 40,000 in 24 hours.

With *hard* waters, on the other hand, the dose of lime must of course be increased considerably, as the bicarbonates render the lime inert as a bactericidal agent. In practice, indeed, it is desirable to add even more lime than would seem to be indicated on theoretical grounds.

With *very soft* waters the bactericidal dose is, as has been shown, very small, but the author has found with hard waters (especially if impure) and with sewage, that to effect sterilisation the amount of active lime left in these liquids, after neutralising the substances which combine with the lime must be in excess of the apparent bactericidal dose.

Table XX illustrates the germicidal action of quicklime (1 in 5,000) in the case of the hard raw Thames River water.

TABLE XX.—STERILISATION OF THAMES RIVER WATER.

Duration of contact.	Number of samples of *raw* Thames water.	Number of tests made.	Results as regards B. coli. + = alive. − = dead.	Remarks.
1 hour	28	43	In 1 case − 10 and 1 c.c. In 2 cases + 10 − 1 c.c. In 40 cases + 10 and 1 c.c.	B. coli alive in 42 out of 43 cases.
5 hours	20	33	In 3 cases + 10 and 1 c.c. In 4 cases + 10 − 1 c.c. In 26 cases − 10 and 1 c.c.	B. coli dead in 26 out of 33 cases.
24 hours	28	43	In 1 case + 10 − 1 c.c. In 42 cases − 10 and 1 c.c.	B. coli dead in 42 out of 43 cases.

It will be seen that in nearly all cases B. coli was killed either in 5 or in 24 hours.

For the purpose of contrast and comparison, a further set of experiments with raw Thames water, purposely inoculated with 1 per cent. of crude sewage was also undertaken. The additional number of B. coli thus added to the river water was estimated to be about 1,000 per c.c.

The results are shown below (Table XXI., p. 69).

It is apparent that the effective dose was 1 in 5,000 (5 to 24 hours' contact), but that a dose of 1 in 7,500 was ineffective.

Speaking generally, the bactericidal dose with hard waters would seem to be rather less than 1 to 5,000 and with *very soft* waters rather more than 1 to 50,000.

Even so grossly impure a liquid as crude sewage can be successfully sterilised by means of lime. According to the author's experiments, London sewage requires a dose varying from 1 to 1,500 to 1 to 2,500.

Neutralisation of the Excess of Lime.—It is obvious that the treated water requires further treatment to get

TABLE XXI.—STERILISATION OF ARTIFICIALLY POLLUTED THAMES RIVER WATER.

Duration of contact.	One part quicklime (about 75 per cent. CaO) in :—	
	5,000 parts sewage-inoculated raw Thames water. *A.*	7,500 parts sewage-inoculated raw Thames water. *B.*
1 hour	B. coli alive in 10 and 1 c.c. in all 10 experiments.	B. coli alive in 10 and 1 c.c. in all 10 experiments.
5 hours	B. coli alive in 10 and 1 c.c. in 2 experiments. B. coli alive in 10 but not in 1 c.c. in 4 experiments. B. coli dead in 10 and 1 c.c. in 4 experiments.	B. coli alive in 10 and 1 c.c. in all the 10 experiments.
24 hours	In 1 experiment B. coli alive in 10 but not in 1 c.c. ; in the remaining 9 experiments B. coli dead in 10 and 1 c.c.	B. coli alive in 10 and 1 c.c. in 4 experiments. B. coli alive in 10 but not in 1 c.c. in the remaining 6 experiments.

rid of the excess of lime. The procedure to be adopted may have to be varied according to the original quality of the water undergoing treatment.

With *very soft* waters the excess of lime in the water, after sterilisation, is so small that it might be found best to treat the whole of the water (instead of only a part) and then to neutralise it with carbonic, sulphuric, or other suitable acid, or possibly it might suffice to filter the water through a percolating filter.

With *hard* waters, it is easy to neutralise the excess of lime by the addition of " untreated " water. For example, in the case of the raw River Thames water (sterilised by adding 1 part of quicklime to 5,000 parts of water) the "treated" portion must receive not less than 25 per cent. of "untreated" water (*stored* water in this particular instance) to effect neutralisation.

Treatment of the water used for neutralisation purposes.—The question naturally arises as to the sterilisation of this water added for neutralisation purposes. According to the author's experience the answer is that *stored* (*i.e.*, unfiltered) water could safely be used for this purpose. Alternatively, and so as to provide the neutralising water, active chlorine (hypochlorites) or ozone could be employed.

The usual objection to ozone is that of cost, but here only a part of the total supply would require ozonisation—the total cost being reduced proportionately. The common objection to "active chlorine" (hypochlorites) is the difficulty of sterilising a water containing a variable amount of oxidisable matter without giving the water a faint taste, and of knowing how best to get rid subsequently of the slight excess of chlorine.

Here also, as only a proportion of the total supply would require chlorination, any question of taste would be practically eliminated and any slight excess of chlorine would be absorbed by the organic matter in the "lime treated" water.

The cost of the process varies according to the degree of temporary hardness of the water. Lime containing at least 75 per cent. CaO can be bought wholesale for about 1d. per 10 lbs., and to sterilise a water like London water, about 1 part would be required per 5,000 parts, or 10 lbs. per 5,000 gallons, or 2,000 lbs. (costing about 16s.) per million gallons. As, however, the lime sterilisation process is applicable only to a proportion of the whole (say three-quarters), the cost would be correspondingly less (say 12s.) The hypochlorite-sterilisation would be considerably cheaper (say 1s. to 10s. per million gallons) than this, but, of course, the advocates of " water softening " might assert (rightly or wrongly) that the saving in soap and fuel consumption more than counter-balanced the apparent economy effected by the chlorine process.

With very soft waters, the cost of lime would be greatly reduced, perhaps to as much as only one-fifth to one-tenth of this estimate. With very hard waters containing very little oxidisable matter the cost of sterilisation by means of hypochlorite is proportionately very small, but with very soft waters containing much oxidisable matter the lime process may turn out actually to be cheaper.

This, however, is only the cost of the lime used. Account would have to be taken for tanks and usually for filtering the finally treated water together with the cost of preparation of the neutralising water. The periodical removal of the sludge from the tanks would also entail additional expense. These are matters which so obviously encroach on the domain of the water engineer that no apology is needed for merely mentioning them in passing.

The circumstances under which the Excess Lime Process appears to be specially attractive are as follows:—

(1) A water, bacteriologically impure, which in any event it is proposed to soften.[1]

(2) A supply hard, as well as impure, situated in a district badly circumstanced as regards alternative supplies.

(3) A river supply contaminated (or liable to be contaminated) having scarcely any available storage accommodation, and necessitating for waterworks purposes the occasional use of flood water, with mere sand-filtration as a safeguard.

(4) Wells not sufficiently pure to be used without some

---

[1] As regards water supplies already undergoing softening treatment, it ought not to prove a very difficult or costly matter so to modify the existing plant as to give effect to the principles laid down in this chapter.

form of treatment, and concerning which some doubt exists as to whether storage *plus* subsequent filtration would prove an altogether satisfactory remedy.[1]

(5) Surface waters unduly "soft" and not free from the risk of undesirable pollution. The River Dee is a case in point, and it is of interest to note that the Medical Officer of Health and the Waterworks Engineer of Aberdeen were so impressed with the results of the author's experiments that they persuaded their Town Council to sanction the carrying out of an experimental trial on the whole of the Aberdeen water supply ($6\frac{3}{4}$ million gallons a day). The experiment lasted three weeks, the dose of CaO being 3 parts per 100,000. The results were so highly satisfactory bacteriologically that the Aberdeen Town Council has now decided on an annual expenditure of £1,270 for liming purposes. An excellent account ("Clarification of Water Supplies by the Excess Lime Method") of the Aberdeen experiments by Dr. James Watt will be found in the *Journal of State Medicine*, August, 1913, No. 8, vol. xxi.

(6) Mixed supplies, part being impure bacteriologically and the rest above suspicion; the former to be lime-treated and the latter used for neutralisation purposes.

Some of the advantages attending the use of lime instead of other sterilising agents may now be mentioned.

One great advantage of the use of lime is that it is "hallowed by precedent" and that practically all drinking waters already contain lime salts. There is, indeed, no objection to the use of this substance either on medical grounds or on the score of taste, or for sentimental reasons.

Personally, the writer sees no objection to the use, under skilled supervision, of hypochlorites, but this view is not shared by a great many persons.

Further, in the case of hard waters (temporary hardness) it decreases markedly the "lime content" of the

---

[1] Well water supplies for a variety of reasons are not always so amenable to purification by storage and filtration as are river water supplies.

finally treated water, thus rendering such waters much "softer," and in the case of very soft water, the treatment may with great advantage be used for an exactly opposite purpose, namely, to "harden" the supply.

TABLE XXII.—"EXCESS LIME" METHOD OF STERILISATION.

(Parts per 100,000) = lbs per 10,000 gallons.
To convert into grains per gallon and "degrees" of hardness, multiply by 7 and divide by 10.

1. Temporary hardness of the water as CaCO$_3$ (soap test).	2. Theoretical amount of CaO required to combine with the bicarbonates.*	3. Theoretical bactericidal dose on the assumption that not less than 2 parts of CaO remain uncombined in the treated water.*
22	12·32	14·32
21	11·76	13·76
20	11·20	13·20
19	10·64	12·64
18	10·08	12·08
17	9·52	11·52
16	8·96	10·96
15	8·40	10·40
14	7·84	9·84
13	7·28	9·28
12	6·72	8·72
11	6·16	8·16
10	5·60	7·60
9	5·04	7·04
8	4·48	6·48
7	3·92	5·92
6	3·36	5·36
5	2·80	4·80
4	2·24	4·24
3	1·68	3·68
2	1·12	3·12
1	0·56	2·56

* N.B.—It will, however, be seen from the text that the figures here given may be found to be too low in practice.

Table XXII may be of some little use in determining the amount of lime required for bactericidal purposes for waters of different degrees of hardness. The first column gives the temporary hardness (parts per 100,000) of the water; the second column shows the theoretical amount of lime required to combine with the bicarbonates, and the last column gives the same figure *plus* 2 parts (per 100,000) of additional lime for bactericidal purposes. For various reasons this amount will be found to be insufficient in practice, especially in the case of hard waters, and about 0·25 part extra for each part of temporary hardness will probably be required.

The following procedure is suggested :—

Determine the temporary hardness in the ordinary way. Inoculate the water with a trace of sewage (say 1 per cent.) to ensure the presence of large numbers of B. coli. To one bottle (A) add the amount of lime indicated in column 3 of the table.

To four other bottles add 10, 20, 30, and 40 per cent. extra lime (B, C, D, E).

Examine the samples (A, B, C, D, E) bacteriologically for B. coli after 1, 5, and 24 hours (1, 10, and 100 c.c. cultures). It will probably be found that after 1 hour all of the five samples (A, B, C, D, E) contain B. coli even in 1 c.c., but that in from 5–24 hours one or more of the samples may be sterile (1, 10, or even 100 c.c.) On the other hand, one or more of the samples will probably yield positive results even in 24 hours (100, 10 perhaps in 1 c.c.)

The following alternative method may also be used :— (1) add to the water a known amount of CaO, but considerably in excess of what is required to combine with the bicarbonates, CO_2, etc. (2) After thorough mixture and settlement estimate the excess CaO in the liquid. (3) The difference between (1) and (2) is the amount of CaO required to combine with the bicarbonates, CO_2, etc., to which must be added 0·002 per cent. extra CaO as this is approximately the *minimum* bactericidal dose (24 hours). (4) Add amount indicated under (3) to the water previously inoculated with 1 per cent. sewage and make B. coli cultures after 1, 5, and 24 hours. (5) Repeat (4), but with slightly larger doses of CaO, until the exact bactericidal dose has been determined.

Having determined the bactericidal dose (let us say that sample C gives the best indication of the bactericidal dose required) it next becomes necessary to find out the percentage of "untreated" water which has to be added to it to neutralise the excess of lime. This is best done by mixing C (after decantation) and the untreated water in stoppered bottles in the following proportions :—

TABLE XXIII.—NEUTRALISATION OF EXCESS LIME.

	C. Treated water. Per cent.	Untreated water. Per cent.		C. Treated water. Per cent.	Untreated water. Per cent.
(a)	90	10	(f)	40	60
(b)	80	20	(g)	30	70
(c)	70	30	(h)	20	80
(d)	60	40	(i)	10	90
(e)	50	50			

After a suitable interval (preferably several hours) the clear liquid (a) to (i) is decanted (or "siphoned" off) and tests made for hardness and free lime.

The sample yielding the lowest results as regards hardness [say (d)] indicates the best proportions of untreated and treated water. This sample will usually be found to give a *slight* pink with phenol phthalein solution, but little or no appreciable brown colour with silver nitrate solution. On the other hand, (c), (b), (a) will be found to give an increasing pink colour with phenolphthlein, and may also show a brown colour with silver nitrate.

As regards hardness, not only will (e), (f), (g), (h), (i) be found harder than (d), but (c) (b) (a) will also be harder owing to excess of CaO.

There are several important, if fairly obvious, points to be borne in mind.

The percentage of CaO in the sample of lime must be determined, and allowance made for its not being of full strength. For example, if it is of 75 per cent. strength an extra 25 per cent. must be added.

Time is necessary for sterilisation purposes, and within certain limits the longer the time allowed the smaller the dose of lime required for bactericidal purposes. *At least 5–24 hours' contact should be given.* The author has actually succeeded in sterilising very soft waters with so minute a dose as 1 part CaO per 100,000 parts of water by prolonging the contact to from three to six days.

A margin of safety should be allowed, particularly in the case of very hard waters, because here an increase in the temporary hardness might use up the excess of lime required for bactericidal purposes, whereas the same *percentage* increase in the temporary hardness of a very soft water would not materially affect the bactericidal dose.

In those cases particularly, in which it is sought to reduce the permanent as well as to remove the temporary hardness, the following modification may be tried.

Sterilise the whole instead of a proportion of the supply, and instead of adding carbonate of soda, use bicarbonate of soda, when the following reactions may be assumed to take place.

$$CaO + NaHCO_3 = CaCO_3 + NaHO.$$
$$NaHO + NaHCO_3 = Na_2CO_3 + H_2O.$$
$$Na_2CO_3 + CaSO_4 = Na_2SO_4 + CaCO_3.$$

It will be seen that 1 molecule of CaO (56) requires 2 molecules of $NaHCO_3$ (84 + 84 = 168) so that if the water after sterilisation contains an excess of CaO of 2 parts per 100,000 (2 lbs. per 10,000 gallons) then 6 parts per 100,000 (6 lbs. per 10,000 gallons) of bicarbonate of soda are required theoretically for the above purpose.

Apart from questions of cost, the chief advantages of this modified procedure are as follows :—

(1) The whole of the supply is sterilised by means of lime.

(2) The water is rendered "softer" owing to the removal of part of the permanent hardness.

The following example illustrates what has been said :—

A well water had a total hardness of 30·32; permanent 9·29; temporary 21·03. The water was inoculated with 1 per cent. of sewage to increase greatly the B. coli content, and then treated with an excess of lime.

Sterilisation took place in 5 hours but not in 1 hour. The excess of CaO at the end of the experiment was 0·0068 per cent.

Bicarbonate of soda was next added in correspondence with the foregoing equation. The result was that the water lost practically all its caustic alkalinity (CaO), and the hardness was reduced to 1·69.

When carbonate of soda was used instead of the bicarbonate, the hardness was found to be 8·86 and the alkalinity 0·00487 per cent.

It is obvious, therefore, that bicarbonate of soda can be used for the double purpose of neutralising the excess of CaO, and of reducing the permanent hardness.

Consideration may now be devoted to the important question of storage, which may be described as Nature's own method of sterilisation.

Note :—The following useful table shows the method employed by American chemists in estimating the alkalinity of waters due to bicarbonates, normal carbonates and hydrates. (*Standard Methods of Water Analysis*, American Public Health Association, 1912) :—

	Bicarbonates	Carbonates	Hydrates
$P = 0$	E	O	O
$P < \frac{1}{2}E$	$E - 2P$	$2P$	O
$P = \frac{1}{2}E$	O	$2P$	O
$P > \frac{1}{2}E$	O	$2(E - P)$	$2P - E$
$P = E$	O	O	E

E = Erythrosine alkalinity.   P = Phenolphthalein alkalinity.

Phenolphthalein does not react with bicarbonates and only with half the carbonates, whilst erythrosine estimates the alkalinity due to both.

[Cochineal or methyl orange might apparently, if preferred, be substituted for erythrosine.]

CHAPTER VI

STORAGE, IN RELATION TO PURIFICATION

THE processes which make for the purification of water under storage conditions are chiefly (1) Sedimentation, (2) Equalisation, (3) Devitalisation.

(1) *Sedimentation.*—In the old days this was regarded as the chief, if not the only, factor of consequence. Though we now know that sedimentation is insufficient *per se* to produce the desired results, yet its importance is clearly indicated in Chapter IV, where it is shown that even less than 24 hours' settlement has a considerable purifying effect.

(2) *Equalisation.*—This factor has never received the attention it deserves. If the water destined to be stored were, to begin with, of uniform composition and contained the microbes of water-borne disease in uniform distribution, no equalisation in the sense here meant could take place.

But, as judged by the usual chemical and bacteriological tests, the quality of a river water varies enormously from time to time; it therefore need scarcely be said that mere storage on purely physical grounds undoubtedly smooths over (levels, as it were) abrupt fluctuations in its quality. Moreover, my observations and experience confirm me in my belief, that even sewage-polluted river waters do not *uniformly*, or of *necessity*, contain (*i.e.* in ascertainable numbers) the microbes generally associated with water-borne disease (*e.g.* the typhoid bacillus).

In support of the truth of this statement reference may be made to Chapter II and to the writer's reports[1] to the London Water Board in which detailed evidence is adduced that when equal volumes (A and B) of *raw* Thames river water, admittedly sewage-polluted, are taken and the one part (A) is purposely infected artificially with the typhoid bacillus or Gärtner's bacillus, and the other part (B) is not so infected, it is comparatively easy to isolate the aforesaid artificially added microbes from (A) whereas it is practically impossible to demonstrate their presence in (B). In the case of the River Thames *raw* water, while it is of course *possible* that the typhoid bacillus may be uniformly present, yet surely it must be in such very few numbers as to be practically non-discoverable. On the other hand, it may be that, although only occasionally present, its numbers on those occasions are nevertheless of serious import.

If the latter view is the correct one, the point to be urged is that, apart from sedimentation and devitalisation, the "levelling" effect of adequate storage would probably so average the infected and non-infected waters as to render the final mixture reasonably, if not demonstrably, safe.

To take a concrete example :—Imagine an individual who has the misfortune to be a typhoid carrier obeying the calls of nature in such a way as unwittingly to contaminate a river water a short distance above the adjacent intakes supplying two towns, A and B. In the case of town A, the water, let us say, is taken directly on to the only line of defence, namely the filter beds, by means of which we can hope to remove, at best, 98 per cent. of the bacteria of all sorts. On the other hand, let us assume that in the case of town B, its main line of defence is

[1] Second, fifth, seventh, and ninth reports on research work.

adequate storage, antecedent to and in anticipation of filtration; it must be obvious that, even apart from sedimentation and devitalisation the probabilities of an epidemic resulting, would be enormously greater in the case of A as compared with B.

(3) *Devitalisation.*—This is a factor of supreme if not paramount importance. Beyond all question the destruction of the microbes of epidemic disease (*e.g.* typhoid fever and cholera) in water is merely a question of time; although the exact time necessary for their deterioration and final disintegration is open to controversy. It is known to vary with the temperature, and no doubt is also influenced by many other factors, such as the prevalence of competitive organisms or their products. According to the writer's experiments, even one week's storage would result in a larger percentage reduction in the initial numbers of typhoid bacilli and cholera vibrios than we could ever hope to achieve by the use of sand filters alone under the usual practical conditions of working.

Without question, however, to secure the *absolute* elimination of these pathogenic bacteria, several weeks' storage *may* be required, but for all practical purposes, provision for 30 days' real storage is ample, that is, when dealing with sources of supply comparable to those of London.

Strong confirmation of the beneficial effect of storage has lately been obtained by the experimental proof that "uncultivated" bacilli succumb in *raw* river water at a more rapid rate than their "cultivated" brethren (pp. 83–86).

Let us now consider the vitality of (1) the cholera vibrio in river water, next that of (2) the typhoid bacillus, and lastly, the bearing of (3) temperature on the question generally.

(1) *Vitality of the cholera vibrio.* Eighteen experiments have been carried out: namely—

Six with *raw* Thames water collected at Hampton.

Six with *raw* Lee water collected at Ponders End.

Six with *raw* New River water collected at Hornsey.

It is important to note that antecedent to inoculating (*i.e.*, seeding) them with the cholera vibrio, the samples of water were *not* sterilised. Subsequent to inoculation with the cholera vibrio, the samples were tested at weekly intervals by various methods, and in different media, for the presence of this microbe. Sometimes one strain, and sometimes a mixture of different strains of cholera, was used for inoculating the samples of water. The experiments were necessarily carried out in the laboratory, and this fact must not be forgotten in interpreting the results.

The chief results are summarised in Table XXIV. (p. 82)

The table shows the number of cholera vibrios added to the water, the number one week later, the percentage reduction in one week and the length of time this microbe persisted in 1, 10, and 100 cubic centimetres of the infected water. The bottles were always vigorously shaken before being tested.

There need be no difficulty in understanding Table XXIV. A glance at column 2 will show that the number of cholera vibrios per c.c. of the artificially infected water varied from a maximum of 13 millions to a minimum of 49,000.

Column 3 shows the enormous reduction of cholera vibrios that occurred as the result of even one week's storage in the laboratory. Column 4 indicates the percentage reduction, which in all the experiments was at least 99·9.

Columns 5, 6, and 7 show the number of weeks the cholera vibrios survived in 1, 10, and 100 c.c. of the infected water, respectively. The outstanding feature was that the cholera vibrios could not be isolated from 100 c.c. of the infected water (column 7) after one week (2 out of eighteen experiments), two weeks (9 out of eighteen experiments) and three weeks (7 out of eighteen experiments).

G

TABLE XXIV.—VITALITY OF THE CHOLERA VIBRIO.

Experiment.	Initial Number of Cholera Vibrios per c.c. of the infected water.	Number of Cholera Vibrios per c.c. one week later.	Percentage Reduction in One Week.	Number of weeks after infection of the water when the Cholera Vibrio could no longer be isolated from 1, 10 or 100 c.c. of water.			Range of Temperature during progress of experiment (deg. Fahr.)
				1 c.c.	10 c.c.	100 c.c.	
Cols. 1	2	3	4	5	6	7	8
1 T. * Nov. 2/08	3,750,000	{ + 1 c.c. ; − 0·01 c.c. }	99·9	2	2	2	50—64
2 L. Nov. 2/08	3,750,000	10	99·9	2	2	3	50—64
3 N.R. Nov. 2/08	3,750,000	20	99·9	2	3	3	50—64
4 T. Nov. 16/08	13,000,000	20	99·9	2	3	3	51—62
5 L. Nov. 16/08	13,000,000	20	99·9	2	2	2	51—62
6 N.R. Nov. 16/08	13,000,000	{ + 1 c.c. ; − 0·01 c.c. }	99·9	2	3	3	51—62
7 T. Nov. 30/08	9,532,500	10	99·9	3	3	3	53—60
8 L. Nov. 30/08	9,532,500	70	99·9	3	3	3	53—60
9 N.R. Nov. 30/08	9,532,500	20	99·9	2	3	3	53—60
10 T. Jan. 18/09	1,775,000	None	99·9	1	1	1	45—55
11 L. Jan. 18/09	70,000	{ + 1 c.c. ; − 0·1 c.c. }	99·9	2	2	2	45—55
12 N.R. Jan. 18/09	3,150,000	{ + 1 c.c. ; − 0·1 c.c. }	99·9	2	2	2	45—55
13 T. Feb. 1/09	680,000	None	99·9	1	1	2	45—60
14 L. Feb. 1/09	510,000	None	99·9	1	1	2	45—60
15 N.R. Feb. 1/09	406,500	None	99·9	1	2	2	45—60
16 T. Feb. 15/09	49,000	None	99·9	1	1	1	48—56
17 L. Feb. 15/09	110,000	None	99·9	1	2	2	48—56
18 N.R. Feb. 15/09	420,000	{ + 1 c.c. ; − 0·1 c.c. }	99·9	2	2	2	48—56

* The letters T, L and N.R. in column 1 refer to *raw* Thames, Lee, and New River water respectively.

In experiments 1–6 a mixture of eleven strains of cholera (known in the laboratory as strains 1–11) were used. In experiments 7–9 a mixture of strains 3 and 4 were employed. In experiments 10 and 18 strain 5 was used. In experiments 11 and 16 strain 6 was employed. Strain 7 was used in connection with experiments 12 and 17. In experiments 13, 14, and 15 strains 2, 3, and 4 were employed respectively.

(2) *Vitality of the typhoid bacillus.* Table XXV. summarises the chief results obtained during an investigation of this subject:—

TABLE XXV.—VITALITY OF THE TYPHOID BACILLUS.

Experiment.	Initial number of typhoid bacilli per c.c. of the infected *raw* river water.	Number of typhoid bacilli per c.c. of the infected *raw* river water, after storage in the laboratory for:— Weeks.					Number of weeks required to effect the destruction of the typhoid bacillus in 100 c.c. of the infected *raw* river water.
		One.	Two.	Three.	Four.	Five.	
1 T.	40	0	—	—	—	—	Five
2 L.	40	0	—	—	—	—	Five
5 L.	170,000	53	2	0	—	—	Five
15 N.R.	525,000	29	3	0	—	—	Five
3 N.R.	40	0	—	—	—	—	Six
4 T.	170,000	9	2	0	—	—	Six
6 N.R.	170,000	40	2	0	—	—	Six
8 L.	470,000	850	11	7	2	0	Seven
9 N.R.	470,000	1,430	14	7	0	—	Seven
14 L.	525,000	32	2	0	—	—	Seven
18 N.R.	475,000	30	3	0	—	—	Seven
7 T.	470,000	480	31	5	0	—	Eight
10 T.	8,000,000	3,000	30	4	0	—	Eight
11 L.	8,000,000	2,900	29	5	0	—	Eight
13 T.	525,000	12	1	0	—	—	Eight
17 L.	475,000	80	11	2	0	—	Eight
12 N.R.	8,000,000	400	22	2	0	—	Nine
16 T.	475,000	210	12	2	1	0	Nine

T. = Thames, L. = Lee, N.R. = New River.

These were all experiments with "*cultivated*" bacilli, *i.e.*, typhoid bacilli, which, after isolation from the excreta or tissues of persons suffering from typhoid fever, had been cultivated in the laboratory on artificial media.

Very different results were obtained with "*uncultivated*" bacilli, *i.e.*, typhoid bacilli as they existed in the urine of typhoid "carrier" cases, and which, of course, had never previously been cultivated in the laboratory.

With the object of demonstrating, at least to his own satisfaction, that his faith was equal to his experimental knowledge, it is now somewhat well-known that the writer, of set purpose, drank, without ill-effect, half a pint of Thames River water, initially contaminated with typhoid urine, known to contain myriads of typhoid bacilli. These personal experiments were made on the 24th, 25th, 26th, 27th, and 28th days, after the date of the original infection of the water in the first test, and on the 23rd, 24th, 25th, 26th, and 27th days in the second test.

In these experiments, the initial number of typhoid bacilli per half-pint was computed at 218,680,000 in the first and 468,000 in the second experiment. In the first case, 770,000 typhoid bacilli per c.c. of the infected water became reduced to only 4 within one week, and subsequent cultures made with 1, 10, and 100 c.c. of the infected water on the 14th, 18th, 21st, 27th, and 29th days after the start of the experiment, all yielded negative results, *i.e.*, as regards the isolation of the typhoid bacillus.

In the second case, the initial number of typhoid bacilli was computed at 1,650 per c.c. of the infected water, and at the end of a week none could be revealed in 1 c.c. Subsequent cultures made with 1, 10, and 100 c.c. of the infected water on the 10th, 14th, 19th, 21st, and 28th day after the start of the experiment, likewise yielded negative results as regards isolation of the typhoid bacillus.

Markedly different results were obtained after the previous isolation and laboratory *cultivation* of the typhoid bacilli derived primarily from the urine of the foregoing " carrier " case. In its " cultivated " state the bacillus was found, indeed, to survive for five weeks in river water, under otherwise comparable conditions of experiment.

Inasmuch as the risk of acquiring typhoid from the drinking of polluted water is mainly due to the possible presence of " uncultivated " typhoid bacilli, these observations would seem to be of far reaching importance.

At a later date, the subject was further investigated and the chief results are summarised in Table XXVI. (p. 85).

TABLE XXVI.—"UNCULTIVATED" TYPHOID BACILLI.

	Experiment 1 A.	Experiment 2 A.	Experiment 3 A.	Experiment 4 A.	Experiment 5 A.	Experiment 6 A.	Experiment 6 B.
Initial number of typhoid bacilli per c.c. of infected river water	0·78	1,480	42	56	37,800	Unknown but assumed to be numerous	89 times fewer than A
Ultimate death of the typhoid bacillus, as judged by inability to isolate it from 100 c.c. of the infected water	one week	second week	one week	one week	third week	one week	one week

"CULTIVATED" TYPHOID BACILLI.

	Experiment 1 B.	Experiment 1 C.	Experiment 2 B.	Experiment 3 B.	Experiment 4 B.	Experiment 5 B	Experiment 5 C.	Experiment 5 D.	Experiment 6 C.	Experiment 6 D.
Initial number of typhoid bacilli per c.c. of infected river water	0·78	0·078	160	42	56	1,460	146	14·6	5,200	52
Ultimate death of the typhoid bacillus, as judged by inability to isolate it from 100 c.c. of the infected water	eight weeks	One week	eight weeks	five weeks	five weeks	five weeks	One week	five weeks	seven weeks	four weeks

For definition of "cultivated" and "uncultivated" typhoid bacilli, see p. 103,

Except as regards the difference between adding "uncultivated," as compared with "cultivated," typhoid bacilli to the water, the following experiments are directly comparable :—1A with 1B and 1C ; 2A with 2B ; 3A with 3B ; 4A with 4B ; 5A with 5B, 5C and 5D ; 6A with 6C ; 6B with 6D.

These results confirm those previously noted, and it would thus appear certain, that "uncultivated" typhoid bacilli die in river water, under conditions of storage in the laboratory, more rapidly than their "cultivated" brethren.

(3) *The question of temperature.*—Ten experiments were carried out at each of the following temperatures :— 0° C. (32° F.) ; 5° C. (41° F.) ; 10° C. (50° F.) ; 18° C. (64·4° F.); 27° C. (80·6° F.) ; and 37° C. (98·6° F.).

The average number of *cultivated* typhoid bacilli added to the samples was 103,328 per c.c. of the artificially infected river water (Thames).

This initial number became reduced, as judged by the tests employed, week by week, at the different temperatures in the way shown in Table XXVII.

Table XXVII.—Influence of Temperature.

Degrees.	Weeks.								
	1.	2.	3.	4.	5.	6.	7.	8.	9.
0°C.	47,766	980	65	34	3	3	2	1	0·0
5°C.	14,894	26	6	3	0·3	0·1	0·0	—	—
10°C.	69	14	3	0·3	0·0	—	—	—	—
18°C.	39	3	0·4	0·0	—	—	—	—	—
27°C.	19	0·1	0·0	—	—	—	—	—	—
37°C.	5	0·0	—	—	—	—	—	—	—

Example :—At 10° C., the average initial number of 103,328 per c.c. was reduced to 69, 14, 3, 0·3, and 0·0 per c.c. in 1, 2, 3, 4, and 5 weeks respectively.

It is strikingly obvious that temperature is an important

factor, bearing on the vitality of the typhoid bacillus in river water, and the lower the temperature, within the limits stated, the longer does this bacillus show evidence of its existence or vitality. It thus becomes a matter of practical importance to consider how far this affects the question of storage.

Table XXVIII. shows the average temperature of the Cherwell which joins the Thames at Oxford :—

TABLE XXVIII.—TEMPERATURE OF THE RIVER CHERWELL, (1892–1903).

(Extracted from Günther's "History of the Daubeny Laboratory")

In Monthly sequence. (Degrees F., at 10 a.m.)		In Temperature sequence. (Degrees F., at 10 a.m.)			
January	38	January	38		
February	39	February	39	say 39	say 41
March	43	December	39		
April	50	March	43	say 43	
May	56	November	44		
June	63	April	50	say 50	
July	65	October	51		
August	64	May	56	say 58	say 58
September	59	September	59		
October	51	June	63		
November	44	August	64	say 64	
December	39	July	65		
Mean, 51					

The critical months apparently are December, January, and February, and these are the months when a river water is usually liable to be rendered specially impure owing to floods; unfortunately, also, they are the periods during which, according to custom, river water is most frequently abstracted for storage purposes in large quantities.

On the other hand, the most critical months as regards the seasonal prevalence or incidence of typhoid fever, are September, October, and November. The water temperature during these months is about the average, and considerably above the average in the immediately preceding months.

Having regard, however, to the enormous number of typhoid bacilli artificially added to river water, in the foregoing experiments and the fact of their being "*cultivated*" (not "*uncultivated*") bacilli, and the circumstance that by the second week, even at 0° C., the reduction was more than 99 per cent. on the average, the results are undoubtedly of a reassuring character.

The influence of low water temperature (32 to 41° F.) in relation to sustained vitality, is largely felt during the first to second week, the big drop in the numbers of typhoid bacilli being delayed until the second to third week. Therefore when water is stored, say for four weeks, the question of temperature becomes, relatively speaking, one almost of secondary importance. Nevertheless, during the five *cold* months, January, February, March, November, and December, it is *specially* desirable that water should be *adequately* stored antecedent to filtration.

In brief, the experiments show the importance of *adequate* storage, not the inutility of storage under conditions of low temperature.

Storage has thus far been considered under the heading of sedimentation, equalisation, and devitalisation. It is now desirable to adduce an example of what has been observed to take place in an actual case.

Storage under practical conditions.—A good example to consider is the storage of Thames River water, in the Chelsea reservoirs, because here the nominal number of days' storage, although only about half the 30 days recommended by the writer, is yet sufficient to show remarkably good results.

The following tables may suffice to show in detail, and by contrast, the beneficial effects of storage :—

TABLE XXIX.—RIVER THAMES *RAW* WATER AT HAMPTON *BEFORE* STORAGE.
Bacteriological results.

Date. 1907-8.	Number of microbes per c.c.			Typical B. coli (lactose + indol +). [+ = smallest volume of water yielding a positive result.]				
	Gelatine at 20-22° C. counted on 3rd day.	Agar at 37° C. 2 days.	Rebipelagar at 37° C. 2 days.	100 c.c.	10 c.c.	1 c.c.	0.1 c.c.	0.01 c.c.
August 9	430	120	32			+		
,, 12	220	160	56		+			
,, 19	500	310	146				+	
,, 26	410	90	33	+				
September 2	220	60	13		+			
,, 9	600	27	73		+			
,, 16	710	166	10				+	
,, 23	800	146	23	+				
,, 30	440	106	21		+			
October 7	620	124	38			+		
,, 10	210	111	5		+			
,, 14	750	168	52				+	
,, 17	1,800	950	152				+	
,, 21	4,000	220	34					+
,, 24	1,400	204	33				+	
,, 28	1,100	270	8				+	
,, 31	6,100	490	185		+			
November 4	4,300	1,120	82				+	
,, 7	1,700	176	34			+		
,, 11	1,400	112	15				+	
,, 14	1,600	190	71			+		
,, 18	1,110	96	5			+		
,, 21	1,700	165	38			+		
,, 25	1,700	226	61				+	
,, 28	21,000	625	100				+	
December 2	4,000	[10]	*				+	
,, 5	16,000	900	120				+	
,, 9	16,000	640	74					+
,, 12	2,800	*1,300*	150				+	
,, 16	5,000	480	46				+	
,, 19	1,600	470	24				+	
,, 27	530	330	60				+	
,, 31	830	500	29				+	
January 2	210	650	52				+	
,, 6	1,500	440	28			+		
,, 9	30,000	1,000	*250*					+
,, 13	*65,000*	230	44				+	
,, 16	7,000	290	40				+	
,, 20	1,800	90	19			+		
,, 23	1,500	82	61					+
,, 27	2,000	210	22				+	
,, 30	2,400	180	46					+
February 3	1,600	150	[0]				+	
,, 6	900	130	21			+		
,, 10	700	73	11				+	

* No record.

TABLE XXIX. (continued).—RIVER THAMES RAW WATER AT HAMPTON BEFORE STORAGE

Date. 1907–8.	Number of microbes per c.c.			Typical B. coli (lactose + indol +). [+ = smallest volume of water yielding a positive result.]				
	Gelatine at 20–22° C. Counted on 3rd day.	Agar at 37° C. 2 days.	Rebipelagar at 37° C. 2 days.	100 c.c.	10 c.c.	1 c.c.	0·1 c.c.	0·01 c.c.
February 13 ...	3,900	164	27				+	
,, 17 ...	1,600	162	13			+		
,, 20 ...	4,500	200	34				+	
,, 24 ...	1,900	110	9					+
,, 27 ...	35,000	180	43			+		
March 2 ...	1,000	544	5			+		
,, 5 ...	4,300	340	15			+		
,, 9 ...	14,000	496	51					+
,, 12 ...	4,900	246	41				+	
,, 16 ...	500	130	13			+		
,, 19 ...	1,700	380	25			+		
,, 23 ...	300	60	3			+		
,, 26 ...	3,100	310	52		+			
,, 30 ...	3,100	296	16				+	
April 2 ...	3,400	356	41			+		
,, 6 ...	800	182	16			+		
,, 9 ...	960	72	11			+		
,, 13 ...	630	128	11					+
,, 23 ...	550	114	10			+		
,, 27 ...	1,400	290	12					+
,, 30 ...	64,000	550	33			+		
May 4 ...	1,140	320	18			+		
,, 7 ...	2,800	210	88			+		
,, 11 ...	1,400	118	36			+		
,, 14 ...	2,000	270	10			+		
,, 18 ...	1,800	110	18				+	
,, 21 ...	600	230	12			+		
,, 25 ...	800	106	11	+				
,, 28 ...	1,900	672	31	+				
June 1 ...	800	184	21				+	
,, 11 ...	290	69	6	+				
,, 15 ...	450	64	1			+		
,, 18 ...	2,800	382	120			+		
,, 22 ...	1,200	210	22			+		
,, 25 ...	800	120	46				+	
,, 29 ...	[200]	93	5		+			
July 2 ...	250	92	20			+		
,, 6 ...	380	194	35			+		
,, 10 ...	1,100	680	104			+		
,, 13 ...	1,600	180	70			+		
,, 16 ...	500	180	33			+		
,, 20 ...	1,200	410	19			+		
,, 23 ...	4,480	56	7		+			
,, 27 ...	1,200	65	14			+		
Average ...	4465·4	279·9	41·4	2·2 %	14·6 %	34·8 %	38·2 %	10·1 %

The figures in italics and figures in brackets refer to the maximum and minimum results respectively.

TABLE XXX.—RIVER THAMES WATER *AFTER* STORAGE IN THE CHELSEA RESERVOIRS.

Bacteriological results.

Date. 1907-8.	Number of microbes per c.c.			Typical B. coli (lactose + indol +). [+ = smallest volume of water yielding a positive result.]				
	Gelatine at 20-22° C. counted on 3rd day.	Agar at 37° C. 2 days.	Rebipelagar at 37° C. 2 days.	100 c.c.	10 c.c.	1 c.c.	0·1 c.c.	0·01 c.c.
August 7 ...	360	9	1	−				
,, 12 ...	45	19	4	−				
,, 19 ...	20	24	9	+				
,, 26 ...	34	16	0			+		
September 2 ...	20	3	0	−				
,, 9 ...	270	63	75	−				
,, 16 ...	350	68	3	+				
,, 23 ...	280	126	15	+				
,, 30 ...	700	154	6	−				
October 7 ...	*2,200*	*510*	*71*	−				
,, 10 ...	150	21	2	−				
,, 14 ...	50	10	0	−				
,, 17 ...	50	20	2	+				
,, 21 ...	110	10	0		+			
,, 24 ...	60	6	0		+			
,, 28 ...	69	180	0	+				
,, 31 ...	60	[2]	0	+				
November 4 ...	80	9	0	−				
,, 7 ..	38	7	1	−				
,, 11 ...	210	48	1	+				
,, 14 ..	130	72	2	+				
,, 18 ...	40	21	0		+			
,, 21 ...	40	11	1	+				
,, 25 ...	90	30	0		+			
,, 28 ...	92	60	0	−				
December 2 ...	30	*	*	+				
,, 5 ...	35	24	0	−				
,, 9 ...	1,200	31	4			+		
,, 12 ...	1,120	192	12		+			
,, 16 ...	600	150	12				+	
,, 19 ...	1,140	460	5			+		
,, 27 ..	60	70	2			+		
,, 31 ...	80	42	4				+	
January 2 ...	5	36	3			+		
,, 6 ...	150	40	4					+
,, 9 ...	160	70	3		+			
,, 13 ...	80	21	1	+				
,, 16 ...	70	10	2	+				
,, 20 ...	1,600	92	2			+		
,, 23 ...	310	43	1		+			
,, 27 ...	170	33	2			+		
,, 30 ...	70	18	0	+				
February 3 ...	140	30	1	+				
,, 6 ...	74	12	1	−				
,, 10 ...	140	13	0	+				

* No record. −Sign denotes negative result.

TABLE XXX (continued).—RIVER THAMES WATER *AFTER* STORAGE IN THE CHELSEA RESERVOIRS.

Date. 1908.	Number of microbes per c.c.			Typical B. coli (lactose + indol+). [+ = smallest volume of water yielding a positive result.]				
	Gelatine at 20–22° C. counted on 3rd day.	Agar at 37° C, 2 days.	Rebipelagar at 37° C. 2 days.	100 c.c.	10 c.c.	1 c.c.	0·1 c.c.	0·01 c.c.
February 13 ...	54	11	0		+			
,, 17 ...	50	9	0	+				
,, 20 ...	32	7	0	+				
,, 24 ...	36	4	0	+				
,, 27 ...	50	10	0	+				
March 2 ...	40	15	0	−				
,, 5 ...	46	15	0		+			
,, 9 ...	20	6	0	−				
,, 12 ...	10	3	0	+				
,, 16 ...	20	9	0	−				
,, 19 ...	50	27	5	+				
,, 23 ...	11	10	0		+			
,, 26 ...	9	3	0	+				
,, 30 ...	5	4	0	−				
April 2 ...	7	10	0	−				
,, 6 ...	80	16	0		+			
,, 9 ...	38	22	0			+		
,, 13 ...	36	11	0		+			
,, 23 ...	2	27	0	+				
,, 27 ...	[1]	4	0	+				
,, 30 ...	11	6	0	−				
May 4 ...	40	23	0	−				
,, 7 ...	80	31	0			+		
,, 11 ...	20	11	0	−				
,, 14 ...	20	36	0	−				
,, 18 ...	22	9	0		+			
,, 21 ...	42	28	0	−				
,, 25 ...	80	22	0	−				
,, 28 ...	54	13	0	−				
June 1 ...	75	17	2	−				
,, 11 ...	1,700	47	2	−				
,, 15 ...	*180*	*114*	*32*	−				
,, 18 ...	900	74	25	+				
,, 22 ...	260	11	2	−				
,, 25 ...	140	13	5	−				
,, 29 ...	100	12	6	−				
July 2 ...	300	22	6	−				
,, 6 ...	140	78	11	−				
,, 9 ...	42	11	6	−				
,, 13 ...	320	92	58	−				
,, 16 ...	40	30	22		+			
,, 20 ...	160	12	1	−				
,, 23 ...	140	23	11	−				
,, 27 ...	250	25	7	−				
Average ...	207·8	43·9	5·1	% 24·7	% 19·1	% 10·1	% 2·2	% 1·

The figures in italics and figures in brackets refer to the maximum and minimum results respectively.

TABLE XXXI.—RIVER THAMES *RAW* WATER AT HAMPTON *BEFORE* STORAGE.

Chemical results.   Parts per 100,000.

Date.	Ammoniacal Nitrogen.	Albuminoid Nitrogen.	Oxidised Nitrogen.	Chlorine.	Oxygen absorbed from permanganate. 3 hrs. at 80°F.	Turbidity, Sacc. carb. of iron.	Colour, mm. brown in a 2 ft. tube.	Total Hardness.	Permanent Hardness.
1.	2.	3.	4.	5.	6.	7.	8.	9.	10.
1907.									
August 7	0·0018	0·0140	*0·20	1·67	0·1751	1·31	46	*21·00	*5·9
,, 12	0·0017	0·0162	*0·17	1·82	0·1601	0·70	34	23·87	4·71
,, 19	0·0051	0·0150	*0·17	1·77	0·1585	1·45	37	20·99	5·43
,, 26	0·0039	0·0132	*0·20	1·70	0·1377	0·80	41	22·30	5·60
September 2	0·0022	0·0136	0·18	1·72	0.1287	0·60	32	21·8	—
,, 4	0·0013	0·0126	*0·18	1·70	0·1238	0·45	33	*21·8	—
,, 9	0·0036	0·0120	*0·18	1·73	0·1204	0·52	36	21·4	—
,, 16	0·0017	0·0118	*0·19	1 72	0·1099	0·45	36	21·6	5·3
,, 23	0·0019	0·0120	*0·19	1·80	0·1079	[trace]	34	21·9	5·8
,, 30	0·0026	0·0100	*0·17	1·79	0·1045	,,	37	21·0	5·0
October 7	0·0030	0·0092	*0·16	1·71	0·1042	,,	32	19·9	5·4
,, 14	0·0038	0·0096	*0·19	1·77	0·1102	,,	[31]	21·1	5·7
,, 21	0·0151	0·0240	*0·15	1·90	0·3484	7·09	90	[17·7]	6·1
,, 28	0·0088	0·0179	*0·18	1·87	0·3596	0·88	74	22·0	6·5
November 4	0·0073	0·0248	*0·17	1·70	0·4930	7·95	140	24·6	7·5
,, 11	0·0077	0·0128	*0·25	1·70	0·2089	0·80	64	26·0	6·8
,, 18	0·0054	0·0088	*0·24	1·65	0·1462	0·57	54	24·2	6·2
,, 25	0·0085	0·0128	0·27	1·80	0·1959	2·43	70	26·0	7·7
December 2	0·0085	0·0304	0 23	1·71	0·5835	17·40	290	22·1	9·4
,, 9	0·0091	0·0300	0·19	1·65	0·6651	*35·00*	360	21·0	5·5
,, 16	0·0052	0·0248	*0·20	1·59	0·5690	19·10	*384*	20·0	9·2
,, 23	0·0088	0·0126	—	1·58	0·2408	4·93	100	—	—
,, 30	0·0106	0·0122	*0·31	1·58	0·1879	2·72	96	26·8	6·5
1908.									
January 6	*0·0169*	0·0098	*0·36	1·66	0·1246	1·40	43	26·2	6·5
,, 13	0·0120	0·0292	*0·33	1 80	0·4737	7·64	180	21·8	9·0
,, 20	0·0126	0·0124	*0·31	1·78	0·1863	2·35	50	25·2	8·0
,, 27	0·0132	0·0094	*0·33	1·63	0·1353	2·07	50	26·9	7·2
February 3	0·0110	0·0086	*0·36	1·70	0·1184	0·81	40	27·4	8·8
,, 10	0·0096	[0·0085]	*0·39	1·60	0·1068	0·52	45	27·8	8·5
,, 17	0·0086	0·0088	*0·31	1·60	0·1083	1·01	—	—	—
,, 24	0·0066	0·0120	*0·34	1·60	0·1421	0·81	60	27·9	6·4
March 2	0·0064	0·0120	*0·32	1·79	0·1329	0·95	66	26·4	6·9
,, 9	0·0122	*0·0332*	*0·25	1·80	0·5046	18·20	200	22·8	8·4
,, 16	0·0074	0·0134	*0 31	1·79	0·1813	1·01	80	*26·6	*8·3
,, 23	0·0040	0·0102	*0·29	1·77	0·1129	[trace]	44	*24·9	*6·1
,, 30	0·0082	0·0300	*0·25	1·66	0·4867	14·10	200	*25·4	*7·0
April 6	0·0053	0·0176	*0·29	1·80	0·1995	1·81	93	*26·1	*7·8
,, 13	0·0037	0·0140	*0·28	1·67	0·1723	0·45	64	*24·8	*6·7
,, 23	[0·0006]	0·0100	*0·28	1·60	[0·1024]	0·47	51	*22·9	*5·7
,, 27	0·0088	0·0228	*0·24	1·62	0·2608	—	135	*19·0	*7·1
May 4	0·0040	0·0236	[*0·13]	[1·39]	0·4915	2·90	208	22·6	8·2
,, 11	0·0038	0·0205	*0·28	1·59	0·2736	2·48	96	24·6	6·5
,, 18	0·0030	0·0130	*0·27	1·60	0·2110	1·77	76	24·1	6·8
,, 25	0·0010	0 0120	*0·29	1·60	0·1340	1·50	48	*24·5	*6·9
June 1	0·0030	0·0110	*0·26	1·59	0·1236	1·58	39	24·2	5·9
,, 12	0·0059	0·0142	*0·25	1·59	0·1452	2·14	47	*24·0	*5·7
,, 15	0·0016	0 0146	*0·28	1·59	0·1392	2·14	45	21·7	5·8
,, 22	0·0016	0·0156	*0 28	1·58	0·1304	2·14	36	21·8	6·0
,, 29	0·0031	0·0156	*0·25	1·59	0·1240	2·22	38	23·2	5·4
July 6	0·0050	0·0162	*0·25	1·60	0·1387	2·22	43	21·6	4·7
,, 13	0·0044	0·0116	0·23	1·46	0·1152	1·36	36	22·5	5·2
,, 15	0·0032	0·0112	*0·23	1·54	0·1230	1·72	42	*22·5	*5·2
,, 20	0·0042	0·0114	*0·25	1·55	0·1301	1·33	43	23·3	[4·3]
,, 27	0·0036	0·0124	0·21	1·56	0·1256	1·09	44	22·5	5·4
Average	0·0060	0·0153	0·26	1·67	0·2127	3·50	83	24·29	6·82

As regards columns 4, 9, 10, the tests are not always carried out on the actual samples collected on the dates shown in column 1. The figures marked thus * are, however, taken from analyses carried out on samples collected within the same week.

The figures in italics and the figures in brackets refer to maximum and minimum results, respectively.

TABLE XXXII.—RIVER THAMES WATER *AFTER* STORAGE IN THE CHELSEA RESERVOIRS. CHEMICAL RESULTS. PARTS PER 100,000.

Date.	Ammoniacal nitrogen.	Albuminoid nitrogen.	Oxidised nitrogen.	Chlorine.	Oxygen absorbed from Permanganate. 3 hours at 80° F.	Turbidity, Sacc. carb. of iron.	Colour, mm. brown in a 2 ft. tube.	Total Hardness.	Permanent Hardness.
1907.									
August 7	0·0016	0·0118	0·17	1·66	0·1212	[trace]	46	[19·4]	6·7
,, 12	0·0011	0·0124	0·17	1·73	0·1285	,,	31	20·4	4·9
,, 19	0·0012	0·0126	0·19	1·72	0·1261	,,	31	22·3	5·9
,, 26	0·0014	0·0110	0·18	1·71	0·1271	,,	26	22·6	6·4
September 2	0·0015	0·0126	[0·16]	1·73	0·1201	,,	27	21·5	—
,, 9	0·0011	0·0112	0·17	1·70	0·1165	,,	27	20·9	—
,, 16	0·0012	0·0098	[0·16]	1·68	0·1009	,,	29	21·7	5·5
,, 23	0·0011	0·0120	0·18	1·70	0·0978	,,	26	21·5	5·1
,, 30	[0·0006]	0·0090	0·18	1·76	0·0955	,,	[18]	20·2	5·3
October 7	0·0013	0·0088	0·17	1·71	0·0925	,,	[18]	20·8	6·7
,, 14	0·0008	0·0080	[0·16]	1·73	[0·0858]	,,	22	21·2	3·3
,, 21	0·0013	0·0096	0·18	1·80	0·0956	,,	24	21·1	5·4
,, 28	0·0017	0·0112	0·18	1·78	0·1851	,,	37	20·0	5·6
November 4	0·0027	0·0126	0·18	1·80	0·2028	,,	43	20·6	6·2
,, 11	0·0025	0·0144	0·18	1·75	0·2587	,,	57	21·1	6·9
,, 18	0·0015	0·0115	0·21	1·67	0·2127	,,	48	22·6	6·6
,, 25	0·0015	0·0100	0·23	1·60	0·1669	,,	41	24·2	5·8
December 2	0·0030	0·0094	0·24	1·65	0·1439	,,	42	24·4	7·6
,, 9	0·0035	0·0141	0·23	1·66	0·2710	2·35	94	24·2	7·1
,, 16	0·0023	0·0168	0·21	1·54	0·3976	6·82	200	21·7	7·6
,, 23	0·0026	0·0154	—	1·60	0·3240	4·00	124	22·2	6·7
,, 30	0·0027	0·0134	—	1·61	0·2577	1·60	80	24·1	8·6
1908.									
January 6	0·0061	0·0108	0·26	1·60	0·1976	0·55	36	25·4	7·3
,, 13	0·0059	0·0122	0·29	1·63	0·2042	[trace]	50	26·8	7·0
,, 20	0·0082	0·0124	0·33	1·60	0·2263	1·35	62	25·2	6·8
,, 27	0·0054	0·0110	0·32	1·62	0·1693	0·86	50	26·9	6·4
February 3	0·0058	0·0100	0·32	1·65	0·1428	[trace]	48	26·1	7·9
,, 10	0·0048	0·0091	0·33	1·69	0·1403	,,	46	26·9	5·6
,, 17	0·0039	[0·0063]	0·33	1·57	0·1059	,,	26	27·2	5·1
,, 24	0·0018	0·0077	0·35	1·54	0·0988	,,	31	28·3	6·2
March 2	0·0022	0·0086	0·32	1·75	0·1206	,,	41	26·9	7·3
,, 9	0·0020	0·0098	0·35	1·69	0·1255	,,	47	26·8	6·5
,, 16	0·0024	0·0098	0·29	1·72	0·1358	,,	41	25·4	6·7
,, 23	0·0017	0·0094	0·27	1·78	0·1516	,,	44	26·4	6·5
,, 30	0·0015	0·0096	0·27	1·70	0·1380	,,	58	26·5	6·8
April 6	0·0020	0·0100	0·24	1·70	0·1635	0·50	46	25·9	6·5
,, 13	0·0025	0·0100	—	1·58	0·1661	[trace]	47	—	—
,, 23	0·0009	0·0086	0·23	1·64	0·1383	,,	46	23·4	6·4
,, 27	0·0009	0·0092	0·24	1·60	0·1420	,,	50	23·8	6·3
May 4	0·0012	0·0080	0·25	1·58	0·1168	,,	50	23·4	5·4
,, 11	0·0016	0·0124	0·21	1·48	0·2238	0·51	62	24·5	6·5
,, 18	0·0014	0·0124	0·21	1·50	0·2110	0·25	52	23·5	6·2
,, 25	0·0014	0·0104	0·24	1·50	0·1691	0·52	56	23·9	7·8
June 1	0·0018	0·0098	0·27	1·49	0·1371	0·67	33	23·8	6·5
,, 11	0·0020	0·0124	0·25	1·50	0·1339	1·33	31	29·3	6·2
,, 15	0·0018	0·0104	0·25	1·50	0·1199	1·09	36	21·7	6·1
,, 22	0·0014	0·0096	0·24	1·48	0·1028	0·50	32	22·7	5·7
,, 29	0·0010	0·0100	0·25	1·49	0·0935	0·52	30	24·0	6·0
July 6	0·0018	0·0100	0·24	[1·45]	0·0915	0·72	32	24·3	5·1
,, 13	0·0012	0·0104	0·21	1·52	0·0931	0·60	27	23·2	4·7
,, 20	0·0016	0·0128	0·22	1·46	0·0995	2·14	30	21·3	[4·4]
,, 27	0·0008	0·0100	0·22	1·46	0·1006	0·77	32	21·6	5·9
Average	0·0022	0·0108	0·24	1·63	0·1536	0·53	45	23·49	6·28

The figures in italics and the figures in brackets refer to maximum and minimum results respectively.

The foregoing results may be summarised as follows:—

TABLE XXXIII. (FIG. 20).—BACTERIOLOGICAL.

	Number of bacteria per c.c.		
	Gelatine at 20–22° C.	Agar at 37° C.	Bile–salt agar at 37° C.
River Thames before storage ...	4465	280	41
Chelsea stored water	208	44	5
Reduction (per cent.)	95·3	84·3	87·8

TABLE XXXIV. (FIG. 21).—B. COLI TEST (LACTOSE + INDOL +).

	Per cent. of samples yielding positive results.				
	+100 c.c. or less.	+10 c.c. or less.	+1 c.c. or less.	+0·1 c.c. or less.	+0·01 c.c. or less.
River Thames before storage	99·9	97·7	83·1	48·3	10·1
Chelsea stored water	57·2	32·5	13·4	3·3	1·1

TABLE XXXV. (FIG. 22).—CHEMICAL (PARTS PER 100,000).

	Ammoniacal nitrogen.	Albuminoid nitrogen.	Permanganate Test.	Turbidity Test.	Colour Test.
Raw Thames before storage	0·0060	0·0153	0·2127	3·50	83
Chelsea stored water	0·0022	0·0108	0·1536	0·53	45
Reduction per cent.	63·4	29·4	27·8	84·9	45·8

Figs. 20–22 (pp. 97–99) illustrate the foregoing results. As regards Fig. 22, the difference between the outside margin of the black area, and the black upper line represents the degree of purification effected by storage.

It is impossible within the compass of this work to do more than condense the chief points showing the advantages accruing from the simple storage of raw river water :—

(1) Storage reduces
    (a) the number of bacteria of all sorts.
    (b) the number of bacteria capable of growing on agar at blood heat.
    (c) the number of bacteria, chiefly excremental bacteria, capable of growing on a bile-salt medium at blood heat.
    (d) the number of coli-like microbes.
    (e) the number of " typical " B. coli.
    (f) the amount of suspended matter, colour, ammoniacal nitrogen and oxygen absorbed from permanganate.
    (g) the hardness.

(2) Storage alters certain initial ratios, for example :—
    (h) it reduces the number of " typical " B. coli to a proportionately greater extent than it does the number of bacteria of all sorts.
    (i) the colour results improve relatively to a greater extent than those yielded by the permanganate test.

(3) Storage, if sufficiently prolonged, devitalises the microbes of water-borne disease, *e.g.*, the typhoid bacillus and the cholera vibrio.

(4) Storage produces a marked " levelling " or " equalising " effect.

NUMBER of BACTERIA per c.c.

BEFORE STORAGE

GELATINE

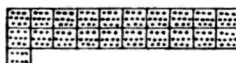

AFTER STORAGE
REDUCTION 95·3 PER CENT

BEFORE STORAGE   BEFORE STORAGE

AGAR   BILE SALT AGAR

AFTER STORAGE   AFTER STORAGE
REDUCTION 84·3 PER CENT   REDUCTION 87·8 PER CENT

DIAGRAM TO ILLUSTRATE THE EFFECT ON RAW THAMES WATER OF STORAGE IN THE CHELSEA RESERVOIRS

Fig. 20.

(5) An adequately stored water is to be regarded as a "safe" water, and the "safety change" which has occurred in a stored water can be recognised, and demonstrated by appropriate tests.

(6) The use of stored water permits of a constant check being maintained on the safety of a water supply *antecedent* to, and irrespective of, filtration.

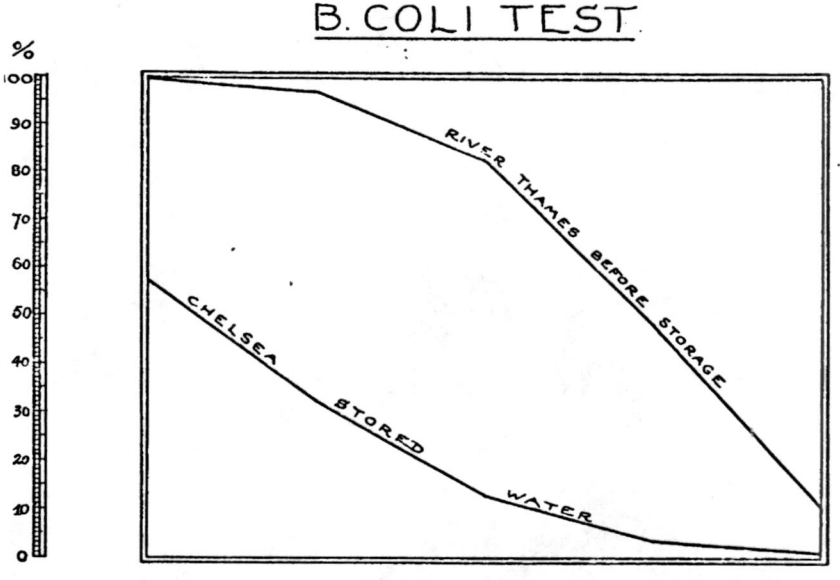

FIG. 21.—THAMES WATER, BEFORE AND AFTER STORAGE (B. COLI TEST).

(7) The use of stored water goes far to neutralise or wipe out the gravity of any charge that a water supply is derived from polluted sources.

(8) The use of adequately stored water renders any accidental breakdown in the filtering arrangements much less serious than might otherwise be the case.

These are some of the chief *advantages* of storage, but it must not be forgotten that there are also real or potential *disadvantages*.

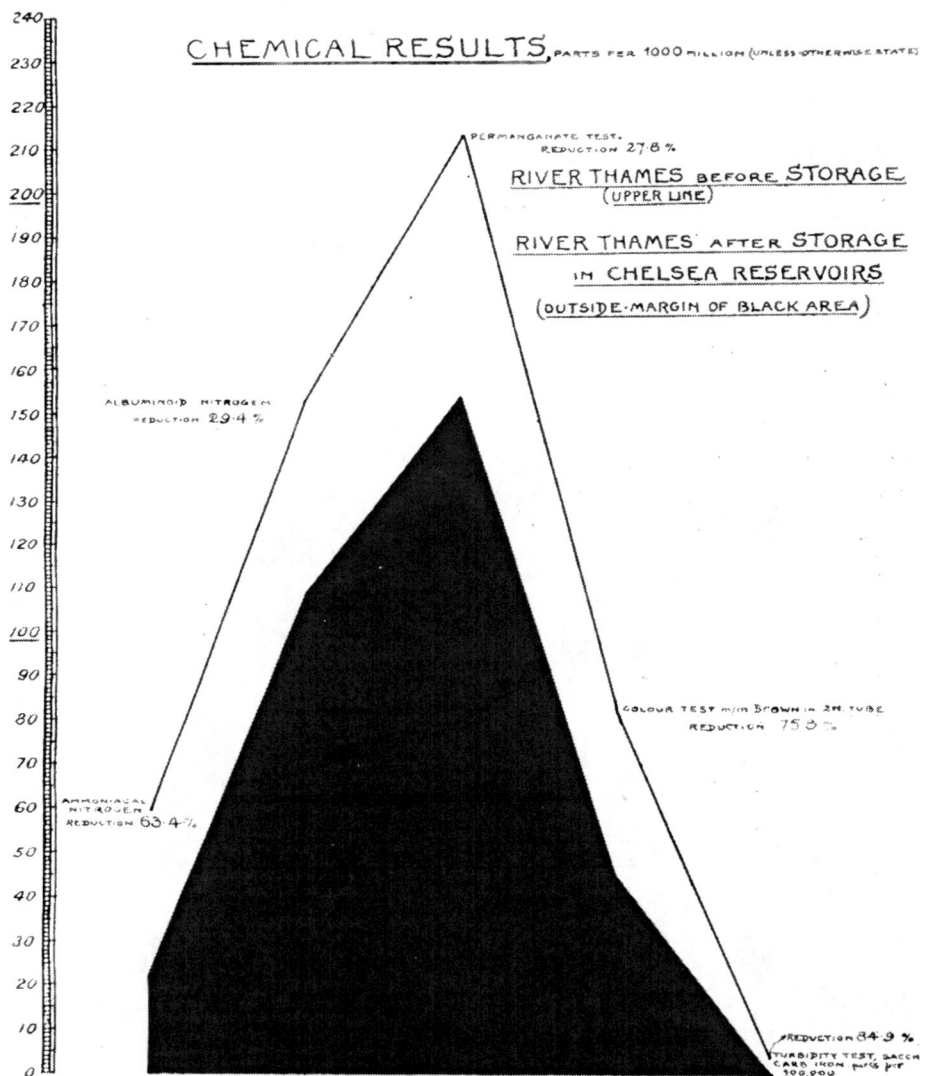

Fig. 22.

Sometimes the river water may be *apparently* so pure that it would seem to be desirable to pass such water directly on to the filter beds instead of pumping it into the storage reservoirs. Nevertheless, from the epidemiological point of view, the purity on such occasions may be more apparent than real.

Again, it sometimes happens that Algæ develop to such an extent in storage reservoirs as to interfere seriously with filtration processes, and in some cases the water may acquire, in consequence, a most disagreeable fishy or oily taste and odour.

At the beginning of the year 1913, part of London (Hammersmith, Kensington, and Hampstead) experienced a somewhat serious "taste visitation"; the algal growth causing the objectionable taste and smell being chiefly composed of Tabellaria, with some Asterionella. Reference may be made to *Nature* (No. 2266, vol. xci. p. 117, April 3, 1913) and to the writer's monthly report for March, 1913. Some figures illustrating these and other algæ will be found at the end of the Monograph (Figs. 38–43, pp. 195–197).

These algal troubles may, it is true, be combated or even overcome by the use of copper sulphate (dose 2 to 10 lbs. per million gallons) but such treatment should never be undertaken in the absence of skilled supervision, and responsible advice.

As a last resort in the writer's experience the objectionable taste of waters, tainted as a result of algal growths can, *in certain cases,* be effectually removed by the addition of minute doses of permanganate of potassium to the water as it passes into supply. The dose naturally varies with the oxidisability of the particular water, but speaking of the London water supply the innocuous dose of about 2·5 to 5·0 lbs. of permanganate per million gallons of water was found to destroy the taste within a few minutes. The very faint preliminary pink tinge imparted by the addition of the permanganate rapidly fades away, and, in practice, the consumer receives a tasteless water with no pink tint, but slightly browner in colour than the normal. Here again, such treatment is only admissible in special circumstances, and when placed under the vigilant control of competent advisers.

In conclusion, it should be noted that the results observed in connection with the storage of Thames and Lee river water must not be read as necessarily applicable to cases in general, especially if the climatic conditions are not comparable.

CHAPTER VII

WATER AND DISEASE.[1]

APART from the question of accident, presently to be dealt with, it is difficult to conceive that a water prepared with such elaborate care as that of London could have any influence on the incidence of water-borne disease.

It has been shown that the typhoid bacillus and Gärtner's bacillus could not be isolated from 1 cubic centimetre and upwards of the raw Thames water, when employing methods which yield positive results in the case of laboratory samples *artificially infected* with even very small numbers of these pathogenic microbes (see pp. 33–36).

It has also been shown that under the conditions of storage of London water, prior to filtration, the typhoid bacillus and the cholera vibrio, when artificially added to raw river water, in numbers inconceivably greater than could ever occur in practice, diminish rapidly in number. It is true that a few bacilli may persist for several weeks, but having regard to the very large initial number added it may be said with assurance that real storage for one month antecedent to filtration confers reasonable, if not absolute, immunity from risk of water-borne disease (pp. 80–86).

Moreover, it has been demonstrated that "unculti-

---

[1] Reference may be made to a paper by the author on this subject, "Water and Disease," *Journal of State Medicine*, January and February, 1912.

vated"[1] typhoid bacilli die more speedily in water than their "cultivated" brethren, and the danger apprehended to the consumers of impure water is solely due to the possible presence of "uncultivated" bacilli (pp. 83–86).

Further, London water is not only stored for several weeks, but is also filtered, and this filtration process removes about 98 per cent. of the largely diminished numbers of bacteria. In the United States, as will presently be shown, improvements as regards water supplies have antedated a diminished incidence of general and particular diseases, but the evidence that the two circumstances are necessarily related, in a causative sense, is not altogether conclusive.

That serious epidemics[2] have been caused by impure water cannot be doubted by any sane person, but the writer is of opinion that if all the facts were known the cause would usually be found to be *accidental* rather than inherent in character.

It is proposed at this stage to deal with the question of *accident*, and later with the evidence which has within recent years led certain authorities to associate in a causative sense the observed diminution in typhoid fever rates with increased purification of water supplies.

The aim of a waterworks authority should be to *prevent the possibility of accident,* and not merely to produce and distribute a water supply of excellent quality on the average. This is an aspect of waterworks policy and procedure which seems to have received only a minimum of attention, owing to an incomplete understanding of the importance of the subject, and due also to the belief that

---

[1] By "uncultivated" is meant typhoid bacilli as they occur in the discharges of typhoid patients or typhoid "carriers." By "cultivated" is meant typhoid bacilli, which as a result of and subsequent to their isolation from such discharges have necessarily been cultivated or grown in the laboratory on artificial media.

[2] For example, Worthing in 1893 (1,315 cases), Maidstone in 1897 (1,847 cases), Lincoln in 1905 (more than 1,000 cases).

filtration is the panacea for all ills connected with water supply.

Yet if a workman suffering unwittingly from typhoid bacilluria micturated on a filter bed, although that bed was working superlatively well, can anyone doubt the probability, if not the immediate certainty, of a disastrous epidemic? For out of the millions of typhoid bacilli voided with his urine two out of every hundred would be likely to pass into supply in a fresh and presumably highly virulent condition.

In truth, filtration is only trustworthy when the unfiltered water is relatively so innocuous that, when 98 per cent. of its bacteria have been removed, the finished article ceases to contain any harmful element.

Strictly speaking, no workman who has ever had typhoid fever should be actively engaged on waterworks.[1] On all works, indeed, adequate and convenient lavatory accommodation should be provided, a watch being kept on all the employees, and notices prominently displayed, forbidding, under the most severe penalties, any nuisance.

In addition, the supply everywhere must be guarded both antecedent and subsequent to filtration.

The filtered water during its passage to the consumer must be "cut off" from the possibility of those pollutions which may occur in a variety of ways, of which the following are but a few instances.

During structural alterations (e.g., laying down new or replacing old mains) the supply may be jeopardised. Filter wells, pumping wells, and service reservoirs may be so situated as not to preclude the entrance of contaminating matters.

It is commonly believed that the mains are secure owing to the water being under pressure, but physicists hold that

---

[1] The time will assuredly come when no workman, who has had typhoid fever will be engaged or retained, unless he has been certified not to be a typhoid carrier.

under certain conditions it is not impossible for "insuction" to occur.

The danger from defective types of hydrants is so obvious as scarcely to need special mention. In February, 1906, the Edinburgh water supply was observed to contain insects ("Springtails," *Collembola*) in abundance occasioning considerable alarm in the minds of the inhabitants. Apparently these minute creatures were not really of aquatic origin, but bred in the hydrant boxes and occasionally, owing to diminished pressure, were sucked into the mains and so reached the citizens' houses. It was proved by direct experiment that, by diminishing the pressure in the street main, the insects could be sucked from the hydrant boxes into the main water supply and so into the house cisterns in the vicinity.

Storage reservoirs should be protected from the inroads and deposits of trippers, picnic parties, and the public generally. Unless the circumstances are exceptional, fishing should be prohibited, and the aim should be to eliminate any and every possible source of contamination. The river above the intakes for waterworks purposes should be guarded from pollution as zealously as is possible under the existing or improved conditions of the law, and if the Conservancy of the river rests in other hands than the waterworks authority, constant pressure, in the interests of the Public Health, should be brought to bear on those directly responsible to fulfil their obligations faithfully and well.

It is especially important that the river as it nears the intakes should receive constant care as regards prevention of pollution.

At the same time, it may here be pointed out that the provision of *adequate* storage accommodation enormously, if not entirely, reduces the risk of disaster following upon any accidental specific pollution just above the intakes. If a typhoid carrier micturated in the river above the intakes (say from a boat) the typhoid germs, in the absence of storage, would be carried directly on to the filters, with consequences which could hardly be other than calamitous.

A similar accident in the presence of adequate storage would probably, if not certainly, be unattended by serious results, owing to the levelling and devitalising effect of storage. It is the bounden duty of every waterworks authority to guard at every stage in the purification process against the possibility of accident, and the one accident above all others which excites supreme dread is the contamination of the water with the urine or dejecta of a typhoid carrier. As compared with this source of *specific* infection, even sewage pollution, although highly objectionable, is much less to be feared for the reason, according to the author's practical experience, that typhoid bacilli are not usually present in ordinary sewages, in any large numbers—certainly fewer than one typhoid bacillus per 0·001 c.c.

At present, it is the aim (if not the compellable duty) of waterworks authorities to control pollutions *in general*, and also to purify the water to as high a standard as is reasonably practicable.

In the future, it is hoped that, superadded to all this, the endeavour will always be to protect the consumer from *chance* infections, and especially from that deplorable form of contamination which is associated with the *specific* pollution of water by the urine and dejecta of typhoid carriers. Even if water is polluted with as much as from 0·001 to 0·0001 per cent. of crude sewage, the chances of typhoid bacilli being uniformly present are extremely remote, according to the author's own personal observations; but a water polluted with extremely small traces of typhoid urine would probably suffice to produce a serious epidemic.[1]

---

[1] The author added 1 part of typhoid urine to 50 million parts of raw Thames river water, and recovered the typhoid bacillus from the mixture, but

In summary of the foregoing observations, the writer ventures to urge that waterworks authorities should pay special attention to the following points :—

Protect as far as possible the river, especially just above the "intakes," from all sources of pollution.

Interpose adequate storage accommodation between the river and the filter beds, and prevent any pollution of the water in these reservoirs.

Guard the filter beds, filter wells, and sand from all sources of contamination, and filter the water as efficiently as is reasonably practicable.

Prevent the possibility of pollution of the water in the pump wells, service reservoirs, and distributing mains.

Remember that accidents open the road to epidemics, and that the worst form of accident is produced by contamination of water with the recent discharges of typhoid carriers.

Although river water supplies alone are here dealt with, the principles laid down apply, in greater or less measure, to all water undertakings.

The writer in confining his remarks almost solely to typhoid fever, assumes that if we render our water supplies safe in this respect, we need, generally speaking, have little fear of any other water-borne disease.

Lest it should be imagined that undue stress has been laid on the duty of preventing avoidable accidental contamination, it seems appropriate shortly to review here the circumstances pertaining to the recent Rockford (Illinois) typhoid epidemic so graphically described by Jordan and Irons in the *Journal of Infectious Diseases* (Vol. XI., No. 1, July 1912).

The City of Rockford, situated on the Rock River in the northern part of the State, has a population of about

on the other hand, he has repeatedly failed to isolate the typhoid bacillus from 1/1000 to 1/10,000 c.c. of crude sewage when using methods which yielded positive results in the case of artificially infected samples.

50,000. The present water supply is obtained from a series of deep wells sunk in the sandstone. *As drawn to the surface it is of unimpeachable quality.*

During January and February, 1912, 10,000 cases of enteritis and 199 cases of typhoid fever occurred in the town. So gross and explosive a winter outbreak could not be adequately accounted for by any of the contributory causes of typhoid fever acting separately or in conjunction, *e.g.*, contact infection, fly-borne infection, polluted shellfish, etc. Probably the only agencies capable of striking a community so suddenly and so extensively are milk supply and water supply.

Milk was excluded as a primary factor because " as many as 49 different milk dealers supplied the families among whom typhoid fever had developed, and in no instance was the number of cases on any particular milk-route disproportionate to the number of customers on that route."

On the other hand, the city water supply was badly implicated. The private well drinkers largely escaped contagion, whereas the incidence on those drinking city water was very marked. For example, in one group of factories using private wells the incidence of enteritis was 5·8 per cent., whereas in a second group of factories supplied with city water the incidence was 70·2 per cent.

A concatenation of circumstances pointed to the probability of infection of the water about January 16th. On Monday night (January 15–16th), a large fire occurred. There was, in consequence, a heavy draft on the water system, and on investigation the following facts were revealed :—

(1) One of the wells which had been out of use for some months was pumped into supply, and used to fill up the storage reservoir, which had become partially depleted owing to the aforesaid fire. The water issuing from the well proper was quite pure, but before passing into supply

was held up in a pit which received contaminating water from the adjoining street.

(2) The storage or balancing reservoir is partly below the ground level and the water in it on January 16th was drawn from a normal range of from 18·7 to 14·0 feet down to 6·6 feet. Under these conditions, it was proved that some "seepage" might occur, but Jordan and Irons came to the conclusion that "the reservoir, although dangerously placed and insufficiently protected, played a very minor part, if any at all, in the outbreak."

(3) The ground water in the neighbourhood of the pumping station is highly contaminated, and it was found that the suction well or pumping pit was pervious, so that whenever the pumps were "speeded up" and the level of the water lowered, ingress of polluted water took place. The porosity of the pumping pit became manifest when it was purposely emptied.

"On first stopping the pumps, the pit level fell about a foot overnight, and when all the water was pumped out about *six feet of refined sewage seeped in before morning.*"

When this discovery was made one of the City officials was led to make the following remarkable admission :—

"We have been sitting on a keg of powder with a sputtering pipe in our mouths. That the explosion was not greater and more harmful than it was passes comprehension. We have had an excellent water source and then handled it as they did several decades ago—put our water storage in the middle of a cesspool, and trusted to chance that it would not be contaminated."

The Rockford case affords a melancholy example of the futility of providing a water supply of excellent quality, unless the water is also protected from accidental contamination, from its source until it reaches the consumer.

Attention may now be invited to current views as regards the incidence of *endemic*[1] typhoid fever in relation to water supply.

[1] Unfortunately, owing to insufficient data, it is practically impossible, in collating statistics to separate endemic from epidemic typhoid fever. This

It is one thing to recognise the danger of *epidemics* being caused by impure water, and quite another to associate the *non-epidemic* prevalence of typhoid fever with water supply as a factor constantly in operation, and of direct causative significance.

Within recent years it has become quite common to hear in connection with, and as a result indeed of, improvements in, the water supply of a town, and the coincident decline of typhoid fever, such expressions as :—" The typhoid fever rate has been cut in two owing to the increased purity of the drinking water."

In the United States of America, there appears to be almost a consensus of opinion that a typhoid fever death rate in excess of 20 per 100,000 population is directly and wholly attributable to impure water supply.

Some writers would even seem to ascribe a definite percentage of the typhoid death rate to water supply almost irrespective of its total amount.

How strong the feeling is may be judged by the following quotation, which incidentally exhibits some remarkable financial considerations [1] :—

" Cincinnati, by the improvement of its water supply, reduced its typhoid fever death rate from 64 to 13 per 100,000 population. This corresponds to a saving of $5·10 per capita per year or one and three-fourths million dollars per year. Columbus City, by installing a water purification plant, reduced the typhoid fever death rate from 56 to 17, corresponding to a gross saving of $700,000 per year or $3·90 per capita per year. Chicago, by extending its waterworks intake four miles, reduced the average typhoid death rate from 80 to 34, corresponding to a per capita saving of $4·60 per year, or a gross saving of seven million dollars per year."

---

is to be regretted, as one might be prepared to accept all *explosive* outbreaks of typhoid fever as being water-borne, subject always to the exclusion of such agencies as milk supply and shell-fish, and yet be very chary of accepting water as the cause of the cases occurring independently of such epidemics.

[1] *Monthly Bulletin: Ohio State Board of Health*, Jan., 1913, Vol. 111, No. 1.

Again, Whipple in his treatise on Typhoid Fever says [1]:—

"When a contaminated public water-supply is suddenly improved in quality by the installation of a filter plant, there is nearly always a decided fall in the typhoid fever death rate. Cities which have pure water have a generally lower death rate than those which have an impure supply. These differences may serve as a rough measure of the amount of typhoid fever due to impure public water supplies. The average typhoid death rate in American cities is about 35 per 100,000. The cities in the North which have safe water supplies have lower rates,—usually as low as 20, and frequently as low as 15 or even 10. Taking the country over, perhaps 20 may be taken as an average figure. The difference between 20 and 35 may be considered, therefore, as being due to infected public water supplies. Of the 'residual typhoid' the most potent causes are probably infected milk, and direct infection by contagion, by flies, etc. Oysters, vegetables and other foods really play a very insignificant part in the general typhoid death rate.

"A number of years ago infected water probably caused more typhoid fever than all the other causes combined. That is not the case to-day when the country as a whole is considered, although it is still, the most important cause, and in some cities, as in Pittsburgh and Philadelphia, it still overshadows all other causes."

"The long-continued struggle for pure water is bearing fruit, and to-day in many American cities, and even in entire States, where the public water supplies are well guarded from pollution, infection by water has come to be a secondary cause of the disease.

"In a general sort of way it may be said that in the cities of the United States, at the present time, about 40 per cent. of the typhoid fever is due to water, 25 per cent. to milk, 30 per cent. to ordinary contagion (including fly transmission), and only about 5 per cent. to all other causes. In cities supplied with pure well water or filtered water, the effect of water is negligible; where the water is impure, it is still the most important cause of the disease. In the case of rural districts there are no data to show the relative effect of the infected wells, infected milk, and direct infection, but, in all probability, the 'honours' are about even.

"While the care of water supplies cannot be in any degree relaxed, efforts for further reducing the disease must be directed to causes other than water."

Professor Dunbar [2] of Hamburg has also thrown the weight of his authority in favour of the views represented by Whipple, Hazen, Sedgwick, and many others.

---

[1] "Typhoid Fever: Its Causation, Transmission, and Prevention," by George C. Whipple.

[2] "Reflections, Old and New, on the Condition of Surface-water Supply Systems," *Journal of State Medicine*, Vol. XXI., No. 2.

Thus he says :—

"Take London, for example; here in consequence of the continuous improvements effected in the waterworks, the mortality from typhoid fever has gradually declined to 5 per 100,000 in 1905 and to 3 per 100,000 in 1909."

Again :—

"What have been the consequences of this condition of affairs [*i.e., improved water supplies*] on the public health ? During the interval between 1901 to 1905 the death rate from typhoid fever in towns of North America was calculated to amount to 46 per 100,000 against 7·6 for Germany during the same period. Fifty years ago the death rate from typhoid fever in North American towns is said to have varied, just as it did in Germany, without any exception, between 50 and fully 100 per 100,000 living. Even in the year 1900, therefore, at a time when 6·30 per cent. of the town dwellers (counting towns with over 2,500 inhabitants) were for the first time provided with filtered drinking water, but when the remainder still consumed unfiltered suface water, the death rate from typhoid fever reached still 46·5 per 100,000. However, in 1910, when 28·20 per cent. of the town dwellers referred to had filtered water available for use this mortality had become considerably reduced.

"In 1900, 24·1 deaths from typhoid fever were notified per 100,000 living in Boston City, while in 1910 only 11·6 were registered.

"The following table will show some more of the statistics concerned with this development of sanitation :—

Town.	Death rate from typhoid fever per 100,000 living.		
	About 50 years ago.	1900.	1910.
Boston, Mass.	more than 60	24·1	11·6
Lawrence	,, 100	—	ca. 20·0
New York City	—	20·4	11·7
Philadelphia	more than 70	37·2	18·0
Washington, D.C.	—	70·7	24·4
Cincinnati	more than 50	—	5·7
Pittsburgh	,, 100	—	Less than 30
Indianapolis	—	41·4	29·9
Richmond, Va.	—	103·0	21·9
New Orleans	—	52·6	31·5

"This comparison shows clearly that the introduction of the sand-filtration system led to a marked lowering of the mortality from typhoid fever, but that, with the exception of Cincinnati, none of the cities show any result even approximately so striking as those achieved in our British and German towns at home."

There can be no question that in a number of American cities improvement of water supplies has antedated a decrease of mortality, but in our present state of incomplete knowledge, to conclude from this circumstance a direct causative connection between the two is perhaps hardly warrantable in all cases.

The Americans, however, attribute the decline of mortality to an "exclusion of disease germs" or an "increase of vital resistance," or a "combination of these factors."[1]

The mere fact that there has likewise occurred a decline in the incidence of tuberculosis, pneumonia, and respiratory diseases generally, none of which can reasonably be regarded as at all likely to be water-borne, throws some doubt on the hypothesis that an improved water supply necessarily tends to produce any marked and continuously operating decrease of mortality from general and particular diseases.

Let us consider Dunbar's statement :—

"Take London, for example: here, in consequence of the continuous improvements effected in the waterworks, the mortality from typhoid fever has gradually declined to 5 per 100,000 in 1905, and to 3 per 100,000 in 1909"

If we accept this as wholly correct, we are faced with the grave reflection that many other cities and towns containing in the aggregate an immense population would seem to be yearly sacrificing many thousands of lives which might be saved by the application, at a not impracticable cost, of the principles of water purification adopted, for example, by the Metropolitan Water Board. Indeed the critic might go further than this and say that, inasmuch as the destruction by sterilisation of *all* the microbes of water-borne disease is quite a feasible and

[1] Massachusetts Institute of Technology, Vol. VI., "Mortality Decrease Following Water Purification," Professor Sedgwick and Dr. J. Scott McNutt.

practicable measure, implicit faith in the above conclusion demands the advocacy of sterilisation for waterworks purposes as the only means of absolutely, finally, and completely safeguarding the interests of the water consumer.

In England, the seasonal prevalence of most of the cases of typhoid fever occurs year after year, *before* the "worst water periods" as judged by the chemical and bacteriological tests at present in use. Assuming these tests to be trustworthy indices of quality, there does not seem *prima facie* evidence that water played any large part in causing the observed seasonal fluctuation in the incidence of the disease. If seasonal variations in quality of water are apparently inoperative, is it wise to conclude that *improved* quality of water as a result of more efficient purification is of necessity a disease-preventing factor, merely because it happens somehow to seem associated with reduction in the typhoid fever death rate?

Again, is it not true that places, the water supplies of which are above suspicion, are affected, as regards the seasonal prevalence of typhoid fever, in much the same way as places less happily circumstanced in this respect?

Further, if we attempt to form a mental picture of the water supplies in the British Isles and try to arrange them in some sort of order of merit, using for this purpose whatever knowledge is available as to source of supply, manner of purification, analytical data, etc., and then proceed to correlate our list with the typhoid death rate pertaining to the places dealt with, we soon reach the conclusion that many towns supplied with apparently very pure water have high *endemic* typhoid death rates, whereas others, supplied with a less pure water, seemingly enjoy comparative freedom from this disease. It would be of interest to know as regards America:

  (1) Whether the curves illustrating the *seasonal* quality of the water as supplied to consumers show

any correspondence with curves showing the *seasonal* incidence of typhoid fever.

(2) Whether the improvements in the supplies associated with the decline of typhoid fever have always brought about a difference in the actual quality (*e.g.*, as judged by the B. coli test) of the water much greater than the difference observed annually during the "worst" and "best" water periods, which difference in England has not, generally speaking, been observed to affect materially the question of the incidence of typhoid fever.

(3) Whether the curves illustrating the actual observed quality (*e.g.*, as judged by the B. coli test) of the water in the various towns coincide with curves setting forth the incidence of typhoid fever in the same towns.

(4) Whether the improvement in sanitary matters generally which so frequently is conjoined with an enlightened policy as regards water supply may not also be a factor in the situation.

The author has carried out an elaborate search for the typhoid bacillus in samples of crude sewage, and finds that it is possible to isolate the typhoid bacillus from 0·01 c.c. of sewage when this microbe has been *added* to it *artificially* in the proportion of 10 per 0·01 c.c. *Strictly comparable experiments, but with sewage not purposely infected, have so far yielded absolutely negative results.* The conclusion would seem to be reasonable that, as it is possible to isolate the typhoid bacillus from sewage if added *artificially* thereto in the proportion of 10 per 0·01 c.c. or of 1 per 0·001 c.c., the failure to find it in the *non-infected* samples, under strictly comparable conditions of experiment, means presumably that it cannot be present in the same proportion (namely, 1 per 0·001 c.c.).

Now the tested samples of sewage contained the enormous number of about 1,000 excremental bacteria (as judged by the bile-salt-agar test) per 0·001 c.c. If we apply the bile-salt-agar test to a sample of water, and even if we *harshly* assume that all the microbes growing in this medium are truly of direct sewage origin, it becomes extremely difficult to imagine the habitual presence of the typhoid bacillus, *even* in samples of *raw* river water, owing to the fact that such waters contain so comparatively few excremental bacteria. For example, the raw River Thames (admittedly a sewage-polluted river) exhibits in this medium, on the average, only about 50 of these excremental microbes per c.c., so that we are forced to conclude that if it were $\frac{1000}{50} = 20$ times worse, the typhoid bacillus would presumably still be absent from 1 c.c.; or to put it the other way round, in its present state it cannot be expected uniformly to contain the typhoid bacillus in 20 c.c. This river supply is purified about 1,000 times before delivery to the consumer, which inferentially signifies the absence of the typhoid bacillus from 20,000 c.c. Even if the purification process improved the water only 100, nay, even barely 10 times, we still are faced with the inferential conclusion of the absence of the typhoid bacillus from 2,000 or 200 c.c. respectively of such water.

Moreover, it is exceedingly difficult to believe that the ingestion of a single typhoid bacillus would be at all likely to cause typhoid fever.

The author is, of course, not suggesting in the face of conclusive evidence to the contrary that serious typhoid epidemics have not resulted from the consumption of *specifically* polluted water, or that any relaxation in the processes of water purification is permissible; but he does venture to express the opinion that the evidence brought forward in favour of the direct causative relationship between the quality of water supplies and the degree of incidence of *endemic* typhoid fever is not always wholly convincing.

The current desire to "cut the typhoid fever death rate in two" should not lead waterworks authorities to assume, without sufficient warrant, that the danger of epidemics has been wholly removed by improved processes of purification, or to forget the vital distinction between specific and non-specific pollution, and the enormous importance of guarding against the possibility of accident.

The author is strongly of opinion that a water of only a moderate degree of purity, but sheltered from accident, is safer, in the long run, than a water normally of superlative purity, but not free from the possibility of accidental specific contamination.

One cannot fail to be struck with the circumstance that cases somewhat like the following have been of not infrequent occurrence. A town, say, in 1910 has a typhoid death rate of perhaps 30 per 100,000. In 1911 it has fallen possibly to 15, subsequently to an improvement in the water service, and it is not improbably eagerly claimed that the improved quality of the water has cut the typhoid death rate in two. In 1912 the figure perhaps reverts to 30 without any proven change in the water supply having taken place.

It is impossible, of course, to accept any theory which associates diminution of the typhoid fever rate as attributable to improved water supplies, but seems to ignore increased incidence of the disease as of water significance. In conclusion, it is apposite to quote the following extracts from the monthly (January, 1913) *Bulletin* of the New York State Department of Health :—

Reduction in Typhoid Fever Rates Resulting from Improved Water Supplies. That the public health of a community is largely dependent upon the purity of its public water supplies hardly needs demonstration in the present day of enlightenment in sanitary science. Furthermore, that of all so-called communicable diseases the typhoid fever death rate has by experience proven to be the best index of this relation, at least in American cities, and especially when the rates are in excess of a certain amount. Owing to the fact, however, that typhoid fever is traceable to other causes than impure water; and that contamination of supplies is generally of progressive occurrence, this relationship, as is well known to students of vital statistics, does not readily nor uniformly appear in the table or charts of typhoid fever rates of municipalities having public water supplies which are or have been subject to contamination. It is of considerable interest therefore to sanitarians to find examples or illustrations in actual practice which shew this relationship, especially where improvements have been made effecting the sanitary quality of the water.

The State Department of Health has for some six years or more been actively engaged in a campaign for pure water supplies through the State. Although hindered greatly by inadequate laws and lack of direct control over public water supplies it has, by means of investigations, reports, and educational measures brought strong and effective pressure to bear upon many municipalities in improving the quality of their supplies. That these efforts have borne fruit will be seen from the following table showing the typhoid fever rates in certain cities of the State where during recent years the Engineering Division has been specially active in this direction.

Accompanying the typhoid statistics for each municipality is a brief statement of the essential facts having a bearing upon the sanitary quality of the supply. This comparison shows with marked clearness in nearly all cases, the lowering of the typhoid rates corresponding to the improvements in the water supplies responsible for them. If the data were plotted this relationship would be all the more apparent. Furthermore, if these cities be taken as a class and typhoid rates arranged for each year a most convincing picture is presented of not only the relationship referred to but as to what can be accomplished in a practical way in the lowering of typhoid fever rates through improvements in the sanitary quality of public water supplies, along inductive lines carried out by the Department.

TYPHOID FEVER RATES.

Albany.	1900–5.	1906.	1907.	1908.	1909.	1910.	1911.	1912.
Typhoid rate (per 100,000)	24·8	20·3	20·0	10·9	18·8	14·9	17·8	17·8

Water filtered since 1899 prior to which typhoid rate was over 80. Preliminary filters installed in 1910. Hypochlorite used at intervals during past three years. Note a great reduction but not marked decline since filters were installed.

Amsterdam.	1900–5.	1906.	1907.	1908.	1909.	1910.	1911.	1912.
Typhoid rate (per 100,000)	22·2	24·8	15·9	—	11·9	22·1	9·0	11·6

In 1908 Department ordered city to inspect watershed, resulting in removal of violations. In 1910 as a result of Departments recommendations, one polluted watershed abandoned. Note general but irregular decline in rate since 1906.

Auburn.	1900–5.	1906.	1907.	1908.	1909.	1910.	1911.	1912.
Typhoid rate (per 100,000)	23·8	12·1	6·0	46·6	17·5	8·6	7·9	11·2

VII WATER AND DISEASE

In 1906 rules and regulations protecting supply were enacted by Department, since which time orders have been issued to local boards covering 170 violations. Water board maintains active sanitary patrol. In 1908 special orders were issued to the water board to remove all violations. With exception of 1908 note reduction and general low rate since 1905.

Binghampton.	1900–5.	1906.	1907.	1908.	1909.	1910.	1911.	1912.
Typhoid rate (per 100,000)	25·6	9·1	18·2	15·2	13·1	12·4	4·0	17·8

Water supply filtered since 1902, prior to which rate exceeded 50. Note as with case of Albany, great reduction but no marked decline since filters were installed.

Cohoes.	1900–5.	1906.	1907.	1908.	1909.	1910.	1911.	1912.
Typhoid rate (per 100,000)	92·9	57·8	78·2	62·0	82·2	76·8	108·5	48·0

In February, 1908, the Mohawk river pollution investigation pointed out high typhoid fever rates and necessity for improved supply. In June, 1908, full investigation was made of water in connection with city investigations and water filtration was strongly urged. In 1911 filter plant was installed. Note reduction in rate in 1912.

Elmira.	1900–5.	1906.	1907.	1908.	1909.	1910.	1911.	1912.
Typhoid rate (per 100,000)	45·5	44·7	28·0	30·7	33·5	26·9	13·3	15·9

In 1896 as result of serious epidemic, filtration plant installed. In 1909 investigation by Department showed continued high rates and recommendations made to abandon local wells and increase efficiency of plant. Operation improved since 1909 and hypochlorite used during past two years. Note reduction in rate since 1909.

Lockport.	1900–5.	1906.	1907.	1908.	1909.	1910.	1911.	1912.
Typhoid rate (per 100,000)	47·8	67·6	50·1	60·7	49·7	11·1	22·0	16·6

In 1906 as result of outbreak of typhoid fever the Department recommended abandonment of polluted Erie canal supply. Since 1909 the supply has been taken from Niagara river. In 1911 Department recommended filtration. Note reduction in rate since 1909.

Middletown.	1900–5.	1906.	1907.	1908.	1909.	1910.	1911.	1912.
Typhoid rate (per 100,000)	24·1	18·8	18·8	42·1	18·1	26·1	59·1	26·5

Mechanical filter plant installed in 1900 and enlarged in 1909. Hypochlorite used recently. In 1908 Department ordered city to inspect and remove violations on watershed. In 1912 outbreak of typhoid due to milk indicated high typhoid rate probably due in part to other causes than water.

New York.	1900–5.	1906.	1907.	1908.	1909.	1910.	1911.	1912.
Typhoid rate (per 100,000)	18·6	15·5	17·4	12·8	12·7	11·6	11·0	9·7

Prior to 1907 practically no violations reported to the Department for a number of years. Since 1907 some 267 violations of water rules examined into and necessary orders issued by Department to local health boards. Since 1907 city very active in patrol of watershed and during past two years hypochlorite plant in use. Note marked decline since 1907.

Niagara Falls. Typhoid rate (per 100,000)	1900–5.	1906.	1907.	1908.	1909.	1910.	1911.	1912.
	141·5	154·5	126·0	87·1	74·9	97·9	187	71·5

An investigation of the sanitary conditions of the city of Niagara Falls was carried on by the Engineering Division during the summer of 1907, following which the Department strongly urged a new or a filtered supply. In 1910 following another investigation, public warned of danger of supply. During 1912 filters installed, with hypochlorite treatment. Note marked reduction in rate in 1912 as result of filtration.

Ogdensburg. Typhoid rate (per 100,000)	1900–5.	1906.	1907.	1908.	1909.	1910.	1911.	1912.
	52·8	67·3	47·1	26·8	26·8	37·5	30·8	36·7

In 1907 as result of investigation the Department urged new filtered supply. Filtration plant installed during 1912. No typhoid deaths occurred during 1912 after filters were put in continuous use in the early fall.

Oswego. Typhoid rate (per 100,000)	1900–5.	1906.	1907.	1908.	1909.	1910.	1911.	1912.
	47·5	58·0	66·0	62·2	26·6	51·2	12·7	21·0

In 1907, as result of investigation, Department recommended new supply or purification. In 1910 new supply from Lake Ontario installed with hypochlorite used at intervals. Note decrease in rate since 1910.

Peekskill. Typhoid rate (per 100,000)	1903–5.	1906.	1907.	1908.	1909.	1910.	1911.	1912.
	22·5	15·2	14·0	202·3	12·9	26·2	19·0	0·0

In 1906, as result of investigation, Department urged removal of violations of water rules. In 1908, as result of typhoid epidemic, Department renewed recommendations and urged water filtration. In 1910 new filters in permanent operation. Note reduction in typhoid rate since 1910, with no deaths in 1912.

Poughkeepsie. Typhoid rate (per 100,000)	1900–5.	1906.	1907.	1908.	1909.	1910.	1911.	1912.
	42·4	39·4	112	34·5	23	17·8	14·0	13·7

In March and April 1907, following a typhoid fever outbreak, Department investigated water supply and recommended improvements in operation of filters. Following special report of Mr. George C. Whipple in April, 1907, improvements undertaken and completed in 1907. Hypochlorite used for past three years. Note marked and continuous reduction in typhoid rate since 1907.

Rensselaer. Typhoid rate (per 100,000)	1900–5.	1906.	1907.	1908.	1909.	1910.	1911.	1912.
	67·5	18·6	58·3	30·0	29·9	28·0	18·7	9·4

WATER AND DISEASE

Water supply filtered since 1901. Following recommendations of the Department, since 1907 improvements in operation have been installed and hypochlorite used for past two years. Note continuous reduction since 1907 and especially in 1912.

Rome.	1900-5.	1906.	1907.	1908.	1909.	1910.	1911.	1912.
Typhoid rate (per 100,000)	21·6	28·2	17·0	26·4	16·0	19·3	9·4	22·9

In 1908 Department ordered city to inspect watershed and abate violation of rules and regulations. In 1910 and 1911 special inspections made by the Department following which city urged to remove violations. Note general but irregular decline in rate since 1908.

Two diagrams (Figs. 23–24, facing p. 122 and p. 123) have been prepared to illustrate the foregoing data. In Fig. 23, each place has been treated as a separate entity, in Fig. 24 the death-rates have been calculated back to the actual numbers, the total numbers have then been divided into the total population and finally expressed as a combined rate per 100,000 persons for the periods stated.

There are considerable difficulties involved in the theory of the causative association of the diminished typhoid fever rates with improvements in the water supplies. For example, Albany does not seem to have benefited materially as a result of the remedial measures employed, yet there is no suggestion that the processes of purification were less efficient than in other cases where the lowered typhoid death rate is definitely attributed to water improvement.

Auburn, despite protective measures introduced about 1906, had a rate of 12·1 in 1906, 6·0 in 1907, and actually 46·6 in 1908.

Binghampton introduced filtration after 1902. In 1910 the rate was 12·4, in 1911 only 4, but in 1912, 17·8.

Cohoes, in 1911 installed a filtration plant. In that year the rate was 108·5; it is true that it fell to 48·0 in 1912, but if the filtration plant was at all effective, it surely ought, on a water-borne hypothesis, to have fallen much lower.

Middleton has an unsatisfactory and fluctuating record despite the improvements in its water service.

Niagara Falls, despite filtration and hypochlorite treatment in 1912, had still an exceedingly high rate; almost the same, indeed, as that for the year 1909.

On a water hypothesis, if filtration and hypochlorite treatment were at all effective, the rate might have been expected to be greatly reduced.

Oswego in 1910 obtained a new water supply from Lake Ontario with intermittent hypochlorite treatment. The typhoid fever rate was 51·2 in 1910, and it fell in 1911 to 12·7; but in 1912 it rose to 21·0, a figure not far short of the 26·6 observed in 1909.

Rome in 1908, and again in 1910–11, was pressed to improve its water supply. It is not quite clear to what extent improvement actually took place, but the typhoid fever rate in 1912 was actually slightly worse than in the period 1900–5.

It may be that these and other discrepancies could be explained away convincingly by a full knowledge of all the local circumstances pertaining to each case. It is now somewhat generally accepted that *gross* typhoid fever rates, especially if they are dominated by explosive outbreaks, can only be attributed to impure milk or water supply. Nevertheless, full recognition of the great importance of providing pure water supplies need not blind us to the fact that it is extremely easy to over-exaggerate the part played by bad water in fostering *endemic* typhoid fever. The facts revealed in the *Monthly Bulletin* (January, 1913) of the New York State Department of Health are of extreme interest as a basis for future discussion, but in the absence of further information they cannot be accepted as finally establishing the hypothesis that the reduction in the typhoid fever rates is to be ascribed *solely* to the improvement of water supplies.

Hypochlorite treatment, if properly applied, ought to be not only relatively but *absolutely* effective in destroying *all* the microbes of water-borne disease. A large number

TYPHOID FEVER DEATH RATE.
PER 100,000 PERSONS LIVING.

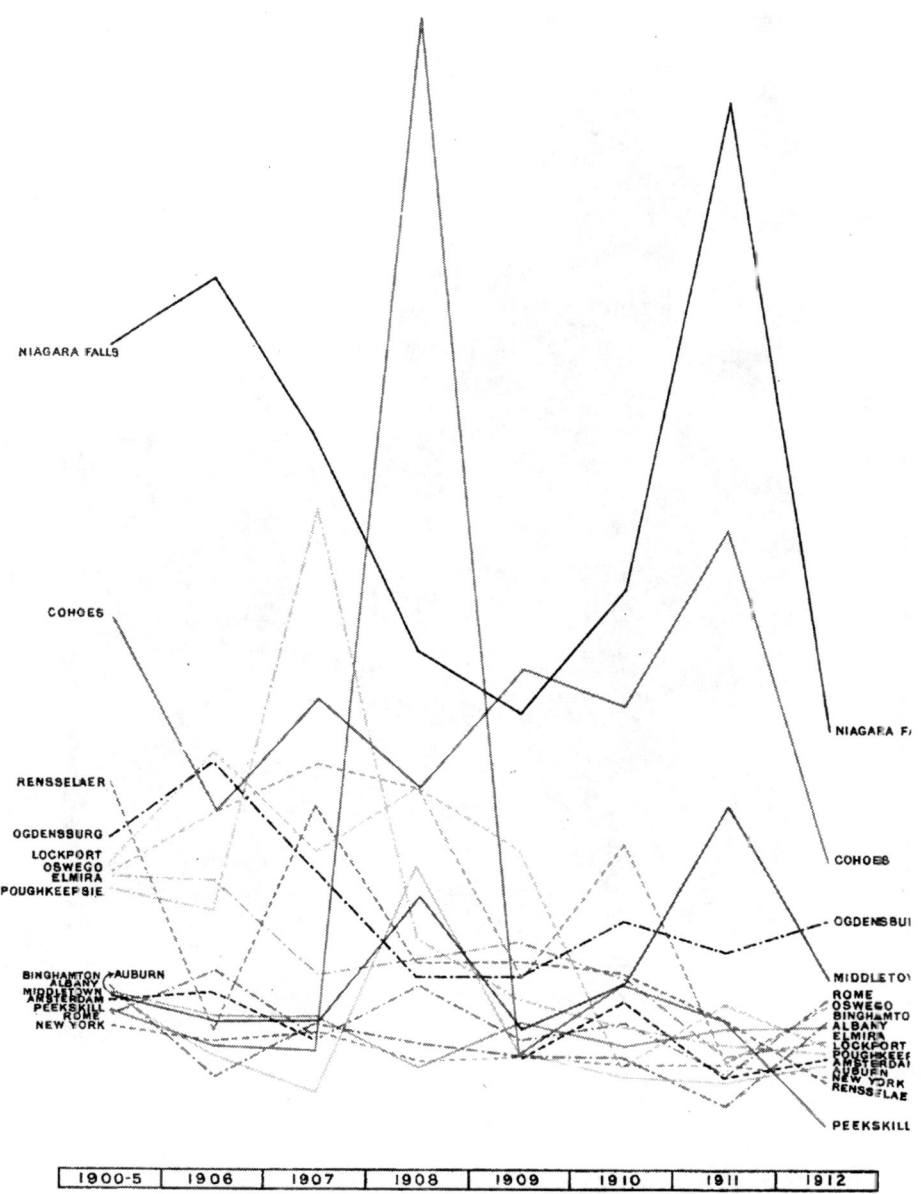

CERTAIN AMERICAN CITIES (NEW YORK STATE).

FIG. 23.

VII WATER AND DISEASE 123

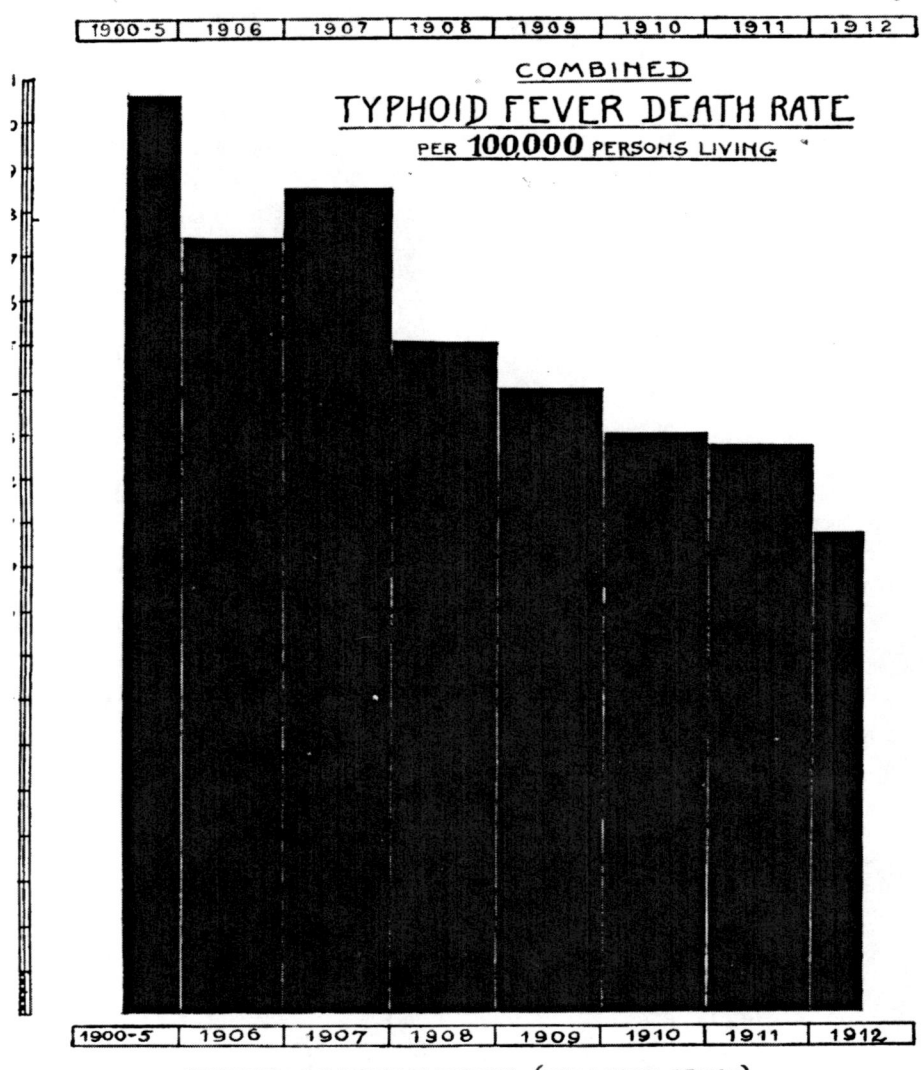

Fig. 24.

of American towns are now applying the hypochlorite treatment and if the typhoid death rate in these towns is above what is known as the "normal"[1] it may be suggested that either the treatment is not being properly carried out or the water-borne hypothesis must be abandoned.

As regards this matter, it would not be either a very difficult or a very costly matter to carry out a demographic test on a vast scale.

A number of large cities might be chosen in the United States in which the typhoid death rate was so considerably above the normal as to give *prima facia* support to the water-borne hypothesis.

Each city could then be divided into two (or more) sections comparable as regards the age, work, and pecuniary and other conditions of its inhabitants, and generally in respect to sanitary matters. By arrangement one section could still receive its old water supply, and as regards the other an *absolutely* sterile water could be supplied year in and year out at a practicable cost, by the hypochlorite or other approved method of sterilisation. If the water contained so large an amount of organic matter and suspended matter as to render sterilisation difficult with moderate doses of hypochlorite, it might first be "rough-filtered" then oxidised by chemical methods or by the use of percolating filters, again filtered through fine material, next treated with hypochlorite in tanks holding not less than *several hours' supply*,[2] and, finally, if found necessary or desirable, passed through filters containing charcoal or other dechlorinating material. Another method would be to use alum antecedent to filtration so as to render the filtrate relatively free from oxidisable matter and then apply the hypochlorite treatment after filtration.

---

[1] The "normal" is that death rate which is assumed to be of non-water origin and caused by such agencies as shell-fish, milk, flies, &c.

[2] Never less than 1 hour and preferably 5, 10, or even 24 hours. This is very important, as it ensures absolute sterilisation with a minimum dose of hypochlorite.

Alternatively, comparable cities might be chosen and the water supplies of a selected number of them sterilised. It must not be supposed that this is a chimerical or impracticable notion. In the first place, we have from the United States the definite suggestion that the formula $D = 2{\cdot}75\,(T-N)$ appraises the monetary loss due to impure water, where $D =$ loss in dollars per million gallons of water used. $T =$ typhoid death rate per 100,000 and $N =$ normal typhoid death rate, *i.e.*, from causes other than water (*see* Chapter VIII.).

Secondly, from the same quarter we are informed that a vast population in the aggregate are in the position of having T greatly in excess of N.

Thirdly, the argument is adduced that, apart from humanitarian considerations, it is much cheaper to purify water efficiently than to bear the burden of disease and death.

Fourthly, it is also averred that there is a well marked causative relationship between improvement of water supplies and diminished incidence of general and particular diseases.

If these contentions are really sound, the logical outcome is that the difference between T and N could be and should be " wiped out " by absolute sterilisation.

CHAPTER VIII

THE FINANCIAL VALUE OF A PURE WATER SUPPLY

Most persons will agree that a pure water supply is not only a great boon, but a sound public asset. It seems an unworthy task to attempt to place the value of human life on a monetary basis, or to argue that the supreme gift of health and attendant happiness can be reduced to a numerical value. Nevertheless, if the result of such calculations is to bring home to negligent waterworks authorities, that an unsatisfactory water supply may not only cause sickness and death, but also lead to financial instability, a good purpose will have been served; if it can also be shown that to remedy matters is a good investment, even from a utilitarian point of view, a good result will have been obtained.

Within recent years a great deal of work has been done on this subject, and though many of the conclusions arrived at are in the highest degree problematical, a very strong case has been established in favour of the financial advantages of a pure water supply.

Perhaps the most ingenious and daring writer on the value of pure water has been Whipple,[1] and the author, although not necessarily endorsing all the views of that authority, feels that the matter is worthy of more than merely sympathetic consideration.

[1] "The Value of Pure Water," by Geo. C. Whipple.

Sanitary value of water.—In estimating the sanitary or health value of water, typhoid fever has been taken as the chief water-borne disease; Whipple, however, considers that improved water supplies also exercise a markedly beneficial effect on diarrhœal diseases.

Albany and Troy are given by him as examples because they are neighbouring towns, and because the former greatly improved its water supply, an example not followed by the latter town.

The percentage reduction of death-rates over comparable periods in the two cases was as follows:—

	Albany.	Troy.
Typhoid Fever	75	0
Diarrhœal Diseases	57	12
Children (under 5)	49	18
Total Deaths	17	6

Although not dissenting from the view that impure water *may* cause diarrhœal diseases, it must not be forgotten there are also other and perhaps more powerful factors which determine the incidence of diarrhœa in this country.

In Fig. 25 (p. 129) is shown the annual death rate per million living, among children, under five years of age from diarrhœal diseases (1891–1900) for England and Wales as a whole, and for twelve towns the water supply of which is derived chiefly from moorland or upland gathering grounds, which, speaking generally, are remote from the possibilities of sewage pollution.

It is surely apparent that we have to look elsewhere than to water supply for the true explanation of this disproportionate incidence of diarrhœa in these northern towns.

A number of American authorities, however, associate, not only typhoid fever and diarrhœal diseases with impure water, but pulmonary and certain other diseases, which we have hitherto always regarded as having no relation to water supply.

The following extract (being a quotation from a paper by Hyde "On the Sterilisation of Water Supplies by the Use of Hypochlorites") from Hooker's treatise on "Chloride of Lime in Sanitation" shows how strong are the views of certain American sanitarians on this point.

"Messrs. Mills (1893), Reincke (1893), Hazen (1904), Sedgwick (1910), and others have shown that when a pure water supply has replaced an impure one in a community, the general death rate therein is generally reduced in a considerably greater degree than would be acccounted for by the reduced prevalence of Typhoid Fever and other recognised typical water-borne diseases. A study of the vital statistics of numerous places where the quality of the public water supply has suddenly been changed from bad to excellent, as for instance, by the construction and proper operation of adequate purification works, has shown that for every person thus saved from death from typhoid fever, approximately three other persons are saved from death from other causes, many of which have probably never been thought to have any direct connection with, or to be especially affected or influenced by the quality of the public water supply. This numerical statement of the reduction in death rate more or less directly due to improved water supplies has recently become known as the HAZEN THEOREM, because Mr. Allen Hazen in 1903–05 was the first to announce in definite terms this interesting and most encouraging phenomenon. Even such unexpected diseases as tuberculosis, pneumonia, bronchitis, and a series of disturbances causing undue mortality among infants seem to be decidedly affected by such changes in the quality of the water supply. From general principles it is to be inferred that the drinking of a polluted and insanitary water supply must surely tend to lower the vital resistance. On the other hand an improved water supply must mean a real improvement in the general health tone of the community, a real uplift and reinforcement, rather than an impairment of the vital resistance of the consumer of such supplies."

Reverting to the less disputable ground of typhoid fever, Whipple calculates that each typhoid death costs the community $10,000[1] and that all typhoid deaths beyond the "normal" are attributable to impure water.

The "normal" is a suppositional figure arrived at by inferring the probable number of cases caused by such agencies as milk, uncooked food, shell-fish, flies, etc. In America 20 is usually taken as the "normal," but this is

[1] To convert dollars into pounds, divide by five. The above sum includes the cost to the community of the non-fatal cases of typhoid fever. Speaking very broadly, each typhoid death represents usually about ten cases of the disease.

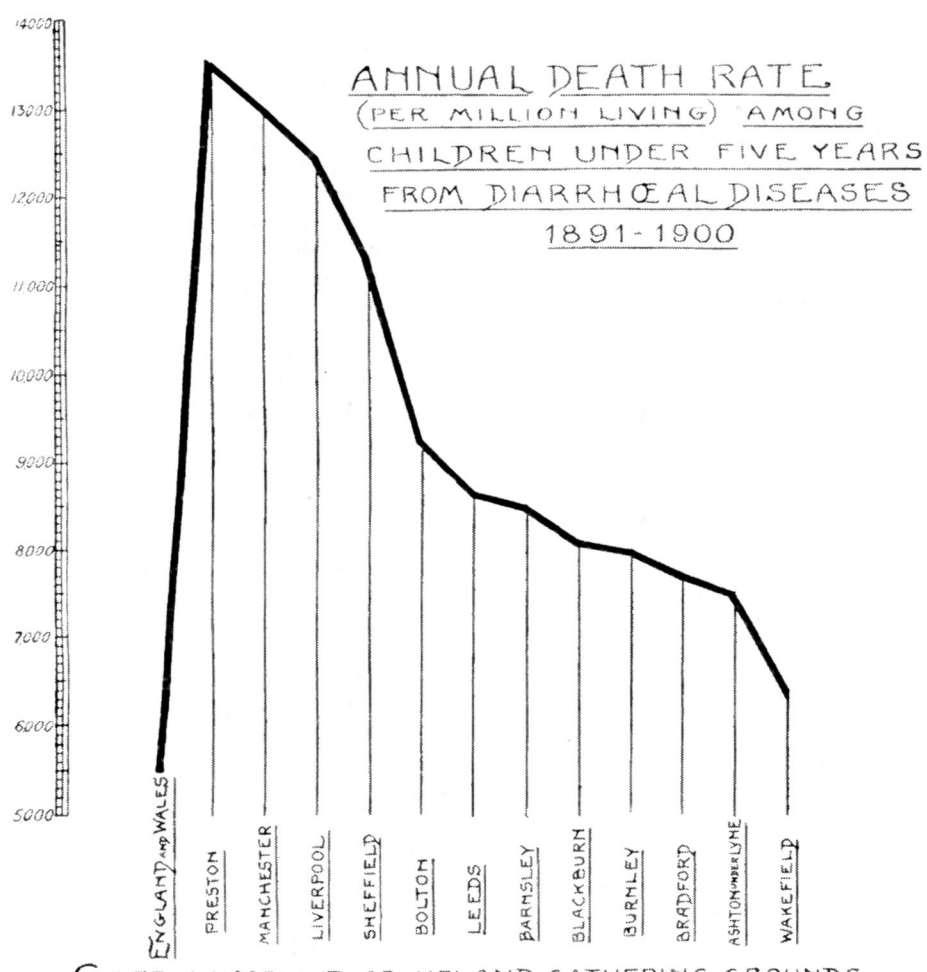

Fig. 25.

sometimes reduced to 15 or lower where the sanitary conditions are good and increased to 25 or more where the converse holds good. Obviously everything depends on the correctness or otherwise of whatever figure is chosen to represent the "normal."

In London the total typhoid death-rate is only about 4 per 100,000 ; so that either we should have to conclude that water played no part in causing the disease, or reduce the American "normal" five times or more.

In order to arrive at the loss in dollars per million gallons of water used, the following formula is applied :—

T = Typhoid death rate per 100,000.
N = "Normal" rate.
Daily consumption taken at 100 gallons per capita.
$(T-N)\,10,000$ = loss to community in dollars for $365 \times 100 \times 100,000$ gallons of water, or $\frac{(T-N)1,000}{365} = 2\cdot75\,(T-N)$, where D stands for loss in dollars per million gallons of water used.

The application of the formula is of considerable interest. Taking the average death-rate from typhoid fever in American cities as 35 per 100,000 and assuming a value of 20 for N.

$$D = 2\cdot75\,(35-20) = \$41\cdot25.$$

On this basis American cities are losing, owing to unsatisfactory water supplies, $41·25 per million gallons or about $15,000 per annum for each million gallons a day of supply.

Whipple gives Pittsburg as an example [1] :—

"In Pittsburg for example, the typhoid death-rate for several years has averaged 120. Here according to formula (1), $D = 2\cdot75(120-20) = \$275$ per million gallons. This is figured, however, on a per capita water consumption of 100 gallons a day. The actual consumption is about 250 gallons per capita per day ; hence D should be taken as $\frac{100}{250}$ of $ 275, or $110 per million gallons.

---

[1] Whipple's book is dated 1907. Many changes have occurred since then, and this fact must not be forgotten in judging the present day value of all the figures and quotations given in this chapter.

Each million gallons of polluted Allegheny water pumped to Pittsburg has therefore reduced the vital assets of the community by $110. This for a population of 350,000, amounts to $3,850,000 per year—a sum enormously greater than the annual cost of making the water pure."

In the British Islands the consumption of water per head is much less than 100 gallons, so that D must be corrected on the basis of $\frac{100}{\text{Daily Consumption}}$. Taking a general average, the consumption would only be about one-third, which involves multiplying D by 3.

Perhaps no very serious exception can be taken to the figure of $10,000 for each death from typhoid fever, but the crux of the whole position is fixing the highly debatable figure for N.

For example, the typhoid death-rates for Edinburgh, London and Glasgow are about 2, 4, and 8 respectively. It would take a very bold controversialist to suggest here the figure 2 for N and to carry into the foregoing formula the figure 2 for London and 6 for Glasgow (T − N).

It is only necessary to compare the widely different typhoid death-rates in European and American cities to realise how delicate a matter it would be to suggest a number for N.

The following diagram (Fig. 26, p. 133) has been constructed from some figures given by McLaughlin in a paper entitled "The Eradication of Typhoid Fever."[1]

The population of all the cities dealt with exceeds 300,000.

A glance at the diagram enables one to realise how difficult, if not impossible, it would be to suggest a non-controversial figure for N.

For example, taking Paris—the *worst* of the European cities given in the diagram—as the normal (namely 5·6), the writer has calculated that on this basis the aggregate

[1] *Boston Medical and Surgical Journal*, Vol. CLXVI., No. 21, pp. 764–771. May 23rd, 1912.

number of deaths from typhoid fever in the 15 American Cities, in excess of the assumed normal of 5·6, totals 1,495, and probably the case rate would be ten times greater. To attribute so much suffering and waste of life to impure water would be a serious step to take.

If it be assumed that bacteriological tests, although indirect and subject to certain limitations, afford a not untrustworthy means of comparing the potential quality of different waters in relation to disease, then the cities dealt with in the diagram ought to show on bacteriological examination results in correspondence with the curve exhibited in the diagram in order to fit in with the water-borne hypothesis. Such an investigation, if carried out by competent observers using precisely the same methods and media, would be of extreme interest. In the absence of an international standardisation of methods and media, it is impossible to institute many comparisons of the gravest importance, alike to bacteriologists and epidemiologists.

Physical Quality of Water.—Too little attention is paid to the physical characters of water from a financial point of view. A water supply which is too highly coloured or turbid, or has an objectionable taste, drives many people to use household filters or to increase the demand for bottled waters.

It may be that a supply unsatisfactory in these respects may be hygienically quite safe, but it is very difficult to persuade complainants that such is the case, and the almost invariable retort is—how can it be pure if it is dirty-looking or " smelly " ?

The formulæ suggested by Whipple for calculating loss due to colour, turbidity, and smell are admittedly open to criticism, and it may suffice to quote the effect of their application to particular instances :—

"For instance, such a water as that now supplied to New York city from the Croton river has a depreciation of $11 per million gallons, or nearly a

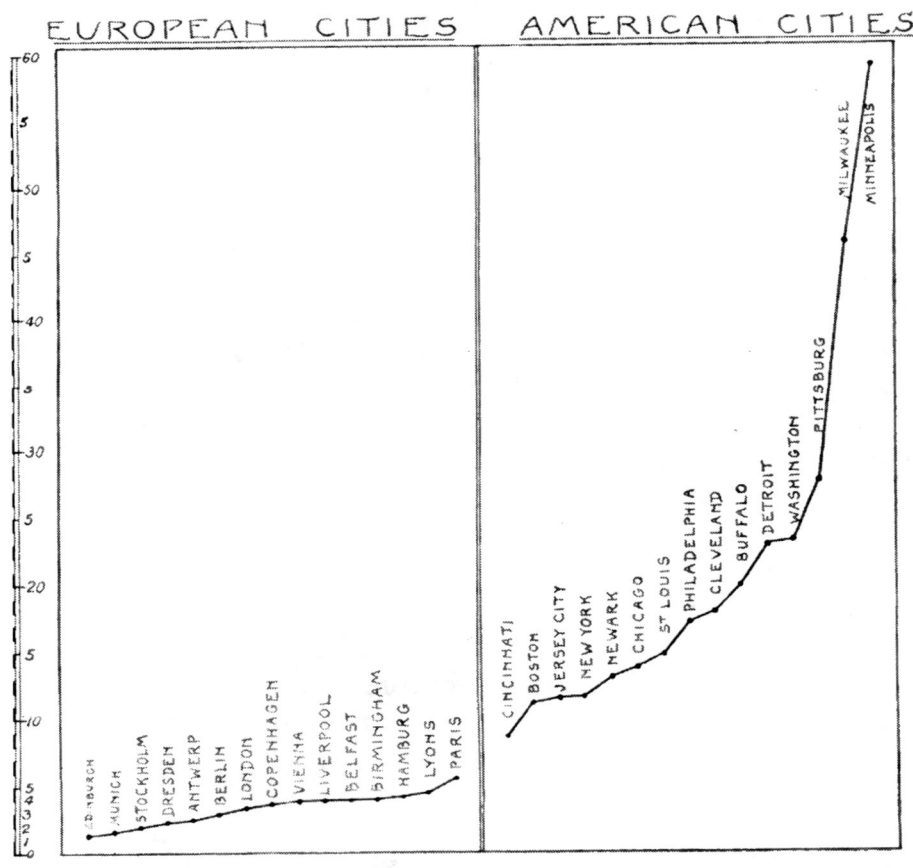

Fig. 26.

million and a half dollars a year for a daily supply of 350 million gallons. At 4 per cent. this represents the interest on about $35,000,000, a sum several times as large as the cost of filtration. An algae-laden water like that of Ludlow Reservoir at Springfield, Mass., has a depreciation of more than $20 per million gallons, because of its odour and turbidity. A coloured water like that of the Black River at Watertown before filtration has a depreciation of $11, while a turbid water like that of the Mississippi River at St. Louis gives $25."

Hardness of Water.—As regards the hardness of water the greatest diversity of opinion exists; and the consensus of medical opinion seems to be that for the general run of people the matter is relatively unimportant.

London, the largest, and one of the healthiest cities in the world, has a decidedly hard water supply.

Glasgow, the second largest city in the British Isles, is exceedingly proud of its very soft supply, derived from Loch Katrine.

On the other hand, a hard water supply undoubtedly means a loss due to increased consumption of soap, waste of fuel, etc. Whipple calculates that for every increase of one part per million of hardness, the cost of soap increased about $10 per million gallons of water completely softened.

All the water used by a community is not completely softened, and Whipple considers that a conservative estimate is one gallon per capita. On this basis, the depreciation of water, on account of its hardness, is $D = H/10$, in which $H =$ the hardness of the water in parts per million, and D the depreciation in dollars per million gallons. Table XXXVI. (p. 135) is given by Whipple in illustration of the application of the formula.

The Aftermath of Water Epidemics.—Whipple does not appear to have taken into account the *ultimate* heavy financial loss accruing when a town loses its fair reputation as a result of a water-borne typhoid epidemic. It may be doubted whether Worthing and Maidstone have yet fully recovered from the effects of their typhoid epidemics in

1893 and 1897, respectively. Lincoln, similarly afflicted in 1905, despite its magnificent new supply introduced in 1911, is likely to suffer financially for many years to come.

The old saying, "Give a dog a bad name," applies with almost brutal force and persistency to the future prosperity of a town which has lost its reputation for health. It is almost useless to urge that the old water supply has been efficiently purified, or even that a new and perfect supply has been obtained. A lost reputation as regards health

TABLE XXXVI.—DEPRECIATION DUE TO "HARDNESS" (WHIPPLE).

State.	City or Town.	Source of Supply.	Total hardness (parts per million).	Depreciation per million gallons.
Maine	Augusta ...	Kennebec River ...	20	$2·00
,, ...	Waterville ...	Messalonskee River	15	1·50
Massachusetts	Boston	Sudbury and Nashua Rivers	12	1·20
,,	Cambridge ...	Storage Reservoir	33	3·30
,,	Pittsfield ...	,, ,, ...	50	5·00
New York ...	New York ...	Croton River	40	4·00
,, ...	Albany ..	Hudson ,, ...	64	6·40
,, ...	Oswego ...	Oswego ,, ...	191	19·10
Pennsylvania	Philadelphia	Schuyekill River ..	179	17·90
Ohio	Toledo	Maumee ,, ...	200	20·00
,, ...	Columbus ...	Scioto . ,, ...	335	33·50
,, ...	Warren • ...	Mahoning ,, ...	578	33·50
England ...	London ...	Chelsea Company ...	215	21·52
,, ...	,, ...	East London ,, ...	243	24·30

affects a town long after the introduction of improved sanitary measures, and persists, despite the publication of reassuring vital statistics.

Summer and holiday resorts, and educational centres, are always very hardly hit, as their welfare depends on what may be called an "optional" population.

Nearly all classes of trade suffer either directly or indirectly to a greater or less extent, and the burden may not be lightened for many years.

No formula can be suggested for estimating the financial

loss attributable to the aftermath of a typhoid epidemic, but that it is very serious cannot be doubted.

Table XXXVII. has been constructed from figures given by Whipple to show to what extent, in his opinion, the *sanitary value* of a polluted public water supply is increased by an efficient system of filtration :—

TABLE XXXVII.—INCREASE IN SANITARY VALUE (IN DOLLARS).

Place.	Per million gallons.	Per year.	Per year per capita.
Lawrence, Mass.	652	665,000	9·50
Albany, N.Y.	130	450,000	4·75
Binghampton, N.Y.	65	160,000	3·80
Watertown, N.Y.	120·34	175,000	6·90

As regards *physical quality*, Whipple calculates that by improving their water supplies, Lawrence, Albany, Yonkers, Poughkeepsie, Binghampton, Watertown, Little Falls, and Brooklyn increased the value of their water supplies by 6·0, 8·4, 9·0, 14·2, 10·4, 12·4, 9·2, 9·0 dollars per million gallons respectively.

Again, the same writer claims that Winnipeg (Manitoba) and Oberlin (Ohio), by *softening* their water improved its value by 38·70 and 12·20 dollars per million gallons respectively. The figures refer only to water used for domestic purposes; if industrial uses were also considered, the gain would be materially greater.

As regards the cost of *purification* (*i.e.*, by filtration), Hazen calculates that :—

"As a general average, with a well-designed modern plant adapted to its work, the cost of filtering water, exclusive of pumping, but including all costs of operating the filters and furnishing the supplies required, and including the interest on the cost of the works and a reasonable allowance for repairs and depreciation, will amount to about $10 per million gallons or one cent per thousand gallons of filtered water."

"In a general way, the purification of the water adds from 10 to 20% to the entire cost of furnishing and supplying water to an American city."

In England the average cost of sand filtration is usually placed at 1d. per 10,000 gallons.

It is open to anyone to challenge and criticise the facts, figures, formulæ, and inferences here presented, but it is impossible to gainsay the broad and general conclusion that, even if we disregard all humanitarian considerations, the provision of a pure water supply is a sound financial proposition.

CHAPTER IX

BACTERIOLOGICAL ROUTINE METHODS

It is proposed in this chapter to deal with the labelling of samples, registration and classification of results, explanation of symbols and variations occurring in connection with the so-called "hektograph" sheets, collection of samples, decimal mode of dilution, the use of racks, coloured wools, labels, and so on.

Sample Collection boxes.—The wooden boxes used for this purpose are made to carry 4, 6, 8, 10, and 12 bottles, each bottle having a capacity of about 180 cubic centimetres.[1]

Figure 29 (p. 141) represents an eight-bottle box and is self-explanatory.

Labels.—The author uses a very simple method for labelling samples. Each sample collector is known by the first letter of his surname, and in cases where two or more names begin with the same letter, some simple device is used to distinguish them, for example, taking the first and last letters of the surname.

Every collector begins each year by labelling his samples 1, 2, 3, and so on to the end of the year, prefixing the number with the first letter of his surname.

An actual example may be given (Fig. 27, p. 139).

---

[1] The American Public Health Association recommends two-ounce bottles, but this small size precludes the possibility of 100 c.c. cultures being made.

· The labels are contained in a book and are printed in triplicate on each page with a perforated division to allow

No. R.1000. Date 22.4.17.
Particulars :— River Thames,
Temp:—13°C. Hampton,
10.40 a.m. Raw Water.
            —"—
Sampler's Name J. S. Ramage.

FIG. 27. Facsimile of a Label used for a water sample.

of two of them being detached, as is indicated in the following figure (Fig. 28) which is of course purposely reduced in size.

The description of the sample is the same on A, B, C. B is torn out and stuck on the sample bottle, C is torn off after the sample collector reaches the Laboratory and is pasted, together with those handed in by the other sample collectors at the end of the day's collection, into a book specially kept for this purpose.

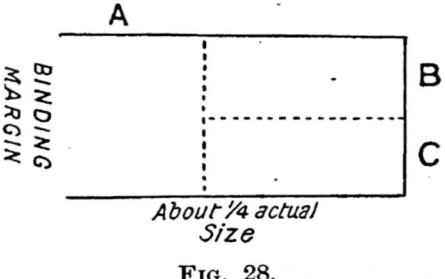

FIG. 28.

The labels in this book are then given " running " numbers, so that the total number of samples collected up to any date can at once be found. As a matter of fact, inasmuch as samples for chemical examination have also to be collected, it is the custom to have red " running " numbers for chemical samples, blue for the bacteriological and black for the aggregate number.

The sample collector retains counterfoil A in his book so

as to guide him in the collection of further samples. In this way, each sample collector is responsible for his own labels and numbers, and if any question arises about any sample, no conflict of opinion can occur between the different sample collectors as to misunderstood instructions, the inquiry being necessarily limited to what a particular man has done or left undone.

Some notes on the registration and classification of results, with particular reference to the B. coli test.—A full copy of the label, together with all the subsequent results, are entered in a book known as the "parent" laboratory book. This book contains all the permanent records necessary for future abstraction and classification purposes.

As the "parent" laboratory book contains, opposite the space left for the results of the analysis of each sample, a full copy of the label referring to it, together with its letter and number, it is only necessary to label all the cultures and sub-cultures relating to the sample with the sampler's number prefixed by the first letter of his surname. Loose working sheets are also used and on these the results obtained are "pencilled" opposite the letter and number from day to day, and so when the final results come out one worker reads out the figures, and another worker records them neatly in the "parent" laboratory book. In addition, records are abstracted on to loose sheets, using hektograph ink for this purpose, and these are arranged under their proper headings, *e.g.*, *raw* Thames water, *raw* Lee water, etc., etc.

At the end of the month several copies are "pulled" off and used for filing, Committee, and other purposes. The foregoing description takes no account of the numerous other ways in which the results are abstracted for special purposes, but the whole system is based on a carefully thought-out plan, which aims at simplicity, accuracy and rapidity. When more than 1,000 samples a month have

IX BACTERIOLOGICAL ROUTINE METHODS 141

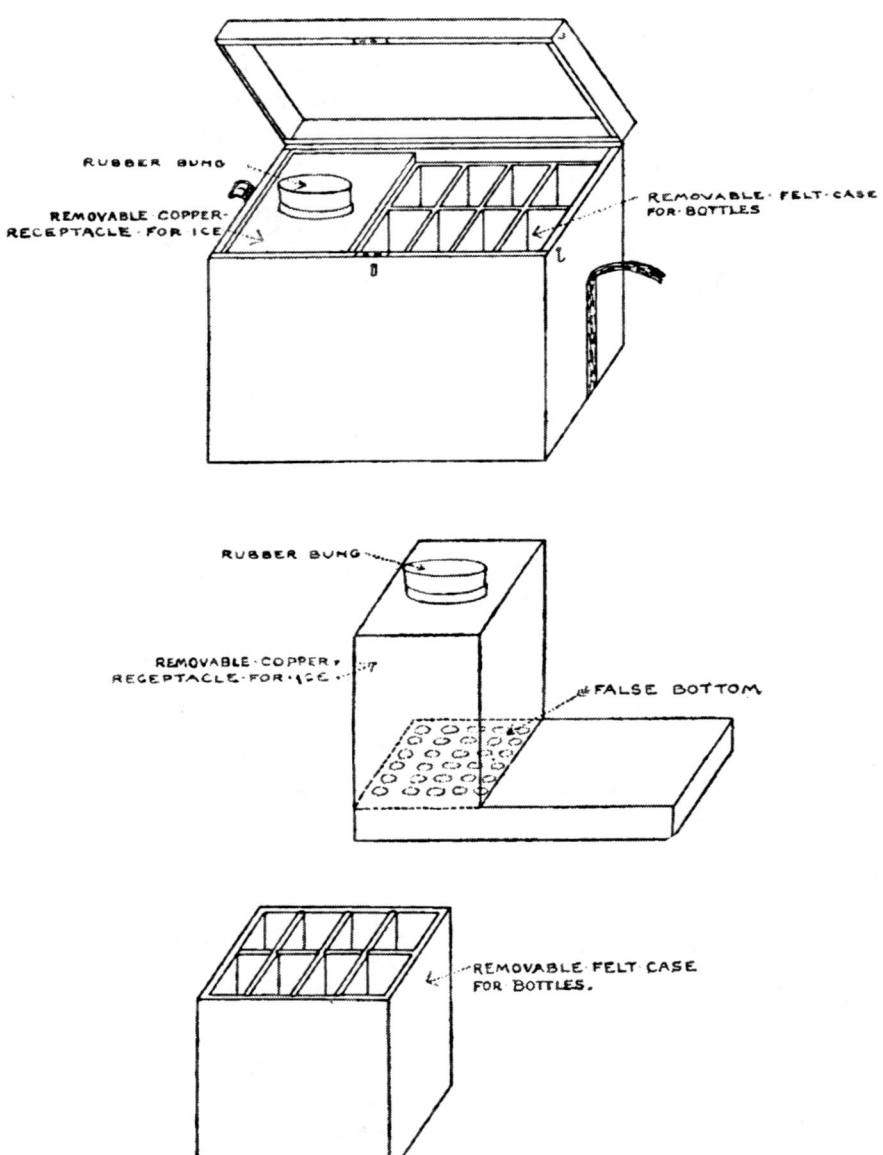

FIG. 29. Sample Collection box.

to be examined minutely, it is a matter of great importance so to organise the work as to prevent errors in entries or any accumulation of arrears of work.

Examples of the "hektograph" sheets already referred to are here given (p. 148). These have been purposely reduced in size, and slightly modified so as to allow of reproduction on a single page. The symbols on the page will be unintelligible to the uninitiated reader, but they enable the observer to register what is technically known as the "farthest out +" for the different B. coli results (presumptive, confirmatory, and typical) for each sample examined. This finally allows percentages to be struck with perfect accuracy owing to the self-checking nature of the method.

By the "farthest out +" is meant the smallest volume of water which yields a positive result on a presumptive, confirmatory and typical B. coli basis. Thus the B. coli results would in practice be summarised in the manner shown on the hektograph sheets, and the results (taking sheet 1 as an example) finally tabulated as follows :—

TABLE XXXVIII.—B. COLI TEST, LAMBETH DISTRICT, GENERAL WELL, JAN., 1907.

(Summary from Sheet 1).

Number of Samples.	−100 c.c. of water.					+100 c.c. of water.					+10 c.c. of water.					+1 c.c. of water.				
	Presumptive.	Confirmatory.		Typical.		Presumptive.	Confirmatory.		Typical.		Presumptive.	Confirmatory.		Typical.		Presumptive.	Confirmatory.		Typical.	
		Gl or Ag.	Ag.	Sagin or Agin.	Agin.		Gl or Ag.	Ag.	Sagin or Agin.	Agin.		Gl or Ag.	Ag.	Sagin or Agin.	Agin.		Gl or Ag.	Ag.	Sagin or Agin.	Agin.
1	2	3	4	5	6	7	8	9	10	11	12	13	14	15	16	17	18	19	20	21
22	13.6% 3	22.7% 5	40.9% 9	45.4% 10	72.7% 16	45.4% 10	40.9% 9	40.9% 9	36.3% 8	9.1% 2	40.9% 9	36.3% 8	18.2% 4	18.2% 4	18.2% 4	% 0	%	%	%	%

It will be noted that the sum of the figures in the following columns corresponds to the number of samples examined, and the sum of the percentages of course in each case is 100.

Presumptive	... ...	columns 2, 7, 12, 17.
Confirmatory	{ gl or ag	columns 3, 8, 13, 18.
	{ ag...	columns 4, 9, 14, 19.
Typical. ...	{ Sagin or agin ...	columns 5, 10, 15, 20.
	{ Agin	columns 6, 11, 16, 21.

To take the presumptive test as a single example:—22 samples of water were examined, 100, 10, 1, 0·1 and 0·01 c.c. cultures of each sample having been made.

3 Samples (13·6%) yielded negative results in all cultures (column 2).
10 Samples (45·4%) yielded positive results with 100 c.c. but not with 10 c.c. of water (column 7).
9 Samples (40·9%) yielded positive results with 100 c.c. and 10 c.c. but not with 1 c.c. of water (column 12).

22 Samples 99·9%.

The same principle governs the classification of the confirmatory and typical B. coli results.

It will also be noted that the B. coli test yields results which may be classified under five separate headings.

Test 1.—*Presumptive B. coli test*, mixed culture gaseous fermentation of primary medium, 48 hours at 37–40° C.

Test 2.—*Confirmatory B. coli test*, on a general basis. Presumptive test has been confirmed by the isolation of either a glucose fermenting ("gl"), or a lactose fermenting ("ag") coli-like microbe.

Test 3.—*Special confirmatory B. coli test*, on a lactose basis ("ag").

Test 4.—*Typical B. coli test*, on either a "sagin" or "agin" basis.

The microbe isolated in pure culture is indistinguishable (on the basis of the tests employed) from the typical B coli of the human intestine. Here the term "sagin" represents a microbe which forms gas in saccharose and in lactose media, and produces indol in peptone water culture. " Agin," indicates fermentation of lactose, and formation of indol, *negative* result with saccharose.

Test 5.—Specially typical B. coli, on an "agin" basis. Here saccharose fermentation excludes an otherwise typical B. coli, from being accepted as specially significant of undesirable pollution.

The two examples of hektograph sheets (*see* end of chapter) are necessarily at first a little difficult of comprehension, but if the reader follows the explanation of the symbols given the matter will become comparatively simple. It may assist somewhat if all the actually occurring variations of results recorded on the two hektograph sheets are explained in detail.

Variation 1.

(M3, M12, M20 (Sheet 1))

Here the presumptive test (black dots) yielded positive results with 100, 10, but not 1 c.c. of water (see columns 4, 9 and 14). Hence the black dots are placed on the farthest out +, namely, in column 9.

The confirmatory test on a general basis (blue bars) yielded positive results with 100, 10, but not 1 c.c. of water (see columns 5–6, 10–11, 15–16). Hence the bars are placed on the farthest out +, namely, between cols. 10 and 11. As regards the special confirmatory test (blue dots on right of blue bars, positive results were obtained with 100, 10 but not 1 c.c. of water (see columns 6, 11, and 16). Hence the dots are placed on the farthest out +, namely, in column 11. No attention need here be directed to the dots on the left side of the bars, as a record of these need only be taken when the more significant special confirmatory test fails.

Next, as regards the typical B. coli test on a general basis (red bars) positive results were obtained with 100, 10 but not 1 c.c. of water (see columns 7–8, 12–13, 17–18). The bars are here placed on the farthest out +, namely, between columns 12–13.

In respect of the specially typical B. coli (red dots on right side of bars) positive results were obtained with 100, 10 but not 1 c.c. of water (see columns 8, 13, 18) so the dots are placed on the farthest out +, namely, in column 13. No attention need be directed to the dots on the left side of the bars, as a record of these need only be taken when the more significant specially typical B. coli test fails.

Variation 2.

M60 (Sheet 1), SS64, SS67 and SS 72 (Sheet 2).

The foregoing description is equally applicable here except that the samples instead of yielding positive results with 100 and 10, only yielded positive results with 100. Hence the dots and bars occur under the columns pertaining to 100 c.c. instead of 10 c.c.

Variation 3.

M68, M75, M123 and M171 (Sheet 1).

Here the only difference from Variation 2 is that no specially typical B. coli could be isolated, "sagin" (col. 7) microbes being obtained instead. The red dot therefore occurs in col. 7 and in column 1 is marked a red dot on the right side of a red bar, signifying that no specially typical B. coli were found even in 100 c.c. of water.

Variation 4.

M27 (Sheet 1).

The symbolic representation here is exactly the same as Variation 1, except that in connection with the 100 c.c. culture a "sagin" instead of an "agin" microbe was isolated, so a + has to be entered in column 7 instead of column 8. This, it is true, does not affect the classification of the B. coli results, and therefore the dot and bar pattern is unaffected; but it does affect the number of specimens (of one or another type) isolated from the different volumes of water dealt with, and of which a record must be kept for a different purpose altogether.

Variation 5

M36 (Sheet 1).

Here we are dealing with a new pattern because the sample although yielding positive results with the presumptive test in 10 c.c. (black dot column 9) failed to yield any typical B. coli in this amount and indeed was only confirmed on a lower "gl" plane. Hence the blue bar although placed between cols. 10-11 has the blue dot to the left (col. 10) and we have to fall back on the 100 c.c. culture to obtain an "ag" microbe (see blue dot in col. 6). Further, the 100 c.c. culture had to be fallen back upon to obtain typical B. coli and as it turned out to be an "agin" microbe the red bar is placed between cols. 7-8 with the red dot in col. 8.

Variation 6.

M140, M147 (Sheet 1) SS. 60 (Sheet 2).

The pattern here exactly corresponds to variation 5 except that the failure to isolate an "agin" microbe necessitated the red dot being placed in column 7 instead of 8 and a red bar with right hand red dot in column 1 which may really be regarded as the negative 100 c.c. column.

Variation 7.

M156 (Sheet 1) SS 68 (Sheet 2).

In these samples the failure to isolate typical B. coli of any kind, even in 100 c.c. of water, calls for a red bar, with red dots on either side of it, being placed in column 1. Otherwise the pattern corresponds to variation 2.

Variation 8.

M44, M51 (Sheet 1)

This corresponds with variation 7 except that as a "gl" instead of an "ag" microbe was isolated, the blue dot comes on the left side of the blue bar (col. 5 instead of 6) and a blue bar with right side blue dot has to be introduced into column 1.

Variation 9.

M168, M116 (Sheet 1).

These samples yielded presumptive positive results in 100 c.c. (black dot column 4) but no confirmation was obtained on sub-culture, so a red triangle is introduced into the picture and the No. 1 column receives a blue and a red bar, each with two dots.

Variation 10.

M132 (Sheet 1).

This sample yielded positive presumptive results in 100 and 10 c.c., so the black dot appears in column 9.

Confirmation was not obtained in the 10 c.c. culture, hence the red triangle. A "gl" microbe, however, resulted from the 100 c.c. culture, so a blue bar appears between cols. 5–6 with a blue dot on its left hand side (col. 5) and the No. 1 negative column receives a blue bar with the blue dot on the right side. As no typical B. coli of any kind were found it became necessary to place in column 1 a red bar with red dots on either side of it.

Variation 11.

M164 (Sheet 1).

This sample yielded similar results except that confirmation was obtained in the 10 instead of the 100 c.c. cultures with corresponding alteration of the pattern.

Variation 12

SS 65 (Sheet 2).

In this sample, both the presumptive and special confirmatory results were positive so far out as the 1 c.c. culture thus leading to the black dot being placed in col. 14, the blue bar between cols. 15–16 and the blue dot in col. 16.

In none of the cultures, however, could a specially typical "agin" B. coli be found, hence the red bar with right hand red dot in column 1. A "sagin" microbe resulting from the 100 c.c. culture, a red bar appears between cols. 7–8 and a red dot in col. 7.

Variation 13.

SS 70 (Sheet 2).

Here the presumptive test yielded positive results even in 0·1 c.c., hence the black dot in col. 19. A "gl" confirmatory result was obtained from the same culture, so a blue bar appears between cols. 20–21 and a blue dot on its left hand side, namely, in column 20.

An "ag" confirmatory microbe being isolated from the 1 c.c. culture, a blue dot is placed in col. 16. Typical B. coli was isolated from the 1 c.c. culture, so a red bar appears between cols. 17 and 18; but as it was a "sagin" not an "agin" microbe, the red dot necessarily falls into col. 17.

As however an "agin" microbe was obtained from the 10 c.c. culture, a red dot is placed in column 13.

Variation 14.

M84, M92, M99 (Sheet 1) and SS62 (Sheet 2).

Here the samples yielded completely negative results, as judged by all the tests, so there will be found in the negative No. 1 column a black dot, a blue bar with blue dots on either side of it, and a red bar with red dots on either side of it.

The foregoing description may appear to be very complicated; in practice, however, this method of recording results is not only extremely simple, but it reduces the chances of error practically to nil.

Decimal mode of dilution.—The author has used for so many years the decimal mode of dilution and has described it so often in his reports that the briefest reference need only be made to it here.

A series of tubes each containing 9 c.c. of sterile water are inoculated from the sample of water as follows:

1 c.c. of water is added to the first tube (1) 1 c.c. is taken from tube (1) and added to a second tube (2)

1 c.c. is taken from tube (2) and added to a third tube (3).

1 c.c. is taken from tube (3) and added to a fourth tube (4) and so on according to the quality of sample being dealt with.

Thus with sewages, it may be necessary to go as far as the tenth dilution to ensure negative results at the extreme end of the scale.

1 c.c. from the various dilutions is then added in the reverse order to appropriate media and their values in terms of the original material are obviously as follows :—

$$
\begin{aligned}
1 \text{ c.c. of tube } (10) &= 0\cdot0000000001 \text{ of sample} \\
(9) &= 0\cdot000000001 \\
(8) &= 0\cdot00000001 \\
(7) &= 0\cdot0000001 \\
(6) &= 0\cdot000001 \\
(5) &= 0\cdot00001 \\
(4) &= 0\cdot0001 \\
(3) &= 0\cdot001 \\
(2) &= 0\cdot01 \\
(1) &= 0\cdot1
\end{aligned}
$$

In addition 1 c.c., 10 c.c., and 100 c.c. cultures are also made and in certain cases the writer has used 1000 and 10,000 c.c. cultures as well.

It may be, and indeed has been, objected that there is a wide gap between 100 and 10, between 10 and 1, between 1 and 0·1, and so on. This is true, but if reference be made to the author's original reports the suggestion will be found that, if time and media allow, intermediate cultures may in special cases be made as follows :—

100, 90, 80, 70, 60, 50, 40, 30 and 20 c.c. cultures.

10, 9, 8, 7, 6, 5, 4, 3, and 2 c.c. cultures.

1, 0·9, 0·8, 0·7, 0·6, 0·5, 0·4, 0·3, 0·2, c.c. cultures, and so on.

It is obvious, however, that in routine work this procedure is impossible, nor if it were attempted would the information obtained be likely to prove of much additional value. As some bacteriologists condemn waters on a 1 c.c. basis and others on a 10 c.c. and yet others again on a 100 c.c. basis, it is apparent that with such wide discrepancies of opinion prevalent, the time is scarcely ripe for insisting on meticulous refinements. The attempt to do so usually ends in curtailing the *range* of the cultures, so that the results are all positive with none negative or all negative with no positives. The writer, however, has often

EXAMPLE OF HEKTOGRAPH SHEET.— No. 1.
Lambeth District.—General Wells.
(January, 1907.)

Sample.	Day of Month.	Total Number of Bacteria per c.c. (gelatine at 20–22° C).	B. Coli test.												
			100 c.c.					10 c.c.					1 c.c.		
			Presumptive.	Confirmatory.		Type.		Presumptive.	Confirmatory.		Type.		Presumptive.	Confirmatory.	Type.
				gl.	ag.	Sagin.	Agin.		gl.	ag.	Sagin.	Agin.		gl. ag.	Sagin.
2	3	4	5	6	7	8	9	10	11	12	13	14	15 16	17
3.	2	23	+		+		+	+		+		+	O		
12.	3	21	+		+		+	+		+		+	O		
20.	4	11	+		+		+	+		+		+	O		
27.	7	11	+		+	+		+		+		+	O		
36.	8	6	+		+		+	+	+				O		
44.	9	1	+	+				O							
51.	10	8	+	+				O							
60.	11	2	+		+		+	O							
68.	14	2	+		+	+		O							
75.	15	1	+		+	+		O							
84.	16	12	O												
92.	17	2	O												
99.	18	5	O												
108.	21	5	+		△			O							
116.	22	6	+		△			O							
123.	23	1	+		+	+		O							
132.	24	4	+	+				+		△			O		
140.	25	3	+		+	+		+	+				O		
147.	28	4	+		+	+		+	+				O		
156.	29	8	+		+			O							
164.	30	6	+		△			+	+				O		
171.	31	11	+		+	+		O							
10. 16.			10	9	9	8	2	9	8	4	4	4			

Explanation of Symbols on Hektograph Sheets Nos. 1 & 2.

Note.
(1.)   •   Furthest out presumptive on positive side, or negative presumptive.
(2.)   •| Furthest out positive "gl." in 100 c.c. or less.
       When the furthest out positive confirmatory is an "ag." this symbol is not required.
(3.) |•   Furthest out positive "ag." in 100 c.c. or less, or negative "ag."
       If furthest out positive in this confirmatory test was "gl." then blue dot is placed on furthest out "ag." if present. This completes the symbol •|• the bar portion of the symbol having been previously allocated in the "gl." symbol. In the event of no positive "ag." being found in any of the cultures, then symbol |• is placed in the negative column, at left side of sample number.
(4.)   •|• Negative "gl." and "ag."
(5.)   •| Furthest out positive "sagin" in 100 c.c. or less.
       When the furthest out positive typical is an "agin" this symbol is not required.
(6.) |•   Furthest out positive "agin" in 100 c.c. or less, or negative "agin."
       If furthest out positive in this typical test was a "sagin" then red dot is placed on the furthest out "agin" if present. This completes the symbol •|• , the bar portion of the symbol having been previously allocated in the "sagin" symbol. In the event of no positive "agin" being found in any of the cultures, the symbol |• is placed in the negative column, at left hand side of the sample number.
(7.)   •|• Negative "sagin" and "agin."
(8.)   △ •= Failure. This indicates that although the primary culture formed acid and gas, failure was experienced in the attempt to isolate coli-like microbes from secondary cultures.
9.) Where the results were negative in 100 c.c. or less, as regards these tests, the symbols occur on the negative side, at the left of the sample number. Each of the symbols must occur in number, corresponding to the number of samples examined.
10.) PRESUMPTIVE TEST:—Add number of black dots in each column on positive side, and number on negative side.
11.) CONFIRMATORY TEST.
     "Gl." and "ag." basis:—Add number of blue bars | in each column on positive side and number of •|• symbols on negative side.
     "Ag." basis:—Add number of • in each column on positive side ("ag." column), and number of |• and •|• on negative side.
12.) TYPICAL TEST.
     "Sagin" and "Agin" basis:—Add number of red bars | in each column on positive side and number of •|• on negative side.
     "Agin" basis:—Add number of • in each column on positive side, ("agin" column) and number of |• and •|• on negative

EXAMPLE OF HEKTOGRAPH SHEET.— No. 2.
River Thames water after Storage in the Staines Reservoirs.

2321 $\frac{v}{17510}$ (June, 1909.)

Description of Sample.	Day of Month.	Number of Microbes per c.c.			B Coli test.																			
		Gelatine at 20-22° c. counted on third day.	Agar, at 37° c. counted 20-24 hours.	Rehlpelagar, at 37° c. counted 20-24 hours.	100 c.c.				10 c.c.				1 c.c.				1 c.c.				01 c.c.			
					Presumptive.	Confirmatory.		Type.	Presumptive.	Confirmatory.		Type.	Presumptive.	Confirmatory.		Type.	Presumptive.	Confirmatory.		Type.	Presumptive.	Confirmatory.		Ty
						gl.	ag.	Sagin. AGIN.		gl.	ag.	Sagin. AGIN.		gl.	ag.	Sagin. AGIN.		gl.	ag.	Sagin. AGIN.		gl.	ag.	Sagin.
Cols. 1	2	3 A	3 B	3 C	4	5	6	7 8	9	10	11	12 13	14	15	16	17 18	19	20	21	22 23	24	25	26	27
S.s. 60.	3	220	20	5	+	+	+		+	+			0												
S.s. 62.	7	270	120	7	0																				
S.s. 64.	10	210	34	0	+	+		+	0																
S.s. 65.	14	200	22	1	+	+	+		+	+			+	+			0								
S.s. 67.	17	72	4	0	+	+		+	0																
S.s. 68.	21	120	19	0	+	+			0																
S.s. 70.	24	340	88	4	+	+	+		+	+			+	+			+	+			0				
S.s. 72.	28	80	10	0	+	+		+	0																

IX BACTERIOLOGICAL ROUTINE METHODS 149

made ten 10 c.c. cultures instead of one 10 c.c. and one 100 c.c. culture, and obtained useful results, although it does not necessarily follow that this is really equivalent bacteriologically to making 100, 90, 80, 70, 60, 50, 40, 30, 20, and 10 c.c. cultures.

Racks, coloured wools, labels and media, wires, etc.—It is desirable, as is done at the Metropolitan Water Board Laboratories, to set up racks (Fig. 30) containing the various dilutions and media. Coloured labels are very convenient, *e.g.*, blue for 100, brown for ten, green for 1, pink for 0·1, yellow for 0·01 red for 0·001, and maroon for 0·0001 c.c. cultures, and so on. Coloured wools should also be used to distinguish the various media, or the media may be tinted with litmus, neutral red, etc. Beads also of various colours may be used in the media itself.

Instead of platinum wires and loops, iron wires may be used with great advantage. These may be sterilised in bulk, and their use saves a great deal of time in sub-cultural work. The straight iron wires used by florists and sold in bundles are best for this purpose (about 175 mm. long and about 1 mm. thick). With a suitable pair of round-nosed pliers, it is easy to make a loop at one end of a number of these wires, and these loop wires then serve admirably for all purposes where loop "cultures" are required.

CHAPTER X.

BACTERIOLOGICAL ROUTINE METHODS (*continued*).

IN this chapter will be found a detailed description of the exact method followed in the examination of a sample of raw river water. The work to be carried out each day is fully explained, and the composition of the media used in connection with the various tests is also given.

Examination of a Sample of Water.

First day.—It will perhaps be best to take the examination of a sample of raw river water as an example, it being understood that when dealing with more impure samples the dilutions, etc., must be carried further, the converse holding good in the case of filtered water samples. The rack shown in Fig. 30 (p. 152) may be used for this examination, and the dilutions, culture tubes, etc., arranged in it in the way explained in the accompanying description. At this stage it may be convenient to describe a piece of apparatus used for keeping ordinary agar and bile-salt-agar cultures at the proper temperature so as to be available at any time for "pouring" purposes. To start with, the tubes are first placed in the retainer shown in Fig. 31 (p. 153); this is then lifted out of the water-bath, and placed in another copper vessel, containing a sufficiency of water, and heat applied by means of a Fletcher burner. After the water has boiled for some time so as to ensure that all the agar in the tubes has been liquefied, the water is cooled down (but not below 50° C.), the retainer is lifted out and transferred back to the copper water-bath (*see* Fig. 31), the water in which is maintained at a temperature of 45° C. by means of a capsule which, by its expansion and contraction, governs the supply of gas to the bunsen used for heating purposes.

Before very long the contents of the tubes and the surrounding water become of the same temperature of 45° C., and the tubes are then *always ready* for " pouring " purposes, either on the same day or subsequent days.

One large and six small sterile Petri dishes are placed conveniently on the laboratory bench and labelled as follows :—

1 large dish with brown 10 c.c. label for bile-salt-agar.
2 small dishes with green 1 c.c. labels (1 for ordinary agar and 1 for bile-salt-agar.
2 small dishes with pink 0·1 c.c. labels (1 for ordinary agar and 1 for gelatine).
1 small dish with yellow 0·01 c.c. label (for gelatine).
1 small dish with red 0·001 label (for gelatine).

After first shaking the sample bottle, the lip is flamed, the stopper withdrawn and held in such a way as to avoid contamination, or it may be placed temporarily on any sterile surface.

If reference be made to Fig. 32 (p. 155), the following description will be easily followed.

One c.c. of water is withdrawn from the bottle by means of a sterile pipette and transferred to dilution (1), the tube being moved one place to the left. One c.c. from dilution (1) is then transferred to dilution (2), 1 c.c. from (2) to (3), and, lastly, 1 c.c. from (3) to (4), the tubes on each occasion being shifted one place to the left (*see* 2 in Fig. 32). One c.c. amounts from dilution (4), representing 0·0001 c.c. of the sample, are next taken and added to the tube behind it in the rack, namely, the 0·0001 bile-salt-peptone tube, with maroon label, and whilst this is being

152 STUDIES IN WATER SUPPLY   CHAP.

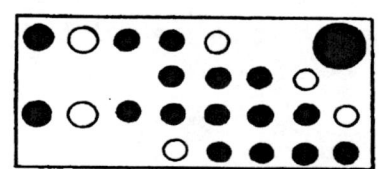

FIG. 30.—Rack, as set up for the Examination of a Sample of *Raw* River Water. As seen in plan.

Reading always from left to right.

Row. 1.—First hole empty. The remaining four contain 9 c.c. dilution tubes.

Row 2.—First hole contains a 10 c.c. double strength bile-salt peptone tube (blue wool). The 2nd hole is empty. The 3rd, 4th, 5th, 6th, and 7th holes contain 10 c.c. single strength bile-salt peptone tubes (pink wool) for the 1, 0·1, 0·01, 0·001, and 0·0001 c.c. cultures. B. coli test. The 8th hole is empty.

Row 3.—The 1st, 2nd, and 3rd holes contain gelatine tubes for the 0·1, 0·01, and 0·001 c.c. cultures. Test for numbers. The 4th hole is empty.

Row 4.—First hole contains a 40 c.c. milk tube for 10 c.c. culture. The second hole is empty. The 3rd and 4th holes contain 10 c.c. milk tubes for the 1 and 0·1 c.c. cultures. The milk tubes are previously boiled to expel oxygen and then rapidly cooled in cold water. These are for B. enteritidis sporogenes test. The last hole is empty. The big hole (right top corner) contains a 50 c.c. treble strength bile-salt-peptone tube, and is for the 100 c.c. B. coli culture.

The 100 c.c. label is blue, and the rest as follows:—10 c.c. (brown), 1 c.c. (green), 0·1 c.c. (pink), 0·01 c.c. (yellow), 0·001 c.c. (red), and 0·0001 c.c. (maroon).

The ordinary agar and bile-salt-agar cultures are made by adding the water direct to the plates and subsequently adding the melted media (*see* text).

done each tube is shifted one place to the right so as to reduce to an absolute minimum any possibility of a mistake (*see* 3 in Fig. 32).

One c.c. amounts from dilution (3), representing 0·001 c.c. of the sample, are next taken and added successively to the tubes behind it in the rack, namely, the 0·001 bile-salt-peptone and gelatine tubes with red labels, the shifting from left to right being again practised (*see* 4 in Fig. 32).

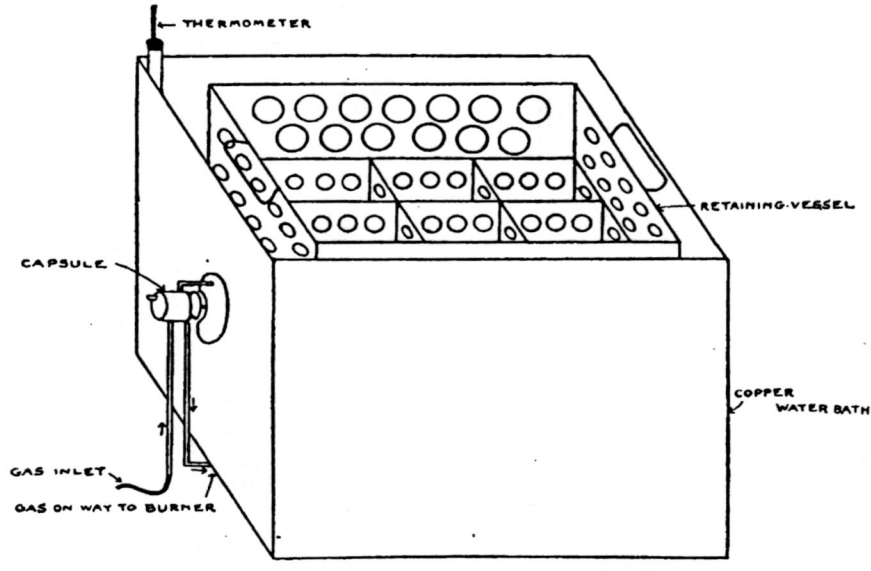

Fig. 31.—Apparatus for Agar Tubes.

One c.c. amounts from dilution (2), representing 0·01 c.c. of the sample, are next taken and added successively to the appropriate tubes, namely, the 0·01 c.c. bile-salt-peptone and gelatine tubes with yellow labels, the shifting process being repeated (*see* 5 in Fig. 32).

One c.c. amounts from dilution (1), representing 0·1 c.c. of the sample, are then added successively to the 0·1 c.c. bile-salt-peptone, gelatine, and milk tubes with pink labels, with the usual shifting operations. In addition, 1 c.c. from the same dilution ($= 0\cdot1$ c.c. of sample) is added to the agar plate with the pink 0·1 c.c. label (*see* 6 in Fig. 32).

We have now come to the end of the dilutions, and have to deal directly with the water in the sample bottle. 1 c.c. amounts are added successively to the 1 c.c. bile-salt-peptone, gelatine, and milk tubes with green labels, each tube, as before, being shifted from left to right as soon as it has been inoculated. In addition, 1 c.c. amounts are added to two of the plates, bearing the green labels, one for ordinary agar and the other for bile-salt agar (*see* 7 in Fig. 32). Next, 10 c.c. amounts of water are added successively to the 10 c.c. bile-salt-peptone (double strength) and milk tubes bearing the brown labels and shifted from left to right, and as well, 10 c.c. are added to the plate with the brown label for bile-salt-agar (*see* 8 in Fig. 32). Lastly, the single 100 c.c. (blue label) culture is made, by pouring the water out of the sample bottle into the tube until it reaches the file mark. The file mark is so placed that the capacity of the tube between the level of the bile-salt-peptone medium (50 c.c. of treble strength) and the file mark is 100 c.c.

The appearance of the rack at each stage of the process is shown in the Fig. 32 (p. 155).

The contents of the bile-salt-agar and ordinary agar tubes, maintained at 45° C., are next poured into the Petri dishes already inoculated with water, and by means of a circular and swaying motion, the medium and the water thoroughly mixed together. After the medium has "set" the following drying operations are required :—

The covers are tilted by means of suitably twisted wire and placed upside down in the incubator at 37° C. until ready for counting.

The milk tubes are placed in a copper vessel containing water at a temperature of 80° C. and left for ten to twenty minutes' heating at 80° C., cooled and then placed in the incubator at 37° C. for two days.

X BACTERIOLOGICAL ROUTINE METHODS 155

FIG. 32.—Rack, during progress of Examination of a *Raw* River Water. As seen in plan.

The open circles are empty and the dark circles contain tubes.

1. Rack, as set up. 2. After making dilutions. 3. After making 0·0001 c.c. culture. 4. After making 0·001 c.c. cultures. 5. After making 0·01 c.c. cultures. 6. After making 0·1 c.c. cultures. 7. After making 1 c.c. cultures. 8. After making 10 c.c. cultures. There remains only the making of the 100 c.c. cultures.

The gelatine tubes are placed in warm water (about 37° C.) until the gelatine is all melted. After shaking, the contents are poured into the Petri dishes waiting to receive them, and which have been already labelled in correspondence. After the gelatine has "set," the plates are placed in the cool incubator (20–22° C.) for three days, after which the colonies are counted.

The liquid bile-salt cultures are placed in the hot incubator; some bacteriologists prefer a temperature of 37° C. whilst others rely on 42° C., others, yet again, on some intermediate temperature.

This concludes the work for the first day, apart, of course, from the work falling due, on account of samples previously examined.

The second day's work (1st day after) may be described as follows :—The colonies in the bile-salt-agar and ordinary agar plates are counted. The results are expressed per c.c., so that if the count is made from a plate bearing the 10 c.c. brown label the numbers must obviously be divided by ten. If the count is from a plate with a 1 c.c. green label, the numbers stand as counted.

Again, if the count is from a plate having a 0·1 c.c. pink label, the numbers must be *multiplied* by ten, and so on. It is obvious that attention to the simple precautions now being described greatly reduces the chances of error.

It may be objected that counting after one day is undesirable inasmuch as all the colonies may not have had sufficient time to develop. On the other hand, if the ordinary agar plates are not counted at this early stage, there is grave risk, despite all drying operations, of the sporing bacteria spreading all over the plates, and rendering accurate counting altogether impossible.

No such danger occurs in connection with the bile-salt-agar plates, but it is not unimportant for comparative purposes that the ordinary agar and bile-salt-agar plates should both be counted on the same day, and we do know that with sewage-polluted waters the excremental bacteria really require no longer period for their development.

Whether any further work falls due on this day depends on circumstances. If for the B. coli work we are dealing with glucose or lactose bile-salt cultures, which require 48 hours[1] in the incubator, there is none, but if we are using the "drop" glucose method associated with a lactose bile-salt medium, then the following procedure is adopted.

All the lactose-bile-salt liquid cultures are removed temporarily from the incubator, which in connection with this method is kept at 42° C.

Those tubes showing no redness or no development of gas associated with the redness, even on smartly tapping the tubes with a flat piece of wood, receive one or more drops of a concentrated sterile glucose solution added by means of a sterile pipette and are then placed in another incubator maintained at 37° C.

The idea underlying this method is either that enfeebled lactose fermenting microbes may be coaxed into activity in the presence of glucose and a lower temperature or, failing this, that the glucose fermenters are, as a last resort, given a chance of asserting themselves. Speaking very broadly, this method is perhaps most useful during the colder months of the year, say October to March. The remaining tubes, namely, those showing gas formation, are replaced in the 42° C. incubator.

The third day's work (2nd day after) will now be described. The milk tubes are examined and those show-

---

[1] Some bacteriologists prefer 20–24 hours or even less. If the writer curtailed the incubation period in the case of the London waters he might lay himself open to the charge of using methods which appreciably affected the results in the direction of placing too favourable an opinion on the quality of the Metropolitan Water Supply.

ing the B. enteritidis sporogenes phenomenon (gas formation, separation of the whey from the casein with precipitation of the latter) are registered as positive results. It may be objected that a variety of microbes may produce these changes, and the writer has always frankly admitted that he regards the test primarily *as a test*, and not necessarily as proving the presence of a particular microbe, and that microbe alone.

The above changes in milk cultures were described by Klein as characteristically typical of the growth of B. enteritidis sporogenes, and so it is both complimentary and convenient to retain the name, although the word *test* should be added as signifying that, in recording a positive result, one is not necessarily committed to the view that the characteristic changes are produced solely by one microbe, and that the one described by Klein. The practically important point is that sewages commonly yield a positive result with 0·001 c.c., and pure water a negative result with 10 c.c. or even more.

The B. coli cultures, whether from a glucose or lactose primary medium (or lactose supplemented with glucose after 24 hours' incubation), are now removed from the incubator, and all those showing gas formation are entered as " presumptive positives."

It is desirable to tap smartly with a flat piece of wood all tubes which show redness but no apparent gas formation, as a small proportion of these may be induced to show visible bubbling.

Each one of the presumptive positive tubes is next subcultured as follows :—

A loopful from the tube is transferred by means of a sterile loop wire into 10 c.c. of sterile water. Alternatively, a straight wire may be used if experience shows that the loop carries with it too much of the culture. In either case, a sterile loop is used to inoculate two slope bile-salt-neutral-red-agar tubes, one of which also contains lactose and the other cane-sugar. The loop should not be allowed to touch the agar until it has reached the base of the slope; the wire is then worked upwards towards the operator slowly and in a to and fro fashion, which ensures separate colonies if carried out with reasonable care.

Of course, plate cultures may be used instead, but the slope cultures are so convenient that no one who has once fairly tried them is ever likely to abandon their use. In making these cultures, it is desirable to use special racks and to shift the tubes one place as soon as each one has been inoculated.

Separate racks should be provided for the 100, the 10, and the 1 c.c. (and less amounts) cultures. It is unnecessary to illustrate these racks, as their exact shape and the size of the holes for the tubes, are matters which may be left to the judgment of bacteriologists individually. It is important to note that the agar slope cultures should be labelled with blue, brown, green, etc., labels in correspondence with the "presumptive positives" from which they were derived. After inoculation, the agar slope cultures are placed in the incubator at 37° C.

The fourth day's work (third day after) comprises the following :—The gelatine plates are counted and the results expressed as number of colonies (or microbes) per c.c. of the sample. The question whether the numbers counted are to be divided by ten or remain as they are, or be multi-divided by ten, one hundred, or more, involves no possible error, as the labels being of a distinctive colour at once determine this point.

Many bacteriologists prefer to count the plates after four, five or more days' incubation. This, however, involves risk of the plates being utterly ruined for counting purposes by the development and spread of liquefying colonies.

The lactose and cane-sugar slope cultures are next

examined, the object being to secure one or more red colonies (if present) from the lactose tube and one or more colourless colonies (if present) from the cane-sugar tube.

The reason for this procedure is that the red colonies on the lactose tube are likely to be, not only " acid-producers," but " gas formers" in a lactose medium, and the colourless colonies on the cane-sugar tube may possibly be non-gas producers in a cane-sugar medium, a negative property associated with the B. coli communis as first described by Escherich. It might perhaps be surmised that this involved risk of losing a lactose fermenter, but the writer's experience is that as many lactose fermenters are derived from the cane-sugar slopes as from the lactose slopes, and there is an increase in the chances of isolating a microbe corresponding to B. coli communis (Escherich). Of course, if the lactose slope shows only colourless colonies, and the cane-sugar slope only coloured colonies, these are sub-cultured, and at the worst one is almost certain to secure at least a glucose fermenter from such slopes.

The number and variety of sub-cultures to be made from the colonies depends on circumstances and the particular views of the individual bacteriologist, but the writer suggests that to save waste of time and to avoid opportunities for error, the principle of his automatic method of inoculation should be practised.[1]

This depends essentially on touching the colony to be sub-cultured only once with a sterile iron wire, transferring the now inoculated wire into a small tube, containing a drop of saline solution, subsequently adding to that tube as many more sterile wires (all of which will be automatically inoculated) as it is desired to make cultures. For example, if it is desired to follow the author's flaginac

---

[1] Described in the Author's Report on the Condition of the Metropolitan Water Supply during the month of January, 1907. Published by the Government Printers.

method, four extra wires would be required for the following cultures :—

Neutral-red-broth	...	...	...	fl. = fluorescence.
Lactose peptone...	...	...	...	ag. = acid and gas.
Peptone water ...	...	...	...	in. = indol.
Litmus milk ...	...	...	...	ac. = acid clot.

Cane-sugar-peptone cultures may be used as well and the symbols C.S.N. or C.S.P. added, according to whether or not there is gas formation.

According to this classification, a flaginac microbe is accepted as a typical B. coli or as a microbe characteristic of excremental matter. Inasmuch as a majority of human fæcal B. coli either do not ferment cane-sugar at all or act on it but feebly, there would seem to be at least arguable reasons for considering a C.S.N. microbe more objectionable than a C.S.P. microbe.

Of course, one could obviously use a peptone water tube instead of a saline tube (as used in the automatic inoculation method) and incubate this until multiplication had proceeded far enough to allow of further sub-cultures being made from it, but this involves practically a wasted day and it is assumed here that any unnecessary delay should be avoided.

The method at present used by the writer may now be described, and one of its essential features is that gelatine solid media instead of liquid media are used, the chief reason being that the former are *much more delicate and rapid indicators of gas production.*

The two little saline tubes are taken from their parent tube (*see* Fig. 33, p. 163) and placed in the holes provided in the rack shown in the same figure. A red (by preference) colony from the bile-salt-agar lactose slope is picked off with a sterile iron wire, and the wire placed in the saline tube on the left-hand side (*a*) and "twirled" round so as to spread the bacilli throughout the medium.

Similarly, a white (by preference) colony from the bile-salt-agar-cane-sugar slope is transferred to the other saline tube (*b*). Two extra iron wires are placed in (*a*) and three in (*b*). The two little peptone tubes are next taken from their parent tube and one marked by means of a red grease pencil with a transverse bar, and inoculated with one of the wires from the (*a*) saline, the other one is inoculated from (*b*) and relates of course to the cane-sugar slope, just as the (*a*) one belongs to the lactose slope. They are then returned to their parent tube.

The five little gelatine tubes are then removed from their parent tube (see Fig. 33) which contains one tube of glucose (not coloured), two tubes of lactose (both coloured with litmus), one of cane-sugar (coloured with neutral red), and one of dulcite (coloured with bismarck brown). These are then inoculated as follows :—

One of the lactose tubes is "barred" to correspond with the "barred" peptone tube for indol and receives one of the wires from the (*a*) saline tube, and the remaining wire is used to inoculate the glucose tube.

The three wires from the (*b*) saline tube are placed separately in the cane-sugar, dulcite, and remaining lactose tubes. All the five wires are then withdrawn from the five gelatine tubes, which are returned to their parent tube and incubated at 37° C. for three hours, and thereafter at 20–22° C. for one or two days. The peptone tubes are, of course, incubated for a similar period but throughout at 37° C.

In practice, it is customary to inoculate a whole series of little saline tubes from the slope cultures and to reverse (*a*) with (*b*), for the reason that when the rack is full it is given a complete half-turn, which, as it were, undoes the reversal and enables the observer to work clear of an army of wires which otherwise would prove a source of embarrassment.

Special racks are provided for the slope cultures and

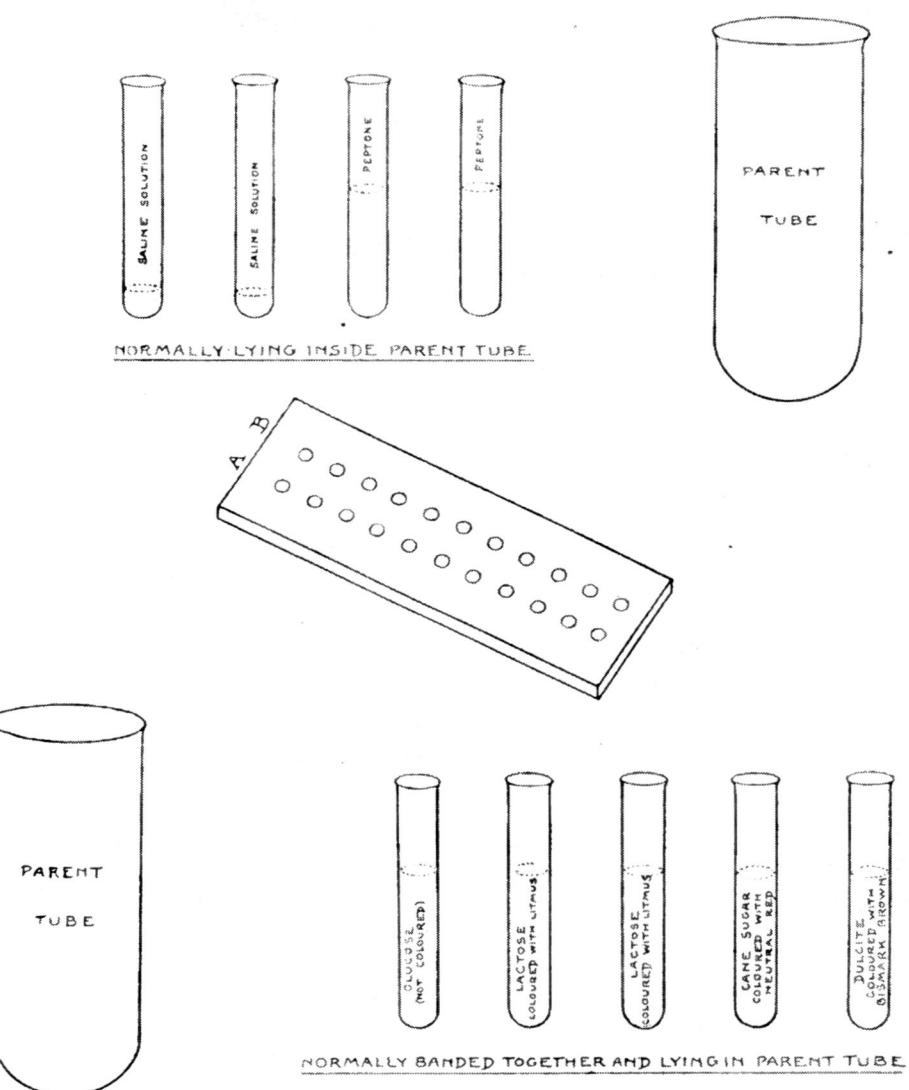

Fig. 33.— B. Coli Tests (The Parent Tubes in Practice, are plugged with Cotton Wool.)

the parent saline peptone and gelatine tubes, and the same principle of shifting a space as each inoculation process is completed is resorted to as has been previously explained. It is far quicker to work in this methodical manner, and it reduces the chances of a mistake to a minimum.

On the fifth or sixth day (4 or 5 days after) the final records are obtained. The fifth day (one day so far as these particular tests are concerned) is certainly not too soon for the glucose, lactose, and cane-sugar results, and suffices, although only barely, for the indol test, but is doubtfully long enough for the dulcite test. In a laboratory where much water work is undertaken, it is desirable to record all the results of the sub-cultural tests on the same day and at the earliest moment; and many, for these reasons, may decide to leave out such tests as demand extra time, particularly when those tests do not after all yield information materially affecting the judgment of the operator, in pronouncing on the hygienic qualities of the water under examination.

This is a matter which must be left to the individual bacteriologist, although most practical workers will agree that those who have suggested a great variety of tests have not brought forward convincingly any intelligible classification enabling one to grade the microbes isolated and studied in the order of their undesirability in a water supply.

At the Water Board Laboratories, the tests are carried out on the fifth day in cases of special urgency and on the sixth day if a rapid diagnosis is not required. The peptone water cultures are tested for indol by the paradimethylamidobenzaldehyde method, the paradimethylamidobenzaldehyde solution being added first and then the potassium persulphate solution, a pink colour developing after the lapse of a few minutes, indicating the presence of indol (*see* page 173).

As regards the gelatine tubes, the presence of gas is

readily seen owing to the medium being split up and fissured with gas bubbles.

The results are then classified as under.—

Typical B. coli (lactose +, indol +) $\begin{cases} \begin{array}{l} 2\text{ A} \\ 2\text{ (A)} \end{array} \} \text{ Saccharose } + \quad \ldots \quad \ldots \quad \ldots \begin{cases} \text{dulcite } 0 \\ \text{dulcite } + \end{cases} \\ \begin{array}{l} 2\text{ B} \\ 2\text{ (B)} \end{array} \} \text{ Saccharose } 0 \quad \ldots \quad \ldots \quad \ldots \begin{cases} \text{dulcite } 0 \\ \text{dulcite } + \end{cases} \\ \text{C} = \text{lactose } + \text{ indol } + \text{ ; other tests not determined.} \end{cases}$

1 = glucose +, lactose 0.   2 = lactose +, indol 0.
+ = gas (or indol).   0 = No gas (or no indol).

This is shown diagrammatically in Fig. 34 :—

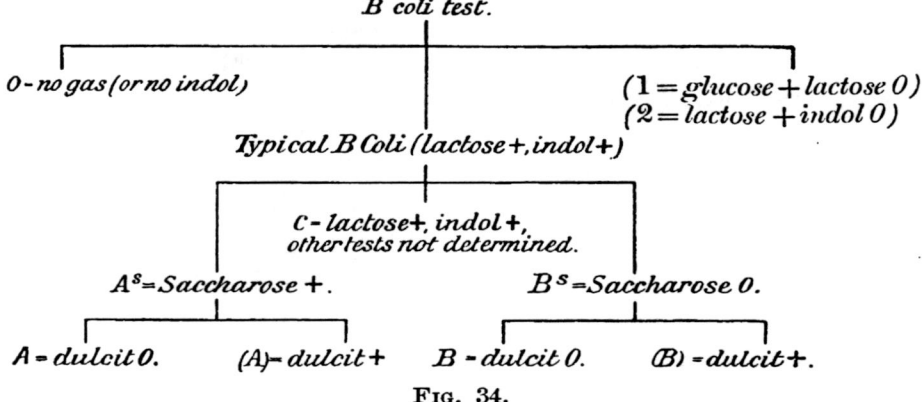

FIG. 34.

As a matter of practice, the rule is to glance at the (*b*) peptone tube first, and if this shows indol, to see whether the non-barred lactose tube is positive. If positive, it remains only to look at the saccharose and dulcite results to determine whether the microbe is to be classed as A (A), B or (B). If however, the lactose result is negative, attention is next turned to the (*a*) indol tube and its corresponding "barred" lactose tube. If both are positive the entry is C, which implies a typical B. coli, but one the characters of which, as regards saccharose and dulcite, remain undetermined.

It very rarely happens that resort has to be made to this entry owing to a failure to isolate an A, (A), B, or

(B) microbe. Suppose however, the (*b*) peptone tube had been negative, attention would equally be directed to the (*a*) series in search for a (C) microbe.

But if all these tests failed, then both the lactose tubes would be examined and if either yielded a positive result the entry would be classed as " 2."

This also having failed, the glucose tube would be observed, and the result if positive would be entered as " 1."

It will be gathered that the object is (1) to isolate if possible a " lactose + indol + microbe " with determined characters as regards saccharose and dulcite. (2) Alternatively to isolate a " lactose + indol + microbe," but with undetermined characters in respect of saccharose and dulcite. (3) Failing these to obtain a " lactose + microbe," and (4) lastly, as a final resort, to fall back upon a " glucose + microbe."

Figs. 35 and 36 (pp. 167, 169) show the results of the application of the B. coli test to the London waters. For full information on " the varieties and significance of B. coli in water supplies," the reader is referred to a paper bearing this title read by the writer at the annual meeting of the British Medical Association, 1912 (*British Medical Journal*, Sept. 21, 1912). It may be worth while here to reproduce the summary of conclusions :—

Typical B. coli (lactose +, indol +) is present in enormous numbers in excremental matters, and is absent from, or present only in small numbers in, substances free from undesirable pollution.

Typical B. coli is a decadent microbe when divorced from the animal body ; hence its presence in a water in any number probably points to fairly recent pollution.

Pure waters, generally speaking, contain no typical B. coli in 100 c.c. in a majority of representative samples ; and incidentally it may be stated that impure waters can be so purified as to yield similar results at a not unreasonable cost.

Even so lenient a standard as "no typical B. coli in 1 c.c." of water in a majority of representative samples implies that the supply is not habitually contaminated with one gallon of sewage or its bacteriological equivalent, even in 100,000 gallons of water. The 10 c.c. and 100 c.c. standards (that is, no B. coli in these amounts) obviously connote the absence of $\frac{1}{10}$ and

x BACTERIOLOGICAL ROUTINE METHODS 167

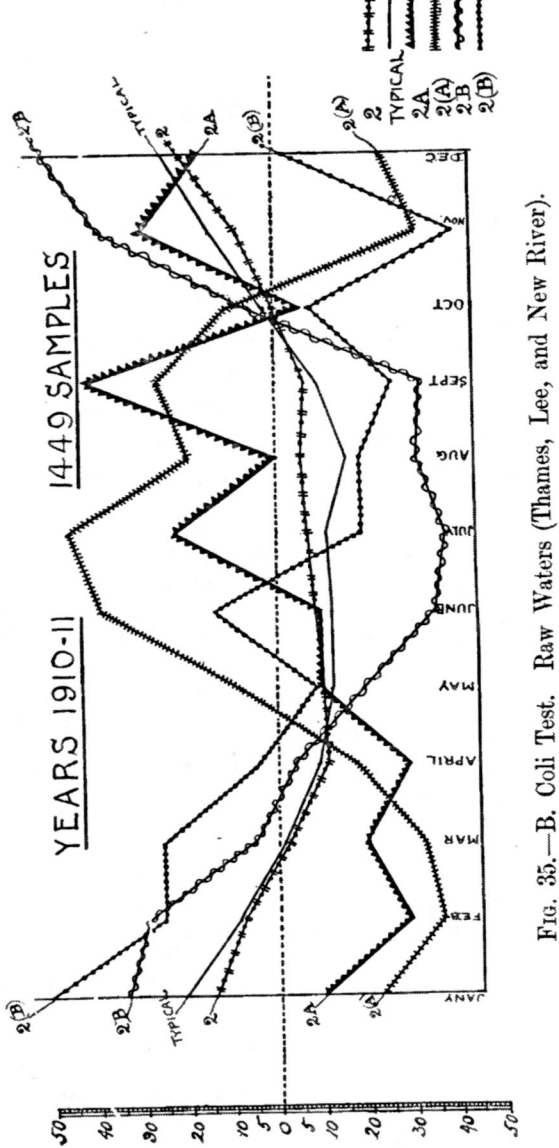

FIG. 35.—B. Coli Test. Raw Waters (Thames, Lee, and New River).

$\tfrac{1}{100}$ gallon of sewage respectively from a like volume of water. With too severe standards there is danger of condemning reasonably safe supplies, and with too lax standards there is the possibility of passing waters which ought properly to be condemned. Always to steer safely between the Scylla of the one and the Charybdis of the other may be difficult or impossible without the aid of a pilot familiar with all the local conditions.

The B. coli test ought primarily to be regarded as a quantitative decimal enumeration of "lactose +, indol +" microbes, but the subsequent grouping, according to certain attributes of the organisms thus obtained, into fairly stable or apparent varieties, may be of real practical or diagnostic importance.

Standards are worse than useless if they are not interpreted with discretion and in relation to local and other conditions. Instances could be quoted where even similar B. coli results ought properly to lead to dissimilar conclusions as regards quality and safety.

The B. coli test even alone is of the greatest value, but a water supply should be finally judged on a summation of verdicts (geological, topographical, physical, bacteriological, and chemical).

The B. coli test is by far the most reliable and speediest method of judging the degree of efficiency of the particular water purification process under investigation, and when a sterilisation treatment is in operation, the certified destruction of B. coli should afford absolute proof, practically speaking, of the devitalisation of all the microbes of epidemic water-borne disease.

The B. coli test having now survived the various vicissitudes of an earlier time, stands to-day as the most practical and delicate and rapid test for excremental filth, and may surely be taken as the most reliable indicator in its positive aspects of possible danger, and in its negative aspects of the almost certain absence of microbes associated with epidemic water-borne disease, and, generally speaking, as the one test which, above all others, it is least excusable for a water analyst to omit.

All the counts in the indictment charged against the B. coli test when fully marshalled amount to no more than this : the test is only, or mostly, of relative, not absolute, value, and therefore the results should be interpreted with discretion.

The working schedule may be summarised as follows :—

First Day :— Examination of Sample.

Second Day (first day after). Agar and bile-salt-agar plates counted and glucose added to the lactose B. coli cultures if this method is in use.

Third Day (second day after). Presumptive B. coli and B. enteritidis sporogenes results recorded, and bile-salt-agar slopes made.

Fourth Day (third day after). Gelatine plates counted and colonies from slopes sub-cultured.

X BACTERIOLOGICAL ROUTINE METHODS 169

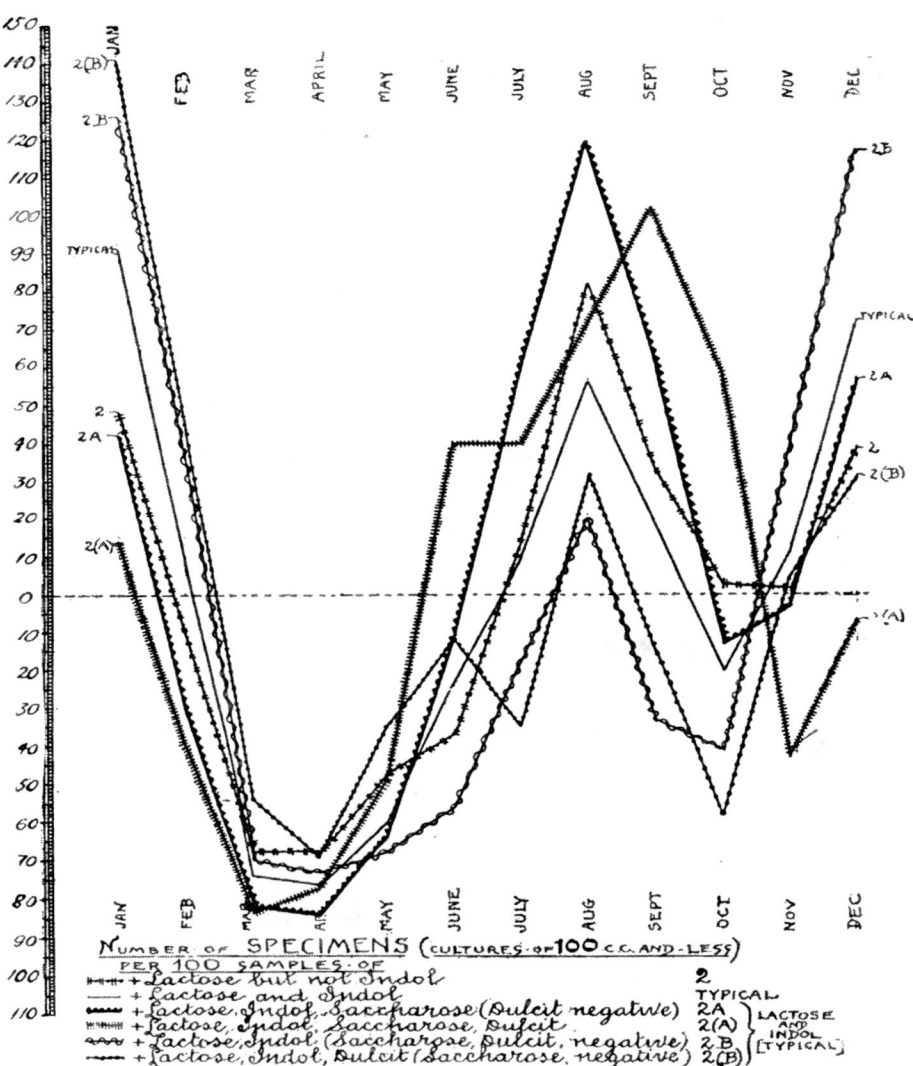

Fig. 36.—B. Coli Test. London Waters. Years 1910–11. 14,149 Samples.

Fifth or Sixth Day (fourth or fifth after). Final B. coli results placed on record.

The composition of the media used in connection with the routine work may be of interest and is here set out as follows :—

COMPOSITION OF MEDIA.

Enumeration of microbes (plate cultures).

Gelatine.
    (a) Standard.
    Gelatine (yellow gold label) 12 per cent.
    Peptone (Witte) 1 per cent.
    Sodium Chloride 0·5 per cent.
    Beef broth (1 lb. beef to 1,000 c.c. of water) to 100 c.c.
    (b) Modified.
    Gelatine 12 per cent.
    Peptone 1 per cent.
    Lemco 0·5 per cent.
    Beef broth 25 c.c.
    Water to 100 c.c.

Made faintly alkaline, till blue litmus paper is rendered slightly more blue, by means of a 20 per cent. solution of potassium hydroxide.

About 10 c.c. in test-tubes $6'' \times \frac{3}{4}''$ with white wool plug for 1 c.c. amounts of water, and 40 c.c. in test-tubes $8'' \times 1''$ with white wool plug for 10 c.c. amounts of water.

Agar
    Agar 2 per cent.
    Peptone (Witte) 1 per cent.
    Sodium Chloride 0·5 per cent.
    Beef broth to 100 c.c.

Make slightly alkaline by means of a 20 per cent. solution of potassium hydroxide 40 c.c. in test-tubes $8'' \times 1''$, with white wool plug, for use in Petri dishes $4\frac{1}{2}''$ diameter.

x BACTERIOLOGICAL ROUTINE METHODS 171

Rebipelagar[1] (*neutral red, bile-salt, peptone, lactose, agar*).

Agar   2   per cent.
Peptone   2   per cent.
Bile salt   0·5 per cent.
Lactose   1   per cent.
Water tinted with neutral red up to 100 c.c.

(4 c.c. of a 1 per cent. sterile aqueous solution of neutral red per litre of medium.) No alkali required. About 40 c.c. in test-tubes 8″ × 1″ with white wool plug.

B. Coli test

Primary Cultures

Dilution Water (decimal method)
9 c.c. of water in tubes 6″ × ¾″, tinted with fluorescin (1 part in a million). White wool plugs.

Bile salt peptone water (MacConkey)

Peptone (Witte) 2 per cent.
Bile salt   0·5 per cent.
Lactose   1·0 per cent.
Tinted with 10 c.c. of a 10 per cent. sterile litmus solution.
Water to 100 c.c.

Above is single strength for 1 c.c. cultures. About 10 c.c. of medium in tubes 6″ × ¾″ with inverted inner tube 2″ × ½″. Pink cotton wool plug.

Double strength for 10 c.c. cultures:—Use twice the percentage of above solid constituents with same size of tubes, but white wool for plugs.

---

[1] This term is merely used for convenience; it will be understood that to MacConkey belongs the credit of the introduction of bile-salt media.

Triple strength for 100 c.c. cultures :—Three times the percentage of above solid constituents. 50 c.c. of medium in tubes 8″ × 1½″, with inner tube 3″ × 1″. White wool plug, covered with sterile paper.

Secondary Cultures

Dilution water.
About 9 c.c. distilled water in tubes 6″ × ¾″. White wool plug.

Rebipelagar.—see supra.
Medium sloped in tubes 6″ × 1″. White wool plug.

Rebipesagar.—Similar composition to rebipelagar, 1 per cent. saccharose being substituted for 1 per cent. lactose. Medium sloped in tubes 6″ × 1″. Red wool plug.

TYPE OF B. COLI.—Attributes determined by

(A) "Flaginac" Test, with additional glucose and cane-sugar test.

fl = fluorescence within two days at 37° C. in *neutral red broth cultures.* Peptone 1 per cent., sodium chloride 0·5 per cent., beef broth to 100 c.c. [2 c.c. of a sterile 1 per cent. aqueous solution of neutral red per litre of medium]. Make faintly alkaline with a 20 per cent. solution of potassium hydroxide. Tubes 6″ × ½″, inner tube 2″ × ¼″. White wool plug.

ag = acid and gas within two days at 37° C. in lactose peptone cultures. Peptone 2 per cent., lactose 1 per cent., 10 c.c. of a 10 per cent. litmus solution, water to 100 c.c. Tubes 6″ × ¾″, inner tube 2″ × ½″. Blue wool plug.

in = indol within five days at 37° C. in peptone water cultures. Peptone 1 per cent., sodium chloride 0·5 per cent., water to 100 c.c. 10 c.c. of medium in tubes 6″ × ⅝″. White wool plug.

ac = acid and clot within five days at 37° C. in litmus milk cultures. 10 c.c. of milk tinted with litmus. Tubes 6" × ⅝". White wool plug.

In addition the two following tests may be applied :—

gl = gas in glucose gelatine (shake cultures). Standard gelatine plus 1 per cent. glucose. 8 c.c. in tubes 6" × ⅝" white wool plug.
cs = acid and gas within two days at 37° C. in cane sugar peptone cultures. Peptone 2 per cent., saccharose 1 per cent., 10 c.c. of a 10 per cent. litmus solution. Water to 100 c.c. Tubes 6" × ¾", inner tube 2" × ½". Red wool plug.

(B) "GLAGINS" TEST, with additional dulcite test. One wide tube 3" × 1", with white wool plug, containing four small tubes 2" × ¼" unplugged.

Saline solution :—Two small tubes each containing one drop of 0·5 per. cent. sodium chloride solution.

Peptone water medium for indol test :—Two small tubes each containing about 0·5 c.c. of medium. Peptone 1 per cent., sodium chloride 0·5 per cent. water to 100 c.c.

Composition of solutions used for testing for indol (Böhme, *Centr. f. Bakt.* Bd. XL. 1905) :—

(1) 8 grammes paradimethylamidobenzaldehyde, 160 c.c. hydrochloric acid, 760 c.c. absolute alcohol.
(2) Saturated cold water solution of potassium persulphate.
One wide tube 3" × 1", containing five small tubes (2" × ¼") of gelatine sugar media of the following stock composition. Peptone 2 per cent. ; gelatine 7·5 per cent. ; 1 c.c. of a 5 per cent. solution of potassium hydroxide per 100 c.c. of medium.

Glucose gelatine medium:—One small tube of above stock medium to which 1 per cent. glucose is added. Medium not tinted.

Lactose gelatine medium:—Two small tubes containing stock medium to which 1 per cent. lactose has been added. Medium tinted with litmus solution.

Saccharose gelatine medium:—One small tube containing stock medium to which 1 per cent. saccharose has been added. Medium tinted with neutral-red.

Dulcite gelatine medium:—One small tube containing stock medium to which 0·5 per cent. dulcite has been added. Medium tinted with bismarck brown.

B. Enteritidis Sporogenes test.

10 c.c. of whole milk in 6″ × ½″ tubes for 1 c.c. cultures.
40 c.c. of whole milk in 8″ × 1″ tubes for 10 c.c. cultures.
} White wool plugs.

CHAPTER XI

BACTERIOLOGICAL SPECIAL METHODS

IT will be convenient next to describe some of the special methods used by the writer in searching for such pathogenic microbes as the cholera vibrio, the typhoid bacillus, and Gärtner's bacillus in samples of water.

The Cholera Vibrio.—No serious cholera epidemic has occurred in this country for many years, and the isolated cases of this disease have been few in number. Although the protection of our water supplies may be thoroughly safeguarded owing to the vigilance of the Local Government Board, Port Sanitary Authorities, Rivers Boards, and Medical Officers of Health, yet the ravages of cholera in the past forbid the belief that our insular position and temperate climate afford us absolute immunity from an importation of this disease.

It is of importance, therefore, to consider what method or methods can be relied on to isolate the cholera vibrio from water if present therein. Without prejudice to the value of other methods, the writer has found the old peptone method, with certain modifications, of great value in the case of impure raw river water, purposely inoculated with only a few cholera vibrios, and so, when the method is successful under these conditions, it is quite certain that with less impure waters still better results could be obtained.

Thirty-seven samples of raw river water (Thames, Lee, and New River) were purposely inoculated with cholera vibrios, and in 23 cases a positive result was obtained. The number of cholera vibrios artificially added to the infected water (in the 23 successful experiments) was as follows :

Per c.c. of infected water.

10·2400	or about	10	0·5000	or fewer than	1
5·2000	,, ,,	5	0·4760	,, ,,	1
4·6400	,, ,,	5	0·3760	,, ,,	1
3·5200	,, ,,	4	0·3540	,, ,,	1
3·5200	,, ,,	4	0·3520	,, ,,	1
2·5600	,, ,,	3	0·2700	,, ,,	1
2·4960	,, ,,	3	0·2380	,, ,,	1
2·4800	,, ,,	3	0·2020	,, ,,	1
1·5840	,, ,,	2	0·1280	,, ,,	1
1·4400	,, ,,	1	0·1060	,, ,,	1
1·2800	,, ,,	1	0·0273	,, ,,	1
			0·0240	,, ,,	1

The delicacy of the test is illustrated by the accompanying diagram (Fig. 37, p. 177). It will be seen that in 12 out of the 23 positive experiments the number of artificially added vibrios was considerably less than 1 per c.c. (about 1 per 4 c.c.) of raw river water.

Of course, it might be said by anyone not conversant with the whole facts that positive results were only obtained when the numbers of cholera vibrios ranged from 10·24 to 0·024 per c.c. of the water, and that a draught of water (say half-a-pint) is equal to about 284 c.c. But the author was dealing with *raw* river water samples, and the B. coli results indicate that the water as supplied to London is at least 1,000 times purer than the raw river water, as judged by this test. For example, nearly as many samples of *filtered* water contain no typical B. coli in 100 c.c. of water, as there are samples of *raw* Thames water containing typical B. coli in 1 c.c. or less of water. In other words, to prove the absence of the cholera vibrio from 1 c.c. of unpurified river water is, one may venture to say inferentially, equivalent to proving its absence from 1,000 c.c. of the same water after its purification.

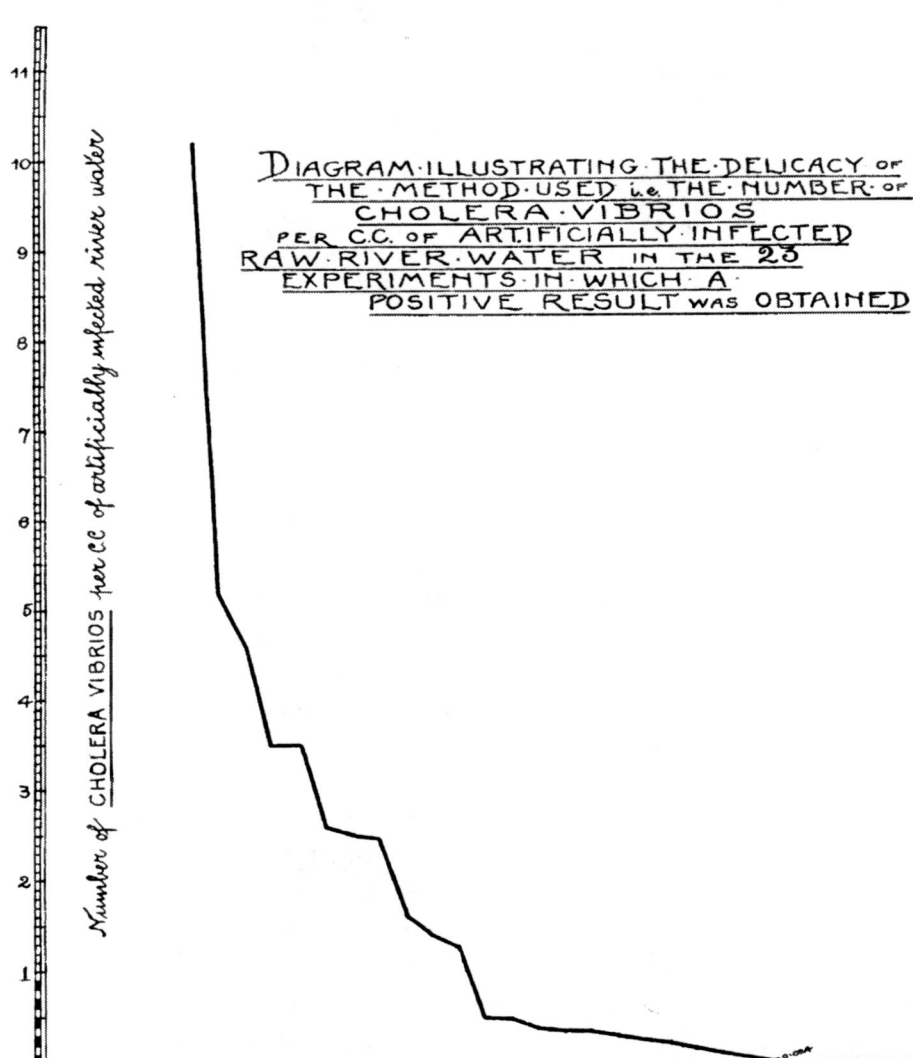

Fig. 37.

The author has worked successfully with as much as 10,000 c.c. of water, but, of course, 1,000 c.c. is a more practicable and yet satisfactory volume to deal with. 1,000 c.c. of the sample are poured into a flask containing 100 c.c. of concentrated peptone water. The culture is incubated at 37° C. and surface agar plate cultures made after 8, 16, and 24 hours, or more frequently, if this be found to be practicable. The plates are also incubated at 37° C. and examined after 24 hours. The author has also worked with bile-salt-agar and Drigalski and Conradi's medium, but his preference is for ordinary agar. The cholera colonies are rather small, and have a characteristic translucent appearance, which, although not exactly diagnostic, is of some *prima facie* value in selecting colonies for sub-culture. It is a good plan to make the sub-culture primarily into cane-sugar peptone water (tinted with litmus). All cultures, which, after 24 hours' incubation at 37° C., show gas formation or absence of acidity are rejected. But those yielding acid, without gas formation, are grown in peptone water. Duplicate cultures should be made, and one set tested with pure nitrogen-free sulphuric acid, for the cholera-red reaction in 24 hours.

If the results are negative all the tubes are rejected. But when positive, further peptone cultures are made and the test reapplied after another 24 hours to the original tubes, which by this time have been incubated for 48 hours. If the test is now negative, all the cultures are discarded; but if positive, further tests must be applied. The reason for this procedure is that some harmless " water microbes " give a slight cholera red reaction in 24 hours, but none in 48 hours; whereas the cholera vibrio gives a reaction as strong (or stronger) in 48 hours as in 24 hours.[1]

It might be supposed that this simple procedure would leave a large proportion out of the total number sub-cultured still requiring to be studied.

---

[1] *Tried* brands of peptone and sulphuric acid are essential for this test.

The contrary, however, is the case, as the following statement clearly shows :—

3120 sub-cultures made from the primary plate cultures.

| 1,790 rejected because no acid change occurred in a cane-sugar medium. | 549 provisionally accepted as they produced acid (without gas formation) in a cane-sugar medium. | 781 were rejected because they gave rise to gas formation in a cane-sugar medium. |

| 532 rejected because they failed to produce the cholera red reaction in peptone water. | 17 provisionally accepted, but finally rejected by a combination of tests. |

It will thus be seen that, by following the above simple method, it is quite easy to reject 3103 out of 3120 colonies subjected to examination.

Of course it will be understood that the author is here dealing with what may be called " normal " cholera vibrios. If any worker desires to include aberrant forms, which do not give acid in a cane-sugar medium, and fail to give the cholera red reaction, but which are nevertheless, rightly or wrongly, considered to be of significance, then he must modify the above methods in such a way as to fit in with his particular plan of campaign.

The few microbes left over after submitting them to the cane-sugar and cholera-red tests may be readily eliminated by employing a combination of tests. In limiting the number of these extra tests, the author does so, because in his experience he has found them trustworthy in practice. Thus he would reject all microbes, which did not conform to the following type.

Acid formation (but no gas) in saccharose, dextrin, and glucose media.

Decided cholera red reaction both in 24 and 48 hours at 37° C. in peptone water cultures.

No apparent change in salicin media.

Reduction of nitrates to nitrites.

Feeble growth and little or no appreciable liquefaction within 48 hours at 20–22° C. on a gelatine (12 per cent.) slope culture.

Minute red colonies on glucose (usually also on saccharose) neutral red bile-salt-agar slope cultures.

Of course, if a microbe did fulfil these characters the likelihood of its being the true cholera vibrio would be so great that resort would naturally be had to all other known tests until its acceptance or rejection ceased to be a matter of speculation.

Of these, the following may be mentioned merely in passing.

"Saturation" and "fixation" tests as well as Pfeiffer's reaction and the hæmolytic and agglutination tests. Morphological appearances, and, in specimens stained for flagella, the presence of only one flagellum.

The composition of the *chief* media used in searching for the presence of the cholera vibrios in water is as follows:—

Primary peptone cultures.
  Peptone 11 per cent.
  Sodium chloride 5·5 per cent.
  Water up to 100.
  100 c.c. of this medium per 1000 c.c. of the sample of water.

Agar plate cultures.
  Agar 2 per cent.
  Peptone 1 per cent.
  Sodium chloride 0·5 per cent.
  Beef broth up to 100.
The beef broth is made in the ordinary way, 1 lb. of beef being used for every 1,000 c.c. of water (rendered slightly alkaline).

Peptone sugar media, tinted with litmus.
  Peptone 2 per cent.
  1 per cent. of whatever sugar or fermentable substance is required, *e.g.*, cane-sugar, glucose, salicin, dextrin, etc.
  Water up to 100.

Peptone water, for cholera-red reaction.
- Peptone 1 per cent.
- Sodium chloride 0·5 per cent.
- Water up to 100.

Nitrate broth for testing reduction to nitrites.
- Potassium nitrate 1 per cent.
- Beef broth 10 per cent.
- Water up to 100.
- The beef broth is made in the ordinary way, 1 lb. of beef being used for every 1,000 c.c. of water (rendered slightly alkaline).

Bile-salt-agar media (MacConkey).
- Agar 2 per cent.
- Bile-salt 0·5 per cent.
- Neutral red Solution } 0·4 c.c. of a 1 per cent. solution of this substance.
- Peptone 2 per cent.
- 0·5 per cent. of whatever sugar or fermentable substance is required, *e.g.*, cane-sugar, glucose, etc.
- Water up to 100.

Gelatine cultures.
- Gelatine 12 per cent.
- Peptone 1 per cent.
- Sodium chloride 0·5 per cent.
- Beef broth up to 100.
- The beef broth is made in the ordinary way, 1 lb. of beef being used for every 1,000 c.c. of water (rendered slightly alkaline).

For additional media and fuller information, the reader is referred to the author's Fourth and Fifth Research Reports to the Metropolitan Water Board.

The Typhoid bacillus and Gärtner's bacillus.—The author has tried many methods, but, in his experience, the method about to be described yields the best results. Any method will yield positive results if a sufficient number of these microbes are added to water, especially when the water is pure; but there are few methods which will stand the test of successful isolation when only a *very few microbes* are added to an *impure* water.

Three series of experiments with artificially infected samples of Thames and Lee *raw* river water yielded results as follows :—

1st Series, 24 samples.

(a) Average number of artificially added typhoid bacilli per c.c. of raw river water = 2·242
(b) Average number of typhoid bacilli recovered = 14·54 [1]
(c) Average number of artificially added Gärtner bacilli per c.c. of raw river water = 0·686
(d) Average nmmber of Gärtner bacilli recovered = 12·417

[1] It should perhaps be explained that the reason why *apparently* more microbes were isolated than were actually added, is, that for purposes of securing a positive result there is no limit, beyond that of practicability, to the number of cubic centimetres subjected to exhaustive examination.

2nd Series, 35 samples.

(e) Average number of artificially added typhoid bacilli per c.c. of raw river water = 0·653
(f) Average number of typhoid bacilli recovered = 11·6
(g) Average number of artificially added Gärtner bacilli per c.c. of raw river water = 0·633
(h) Average number of Gärtner bacilli recovered = 7·86

3rd Series, 42 samples.

(i) Average number of artificially added typhoid bacilli per c.c. of raw river water = 0·993
(j) Average number of typhoid bacilli recovered = 7·524
(k) Average number of artificially added Gärtner bacilli per c.c. of raw river water = 0·728
(l) Average number of Gärtner bacilli recovered = 20·45

If we divide (b) by (a); (d) by (c); (f) by (e); (h) by (g); (j) by (i) and (l) by (k) we get an approximate idea of the number of cubic centimetres of river water, which might be expected to yield a *positive* result, even if only one typhoid bacillus and one Gärtner's bacillus were present.

1st Series.   1 typhoid to 6·485 c.c. of river water.
2nd Series.   1 typhoid to 17·7 c.c. of river water.
3rd Series.   1 typhoid to 7·58 c.c. of river water.
1st Series.   1 Gärtner to 18·10 c.c. of river water.
2nd Series.   1 Gärtner to 12·4 c.c. of river water.
3rd Series.   1 Gärtner to 28·10 c.c. of river water.

Inferentially, it may be concluded that failure to isolate these microbes under comparable conditions of experiment suggests the absence of the typhoid bacillus from about 7 to 18 c.c. of water, and the absence of Gärtner's bacillus from about 12 to 28 c.c. of water.

The significance of this will be readily understood, when the reader is reminded that the raw river water before delivery to the consumers is purified about 1,000 times, as judged by the B. coli test.

500 c.c. of the sample of water are centrifugalised and the deposit spread over 16 malachite green bile-salt agar plates (Medium A).

If the water does not contain an appreciable amount of suspended matter, a little alumino-ferric (5 parts per 100,000 parts) may be added just before centrifugalisation.

After 24 hours' incubation at 37° C., 250 of the colourless colonies are picked off, if so many are obtainable, and sub-cultured into Proskauer and Capaldi's medium No. 2 (Medium B). After 48 hours' incubation at 37° C., the tubes are examined, and those showing no change are discarded. Those tubes showing gas formation are followed up on the Gärtner side, and those showing acidity, without gas formation, are followed up on the typhoid side.

Gärtner part of experiment.—The cultures showing gas formation (Medium B) are sub-cultured into a dulcite medium (Medium C). After incubation for five days at 37° C., they are dealt with as follows:

All those showing no change or no gas formation are discarded. Those showing gas formation are next sub-cultured into a gelatine medium (Medium E). After incubation at 37° C. for three hours, and thereafter for about 45 hours at 20–22° C., the tubes are examined. All those showing gas formation are discarded. The remainder are sub-cultered into peptone water, litmus whey, and litmus milk (Media H. F. G.)

Those cultures giving rise either to indol formation in

peptone cultures or to acidity (instead of alkalinity) in litmus whey (or litmus milk) cultures, after five days' incubation at 37° C., are discarded.

The author's experience, founded on the examination of many thousands of colonies, leads him to assert that these few simple tests suffice for the exclusion of all, or practically all, ordinary " water microbes."

Of course, in the event of a microbe passing the barriers set up by these tests, every known test for Gärtner's bacillus should be superadded (*e.g.*, the agglutination test, Pfeiffer's reaction, etc.

Typhoid part of experiment.—The cultures showing acid, but no gas formation (Medium B) are next sub-cultured into a gelatine medium (Medium D). After incubation for three hours at 37° C., and thereafter for about 21 hours at 20—22° C., they are dealt with as follows :

All those showing gas formation are discarded. Those showing acid formation without gas production are further studied. Not uncommonly cultures are met with which fail to produce gas, but are otherwise not characteristic. These are given the benefit of the doubt, and further subcultured. Comparatively so few microbes are left at this stage that usually it is found best to employ the following multiple tests for their final acceptance or exclusion, viz. :—

(*a*) Neutral red broth medium (I) purplish tint = satisfactory; fluorescence or gas production allows of final rejection.

(*b*) Peptone water for indol, medium (H). No indol = satisfactory; indol formation allows of final rejection.

(*c*) L.S.D.S. medium (J). No change = satisfactory; acid or bleached change or gas formation allows of final rejection.

(*d*) P and C No. 1 (modified) medium (K). No change = satisfactory; acid or bleached change or gas formation allows of final rejection.

(*e*) Litmus milk medium (G). Slight acid change, but no clot = satisfactory; alkaline change or clot allows of final rejection.

The foregoing tests (2 days at 37° C.) in nearly all cases suffice, but it is desirable to supplement them with two extra tests. Growth on gelatine slope cultures and on potato cultures [see media (M) and (L)].

Occasionally cultures pass the ordeal of tests (*a*), (*b*), (*c*), (*d*), (*e*). In all, or nearly all, cases these will be found either to liquefy gelatine or to produce a non-characteristic bluish opaque (instead of a filmy reddish transparent) growth on gelatine slope cultures [medium (M)]; usually also, they produce a dirty fawn-coloured growth on potato cultures [medium (L)] instead of a transparent invisible growth.

Speaking of thousands, and even tens of thousands, of cultures of water microbes, the foregoing procedure is, for all practical purposes, absolutely satisfactory, for the purpose of exclusion, but as a counsel of perfection, tests for agglutination, etc., should also be employed.

The chief reason why this method is so effective as a means of excluding "water microbes" is very simple. Microbes which yield acid in liquid sugar media, but no *apparent* gas, are constantly to be found in water, and they bear a superficial resemblance to the typhoid bacillus, morphologically and culturally. In nearly all cases, they can be shown to be feeble gas producers, by using a gelatine sugar medium (Medium D). In the past these microbes were undoubtedly at times confused with typhoid, and not improbably elaborate experiments were sometimes undertaken to prove their identity; and it is even to be feared that in some cases the final diagnosis was erroneous.

Assuming, as the author believes, it to be true that these tests and plans of procedure do not exclude any microbes which can strictly be classed under the terms typhoid and Gärtner, the methods recommended have the merit of simplicity and they have stood the test of practical experience. The composition of the various media is as follows :—

(A) *Bile-salt agar medium for plate cultures* (both for typhoid and Gärtner).
Agar, 2 per cent.
Peptone, 2 per cent.
Bile-salt, 0·5 per cent.
Lactose ⎫
Saccharose ⎪
Adonite ⎬ 0·2 per cent. of each.
Raffinose ⎪
Salicin ⎭

Water tinted with neutral red (4 c.c. of a 1 per cent. solution of neutral red per litre of medium) up to 100.

Just before pouring the plates, malachite green is added in the proportion of 1 per 10,000 of medium.

Remarks:—Both typhoid and Gärtner form colourless colonies.

(B) *Proskauer and Capaldi's No. 2 medium* (both for typhoid and Gärtner).
    Peptone, 2 per cent.
    Mannite, 0·1 per cent.
Distilled water tinted with litmus up to 100.
Remarks:—Typhoid, acid, no gas; Gärtner gas formation.

(C) *Dulcite medium* (for Gärtner only).
    Peptone, 2 per cent.
    Dulcite, 0·2 per cent.
Water tinted with litmus up to 100.
Remarks:—Gärtner produces gas.

(D) *Glucose gelatine medium* (for typhoid only).
    Peptone, 2 per cent.
    Lemco (Liebig's Extract of Meat), 1 per cent.
    Gelatine, 7·5 per cent.
    Glucose, 1 per cent.
(Potassium hydrate, 10 c.c. of a 5 per cent. solution per litre of medium).
Water tinted with litmus, up to 100.
Remarks:—Typhoid produces acid but no gas.

(E) *Mixed sugar gelatine medium* (for Gärtner only).
    Peptone 2 per cent.
    Gelatine 7·5 per cent.
    Glycerine
    Raffinose
    Saccharose
    Adonite   0·2 per cent. of each.
    Salicin
    Lactose
(Potassium hydrate, 10 c.c. of a 5 per cent. solution per litre of medium).
Water tinted with litmus, up to 100.
Remarks:—Gärtner bleaches but produces no gas.

(F) *Litmus whey medium* (for Gärtner only).
Milk clotted with Hydrochloric acid, filtered, heated and neutralised with caustic soda tinted with litmus and filtered. Or the milk may be clotted with rennet, strained, heated, filtered, and tinted with litmus.
Remarks:—Gärtner produces faint acid, and then an alkaline change.

(G) *Litmus milk medium* (both for typhoid and Gärtner).
Milk steamed allowed to cool and siphoned off to avoid the coagulum. Tinted with litmus.
Remarks:—Typhoid, faint acid no clot; Gärtner, faint acid, later alkaline change, no clot.

(H) *Peptone water* medium for indol test (both for typhoid and Gärtner).
   Peptone 1 per cent.
   Sodium Chloride 0·5 per cent.
   Water up to 100.
Remarks :—Typhoid, no indol ; Gärtner, no indol.

Composition of solutions used for testing for indol (Böhme, *Centr. f. Bakt.* Bd. XL. 1905) :—

(1) 8 grammes paradimethylamidobenzaldehyde, 160 c.c. hydrochloric acid, 760 c.c. absolute alcohol.
(2) Saturated cold water solution of potassium persulphate.

(I) *Glucose neutral red broth* medium (for typhoid only).
   Peptone, 1 per cent.
   Sodium Chloride, 0·5 per cent.
   Lemco, 0·5 per cent.
   Glucose, 0·5 per cent.
Water tinted with neutral red (2 c.c. of a 1 per cent. solution per litre of medium) up to 100.
Remarks :—Typhoid, a purplish tint, no gas, and no fluorescence.

(J) *L.S.D.S.* medium (for typhoid only).
   Peptone, 2 per cent.
   Lactose
   Saccharose
   Dulcit   } 0·25 per cent. of each.
   Salicin
Distilled water tinted with litmus up to 100.
Remarks :—Typhoid, no change.

(K) *Proskauer and Capaldi's* No. 1 (modified) medium (for typhoid only).

Asparagin	0·2 per cent.
Calcium chloride	0·02 per cent.
Galactose	0·2 per cent.
Glucose	0·2 per cent.
Laevulose	0·2 per cent.
Magnesium sulphate	0·01 per cent.
Maltose	0·2 per cent.
Mannite	0·2 per cent.
Potassium monophosphate	0·2 per cent.
Sodium chloride	0·02 per cent.

Distilled water tinted with litmus, to 100.
Remarks :—Typhoid, no change.

(L) *Potato* medium (for typhoid only).
Half cylinder of potato cut obliquely, placed in tubes and sterilised.
Remarks :—Typhoid, colourless growth.

(M) *Gelatine medium, slope cultures* (for typhoid only).
   Peptone, 10 grammes.
   Gelatine, 100–120 grammes.
   Sodium Chloride, 5 grammes.
   Sorbite, 2 grammes.
   Beef broth up to 1,000 c.c. (1 lb. beef per litre).
   Medium rendered faintly alkaline and tinted with litmus solution.

Remarks:—Typhoid, filmy transparent growth, no liquefaction; the medium acquires a faint pinkish tinge.

MISCELLANEOUS INFORMATION.

Weather of London (Camden Hill).—Average temperature and rainfall for 50 years equals 50° F. and 25 inches respectively.

"Absolute drought" = *more than* 14 consecutive days, no one of which is a rain day.

(A rain day = 0·01 inch or over; anything over 0·005 being calculated as 0·01, and 0·005 and under being ignored.)

"Partial drought" = *more than* 28 consecutive days, the mean rainfall of which does not exceed 0·01 inch per day.

One inch of rain per acre = 22,622 gallons (about 101 tons).

Some extremes of rainfall attained in the British Isles—Symons's "British Rainfall," 1884.

0·55 inch in 5 minutes.	1·50 inches in 45 minutes.	
1·10 inches in 15 ,,	1·80 ,, ,, 60 ,,	
1·25 ,, ,, 30 ,,	2·20 ,, ,, 120 ,,	

HYDRAULIC EQUIVALENTS.

One.	Gallons.	Litres.	Cubic Centimetres.	Lbs.	Fluid Ounces.	Cubic Inches.	Cubic Feet.
Gallon	1	4·5459	4545·9	10	160	277·463	0·16
Litre	0·22	1	1000	2·2	35·196	61·024	0·0353
Cubic cent.	0·00022	0·001	1	0·0022	0·0352	0·0610	0·000035
Pound	0·1	0·454	454·6	1	16	27·746	0·016
Ounce	0·00625	0·0284	28·412	0·0625	1	1·728	0·001
Cubic inch	0·0036	0·0164	16·387	0·036	0·5766	1	0·00057
Cubic foot	6·228	28·317	28317	62·3	1000	1728	1

United States gallon = 231 cubic in. = 3·7854 litres.
1 pint = 20 fluid oz. = 0·568 litre.   1 centimetre = 0·3937 inch.
1 litre = 1·759 pints = 35 fluid oz.   1 inch = 2·54 centimetres.
1 lb. = 7,000 grains = 453·59 grammes.   1 cwt. = 112 lbs.   1 ton = 2,240 lbs.
1 micron = 10^{-6} metre = 0·001 mm.

CONVERSIONS :—

Grammes (or c.c.) into grains, ounces, or pounds multiply by 15·432, 0·03528, and 0·0022046 respectively.

Grains, ounces, or pounds into grammes (or c.c.) multiply by 0·0648, 28·35, and 453·6 respectively.

Metres into inches, feet, or yards, multiply by 39·3701, 3·2808, and 1·0936 respectively.

Inches, feet, or yards into metres, multiply by 0·0254, 0·3048, and 0·9144 respectively.

Degrees Centigrade into degrees Fahrenheit, multiply by 9, divide by 5, and add 32.

Degrees Fahrenheit into degrees Centigrade, subtract 32, multiply by 5, and divide by 9.

Parts per 100,000 into grains per gallon, multiply by 7, and divide by 10.

Grains per gallon into parts per 100,000, multiply by 10, and divide by 7.

"Hardness," parts per 100,000 ($CaCO_3$) into degrees of hardness = Clark's scale = grains per gallon, multiply by 7, and divide by 10.

Cubic capacity of cylinder = square of diameter × 0·7854 × length.
Circumference of circle = diameter × 3·1416.
Area of circle = square of diameter × 0·7854.
Capacity in gallons of rectangular vessels :—Multiply length by breadth, by depth in inches, and divide by 277·463 (say 277·5).
Capacity in gallons of cylindrical vessels :—Square of half the diameter in inches, multiplied by 3·1416, multiply product by depth in inches, divide answer by 277·463 (say 277·5).

Rate of filtration :—1 inch per hour = 2 feet per day = 2 cubic feet per square foot per day = 12·5 gallons per square foot per day = 544,500 gallons per acre per day.

Number of gallons per square foot per hour × 1,045,440 = number of gallons per acre per 24 hours.

The following values are given by Baldwin-Wiseman (Proc. Inst. C.E. 1910 for 86 installations in Great Britain :—

Maximum rate of discharge, 1·444 cubic ft. or 9·028 gallons per sq. ft. per hour.
Minimum ,, ,, 0·083 ,, ,, 0·521 ,, ,, ,,
Mean ,, ,, 0·372 ,, ,, 2·322 ,, ,, ,,

METROPOLITAN WATER BOARD.—STATISTICAL INFORMATION (1913).

Population supplied, about 6,630,000 (census, 1911).
Daily supply, 244 million gallons.
Gallons per head per day, 36·5.
Total storage capacity, 13,000 million gallons.
About 60 per cent. of London water is derived from the River Thames, about 20 per cent. from the River Lee, and the remainder from wells, etc.

CLASSIFICATION OF ODOURS CAUSED BY ORGANISMS IN POTABLE WATERS (*after* WHIPPLE).

Group.	Organism.	Natural Odour.
AROMATIC ODOUR.	*Diatomaceæ:*— Asterionella Cyclotella Diatoma Meridion Tabellaria	Aromatic—geranium—fishy Faintly aromatic ,, ,, Aromatic ,,
	Protozoa:— Cryptomonas Mallomonas	Candied violets Aromatic—violets—fishy
GRASSY ODOUR.	*Cyanophyceæ:*— Anabæna Rivularia Clathrocystis Cœlosphærium Aphanizomenon	Grassy and mouldy—green corn—nasturtiums, etc. Grassy and mouldy Sweet, grassy ,, ,, Grassy
FISHY ODOUR.	*Chlorophyceæ:*— Volvox Eudorina Pandorina Dictyosphærium	Fishy Faintly fishy ,, ,, ,, ,,
	Protozoa:— Uroglena Synura Dinobryon Bursaria Peridinium Glenodinium	Fishy and oily Ripe cucumbers—bitter and spicy taste Fishy, like rock weed Irish moss—salt marsh—fishy Fishy, like clam-shells Fishy

Figs. 38–43 show the microscopic appearances of certain algal growths (Asterionella, Oscillaria, Tabellaria, and Dinobryon).

Copper sulphate treatment for Algal growths.—Usual dose 0·2 to 1 part per million parts (lbs. per 100,000 gallons).

BROAD "STANDARDS" *for guidance and working purposes only.*

Bacteriological. River-derived samples (London).

It is assumed that conclusions are based on the examination of a sufficient number of representative samples.

Less than 20 microbes per c.c. (Gelatine at 20–22° C., counted on 3rd day).
,, ,, 5 ,, ,, (Agar at 37° C., counted after 24 hours).
,, ,, 0·5 ,, ,, (Bile-salt Agar at 37° C., counted after 24 hours).

Speaking generally, these standards may be considerably relaxed if the B. coli results are favourable. In striking the gelatine and agar averages it is customary in the case of the London waters to exclude samples containing 100 or more microbes per c.c.

Less than one-half the samples should contain typical B. coli (lactose +, indol +) in 100 c.c.

Chemical (parts per 100,000). River-derived samples (London).

Oxygen absorbed from permanganate at 80° F. } less than { 0·1 in 4 hours. 0·038 in 5 minutes.

Albuminoid nitrogen, less than 0·01.
Ammoniacal nitrogen, less than 0·001.
Colour, less than 20 mm. brown in a 2-foot tube.

WATER-BORNE EPIDEMIC DISEASES.—TYPHOID FEVER, CHOLERA, POSSIBLY DIARRHŒAL DISEASE.

AVERAGE DEATH-RATE FROM ENTERIC FEVER (TYPHOID FEVER) PER 100,000 OF POPULATION.

	1871–80.	1881–90.	1891–00.	1901–10.	1911.
England and Wales...	33	20	17	9	7
London	24	19	14	6	3

Seasonal incidence of typhoid fever.—Minimum about May, June, and July. Maximum, about October and November.

Incubation period of typhoid fever, about 10-14 days.

For information as to suspected connection between water supplies and outbreaks of enteric fever (1867–1892), extracted from reports of Inspectors of the Local Government Board and others, see Appendices to "Evidence of Royal Commission on Metropolitan Water Supply," 1893, page 532.

Chief English typhoid epidemics of recent date attributed to water supply.—Worthing, 1893 (1,315 cases); Maidstone, 1897 (1,847 cases); Lincoln, 1905 (more than 1,000 cases).

Hypochlorite sterilisation.—Usual dose in terms of available chlorine, from 0·2 to 1 part per million parts (lbs. per 100,000 gallons).

METROPOLITAN WATER BOARD.

Notable Events.

Appointed Day (Amalgamation of old Companies).—June 24th, 1904.

Staines Reservoirs.—Water first used, Dec. 28th, 1904. Combined capacity, 3,338 m. g.

Walton Reservoirs.—Opened June 10th, 1911. Combined capacity, 1,198 m. g

MISCELLANEOUS INFORMATION 193

Island Barn Reservoir.—Opened Nov. 4th, 1911. Capacity, 922 m. g.
Beachcroft *Service* Reservoir at Honor Oak.—Opened May 5th, 1909. Capacity, 56·3 m. g. First used, March 14th, 1910.
Metropolitan Water Board (New Works) and Thames Conservancy Acts, 1911.
Humphrey pumps installed, and Chingford Reservoir opened by His Majesty King George the Fifth, March 15th, 1913. Capacity, 3,000 m. g. Now known as King George's Reservoir.

LIST OF PUBLISHED WATER BOARD REPORTS.

The following is a list of the published reports relating to the quality of the Metropolitan Water Supply, since the work commenced on November 1st, 1905 :—

(1) A report each month from November, 1905, onwards. [An unabridged version of the November, 1905, report, giving all the results in great detail was published by the Water Board.] These monthly reports form part of the Government Water Examiner's Monthly Report on the Metropolitan Water Supply, and are published by the Government Printers.

All other reports are published by the Water Board.

(2) First Annual Report, for the year ended March 31st, 1907. (A report dealing with the results for the 12 months ended October 31st, 1906, had previously been issued.)

(3) Second Annual Report, for the year ended March 31st, 1908.

(4) Third Annual Report, for the year ended March 31st, 1909.

(5) Fourth Annual Report, for the year ended March 31st, 1910.

(6) Fifth Annual Report for the year ended March 31st, 1911.

(7) Sixth Annual Report for the year ended March 31st, 1912.

(8) Seventh Annual Report for the year ended March 31st, 1913.

(9) First Report on Research Work. The Vitality of the Typhoid Bacillus in artificially infected samples of *raw* Thames, Lee, and New River Water with special reference to the question of storage.

(10) Second Report on Research Work. The Negative Results of the examination of samples of *raw* Thames, Lee, and New River Water for the presence of the Typhoid Bacillus.

(11) Third Report on Research Work. The storage of *raw* River water antecedent to filtration.

(12) Fourth Report on Research Work. The vitality of the Cholera Vibrio in artificially infected samples of *raw* Thames, Lee, and New River Water, with special reference to the question of storage.

(13) Fifth Report on Research Work. I. The Results of the examination of samples of *raw* Thames and Lee Water for the presence of the Typhoid Bacillus and Gärtner's Bacillus. II. The Results of the examination of the *raw* River Waters (Thames, Lee, and New River) for Fæcal Streptococci. III. The Results of the Examination of the Pre-filtration Water, *i.e.* representative samples of practically all the London Water (*raw*, stored, gravel, well, and mixed water) *antecedent* to filtration. IV. The Negative Results of the Examination of Samples of *raw* Thames, Lee, and New River Water for the presence of Morgan's (No. 1) Bacillus. V. The Isolation of Cholera Vibrios from samples of *raw* River Water *artificially* infected with only a few Vibrios.

O

(14) Sixth Report on Research Work. The Comparative Vitality of "Uncultivated" and "Cultivated" Typhoid Bacilli in artificially infected, samples of *raw* River water with special reference to the question of storage.

(15) Seventh Report on Research Work. I. Search for Pathogenic Microbes in *raw* River water. II. The comparative vitality of "Cultivated" and "Uncultivated" Typhoid Bacilli in artificially infected samples of *raw* River water. III. The Comparative Vitality of the Typhoid Bacillus in *raw* Thames water at different temperatures. IV. On the biological characters of B. coli in *raw*, stored and filtered water. V. On the advantages of passing *raw* River water through small reservoirs antecedent to storage in large reservoirs. VI. On the advantages of occasionally using precipitation methods, antecedent to the storage of *raw* River water in large reservoirs.

(16) Eighth Report on Research Work. The softening, purification, and sterilisation of water supplies.

(17) Ninth Report on Research Work. Search for certain pathogenic microbes in Raw River Water and in Crude Sewage.

SOME ROYAL COMMISSIONS, BOOKS, AND REPORTS ON THE METROPOLITAN WATER SUPPLY

Scratchley, P. A.—"Bolton's" London Water Supply, 1888.
Sisley, R.—The London Water Supply, 1899.
Shadwell, A.—The London Water Supply, 1899.
Richards and Payne.—London Water Supply, 1899.

For a complete bibliography of 629 principal reports and papers (up to 1903) relating to the Water Supply of London, *see* "London Water Supply" issued by the London County Council, 1905.

The following are the titles of a few reports containing information specially concerned with the *quality* of the Water Supply :—

1850. Report by the General Board of Health on the Supply of Water to the Metropolis.

1851. Report by the Government Commission on the Chemical quality of the Supply of Water to the Metropolis.

1868. Rivers Pollution, Royal Commission of 1868 (Sixth Report, 1874). The Domestic Water Supply of Great Britain.

Royal Commissions—Reports, Minutes of Evidence, and Appendices :

1867. Shortly cited as Duke of Richmond's Commission, reported 1869.

1892. Shortly cited as Lord Balfour of Burleigh's Commission, reported 1893.

1897. Shortly cited as Lord Llandaff's Commission, reported 1899.

ALGAL GROWTHS

FIG. 38.—Asterionella × 320.

FIG. 39.—Oscillaria × 250.

Fig. 40.—Tabellaria (front view) × 280.

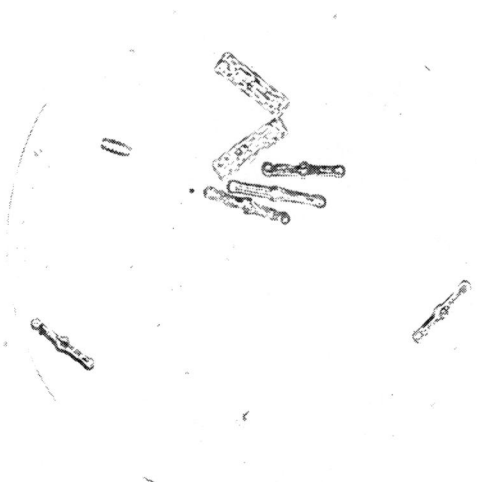

Fig. 41.—Tabellaria (front and side view) × 280.

ALGAL GROWTHS

Fig. 42.—Dinobryon × 180.

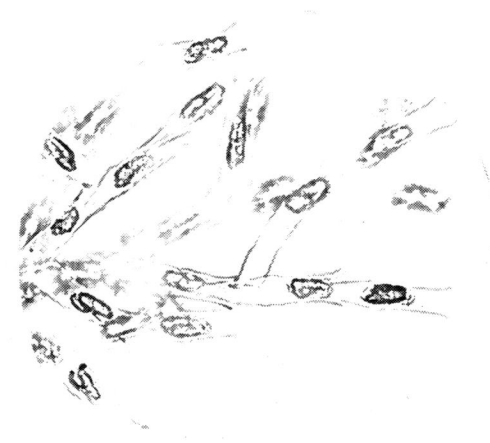

Fig. 43.—Dinobryon × 450.

INDEX

ABSTRACTION, different methods of, 40
  knowledge of current quality as guide to, 44
  relation of colour results to, 40–47
Accidental pollution, importance of safeguards against, 104
Agar, medium, composition of, 170
  plates, method for drying, 154
  tubes, constant temperature water bath for, 150–151
Albuminoid nitrogen, in Chelsea stored water, 94–95
  in River Lee water, 5–7
  in River Thames water, 5–6, 93
Algæ, development of, in storage reservoirs, 100
  microphotographs of, 195–197
  remedy for destroying growth of, 100, 191
  remedy for taste due to, 100
Alumino-ferric, composition of, 56
  cost of, 58
  dose required as coagulant, 59–60
  results of experiments with, 54–58
American Cities, typhoid death rate in, 110–112, 117–121, 133
Asterionella, a cause of taste and smell in water, 100, 191
  microphotograph of, 195
Automatic inoculation, method of, 160

BACILLI, "uncultivated" and "cultivated," definition of, 103
Bacteria enumeration of, average standards for, 191
  in River Lee, 16, 22
  in River Thames, 15–16, 18, 89–90
  in sewage, 116
  in stored water, 91–92, 95
  media for, 170–171
Bacteria, excremental, classification of, 161, 165
  significance of, 166, 168
Bacterial efficiency of mechanical filters, 51
  of sand filtration, 103

Bacteriological examination, bottles and sample cases for, 138
  media rack used in, 152, 155
  quantity of water required for, 138
  routine methods for, 151 *et seq.*
  time required for, 168, 170
Bacteriological results, methods of registration of, 142
  of examination of River Lee, 16, 22
  of examination of River Thames, 15–16, 18, 89–90
  of examination of stored water, 91–92, 95
Bacteriological standards, 168, 191
Bacillus coli, isolation of by "flaginac" method, 161
  isolation of by "glagins" method, 161–164
  media used in isolation of, 170–4
  significance of in water, 166, 168
  types of, 165
Bacillus Coli test, classification of results, 165
  description of presumptive, confirmatory and typical, 143
  results of examination by,
    of filtered water, 1, 49, 169
    of Kent wells, 2
    of River Lee, 16, 22
    of River Thames, 15–16, 18, 89–90
    of stored water, 91–92, 95
Bacillus Enteritidis Sporogenes test, description of, 154, 158
  media for, 174
Bacillus Typhosus. *See* Typhoid.
Bacteria pathogenic, delicacy of method used in search for, 35
  methods for isolation of, 33
  results of experiments, 34–35
  search for, in raw water, 33
    in sewage, 36
Bile-salt peptone water, composition of medium, 171
Bleaching powder, composition of, 62
Boxes, for sample collecting, 138, 141

CHELSEA reservoir, results of storage in, 91–92, 94–95
Chemical examination, of Chelsea stored water, 94
　of River Lee, 5, 7
　of River Thames, 5, 6, 93
Chemical standards, 15, 192
Cherwell, temperature of, at Oxford, 87
Chicago water supply, sterilisation of, 64
Chloros, composition of, 62
　dose for sterilisation, 62
　results obtained at Lincoln, 62
　with wells, 63
　sterilisation by, 62–63
Cholera Vibrio, characters of, 178–188
　delicacy of method employed in isolation of, 176
　media for isolation of, 180–181
　method for isolation of, 178
　vitality of in river water, 80–81
Classification of odours caused by organisms in potable water, 191
　types of *B. Coli*, 165
Coagulants, advantages of use antecedent to storage in large reservoirs, 54
　dose required, 59–60
　results of experiments with, 54–59
Coli. B, see *B. Coli*
Collembola, in hydrants at Edinburgh, 105
Colour results: comparison of river and stored water, 46
　Chelsea stored water, 94-95
　method used for determining, 40
　relation to abstraction, 40–47
　River Lee, 5, 7
　River Thames, 5, 6 ; diagram of, 41
　tables showing number of days results were over 200 and over 100, 46
Confirmatory test for *B. Coli*, definition of, 143
Conradi and Drigalski's medium, composition of, 28
Copper sulphate treatment for Algal growths, 100, 191
Cultivated bacilli, definition of, 103

DEATH rate, definition of normal, 124
　average from enteric fever, England and Wales, 192
Decimal mode of dilution, description of, 147–148
Definition of drought, 189
　normal death-rate, 124
　"uncultivated" and "cultivated" bacilli, 103
Devitilisation as a factor in purification by storage, 80

Diarrhœal diseases, annual death rate from, 129
Dilution, description of decimal mode of, 147–148
Dilutions, coloured labels for, 149
Dinobryon, a cause of taste and smell in water, 191
　microphotograph of, 197
Drigalski and Conradi's medium, composition of, 28
Drinking experiment as proof of devitalisation, 83–84
Drought, definition of, 189

ENDEMIC typhoid fever, current views on, 109–114, 116–117
English typhoid epidemics of recent date, 192
Enteric fever, average death rate, England and Wales and London, 192
Enteritidis Sporogenes. B test, description of, 154, 158
　media for, 174
Enumeration of microbes, media for, 170–171
Epidemic, typhoid, description of Rockford (Illinois), 107–109
　water borne diseases, 192
Epidemics, caused by impure water, 103
　financial loss from water, 134–135
Equalisation, nature of, as a factor in purification of water, 78–80
Equivalents, table of hydraulic, 189
"Excess lime," advantages of process, 72
　cost of process, 70–71
　dose for hard and soft waters, 67–68
　method for determining amount of lime required, 74–75
　method of sterilisation, 65–77

FAECES, results of examination for streptococci in, 29–30
Filtered water, possible causes of pollution of, 104
Filters, mechanical, see Mechanical filters
Filtration of water, cost of sand, 59, 136–137
　efficiency of, 103
　rate of, 190
　trustworthiness of, 104
Financial advantages of pure water supply, 126 *et seq.*
Fishing, prohibition of, 105
Fishy odour, list of organisms causing, 191
"Flaginac" method for isolation of *B. Coli*, description of, 161
　media for, 172–173
Flood water, quality of, 39
　reason for excluding, 47–48

INDEX

Flow of river, in relation to quality, 39
Fluorescent water, composition of, 172
Formula, for monetary loss due to impure water, 125

GÄRTNER'S bacillus, characters of, 183–184
  delicacy of method used, reasons for, 185
  media for isolation of, 185–187
  method of isolation, 183
  results obtained, 182
Gelatin shake test, composition of medium for, 173
"Glagins" method for isolation of *B. Coli*, description of, 161–164
  media for, 173–174
Glucose, drop method for isolation of *B. Coli*, 157

HARDNESS, financial loss from, 134
  method for reduction of permanent, 76
  permanent, removal of, 76–77
  of River Lee, 5, 7; of River Thames, 5–6, 93; of stored water, 94–95
  table of, in American Cities and London, 135
Heat, as a method of sterilisation, 65
Hektograph sheets, description of symbols on, 144–147
  examples of, 148 *et seq*
Hydrants, defective, danger from, 105
Hydraulic equivalents, table of, 189
Hypochlorite sterilisation, dose for, 192

IMMUNITY, from risk of water-borne disease, 102
  of towns from typhoid fever, reasons for, 37
Impure water, epidemics caused by, 103
Indol test, method employed in, 164
  solutions used in, composition of, 173
Inoculation, automatic method of, 160; wires, description of, 149
Inspection of rivers, importance of, 105, 107
Insuctions into mains, possibility of, 105
Intakes, closing of, 39
  importance of safeguarding, 105
Interpretation of results of bacteriological examination, 168
Intestinal type, organisms of, *see B. Coli*

KENT Wells, result of bacteriological examination of, 2

LABELS, use of coloured, 149
  method of labelling samples, 138–140
Laboratory book, description of, 140
Lee River, as a source of supply, 26
  results of bacteriological examination, 16, 22
  results of chemical examination, 5, 7
Lincoln water supply, sterilisation of, by chloros, 62
Litmus whey and milk media, composition of, 186
London water supply, sources of, 2
  arguments against use of rivers, 4
  volume of water required for, 44, 190

MAINS, defective, danger of pollution from, 104–105
Mechanical filters, efficiency of, 51
  as alternative to storage, 51
Media, for isolation of cholera vibrios, 180–181
  for isolation of streptococci, 28–29
  for isolation of typhoid and Gärtner bacilli, 185–188
  for routine bacteriological analysis, 170–174
Methods of abstraction, different, 40
Metropolitan Water Board, list of published reports, 193
  notable events, 192–193
  statistical information, 190

NITRATE broth, composition of, 29
Normal death rate, definition of, 124
Notable events,—Metropolitan Water Board, 192–193

ODOUR, of potable water, classification of organisms causing, 191
  method of destroying, 100–101
Oscillaria, microphotograph of, 195
Oxygen absorbed from permanganate, by Chelsea stored water, 94–95
  by River Lee, 5, 7
  by River Thames water, 5–6, 93

PATHOGENIC bacteria, delicacy of test for, 34–35, 176, 182
  more likely presence during floods, 47
  search for in river water, 32, 175–185
  search for in sewage, 36, 115
Physical quality of water, formula for, 132
  from financial point of view, 132
  importance of, 47
Pollution, accidental, methods of guarding against, 107
  of filtered water, possible causes of, 134
  of rivers, examples of, 2

Potable water, classification of organisms causing odours in, 191
Prefilters, Puech-Chabal multiple system of, 60
Pressure filters, as alternative to storage, 51
efficiency of, 51
Pre-storage settlement reservoirs, advantages of, 52
results of, experiments, 52-54
Presumptive test for *B. Coli*, definition of, 143
Primary cultures, *B. Coli* test, method of making, 151-154
media for, 171
Proskauer and Capaldi's media, composition of, 186-187
Puech-Chabal multiple system of prefilters, 60
Purification of water by storage, factors in, 78
Purity of reservoir water, safeguarded by closing intakes, 39
safeguarded by storm-water courses, 39

QUALITY, knowledge of, as an aid to abstraction, 44
of flood water, 39
of river water, in relation to flow, 39
Quantity of water, per capita daily supply, 130-131, 190
required for bacteriological examination, 138

RAINFALL, extremes of, in British Isles, 189
average at Camden hill, 189
Rate of filtration, 190
Rebipelagar medium, composition of, 171
Registrar-General's returns (extracts for 1905-1911), 3
Registration of bacteriological results, methods of, 142, 144-147
Research reports, list of, 193-194
Reservoirs, algal development in storage, 100
Chelsea storage, results obtained, 91-92, 94-95
method to be adopted if storage inadequate, 50
pre-storage settlement as supplementary, 52
River Lee, bacteriological examination of, 16, 22
results of chemical examination of 5, 7
River Thames, results of chemical examination of, 5-6, 93
results of bacteriological examination, 15-16, 18, 89-90

River Thames, table of colour results of, 5, 46, 93
River water, arguments against use of, as source of supply, 4
colour results compared with stored water, 46
flow of, in relation to quality, 39
isolation of typhoid-like microbe from, 34
method of gauging quality of in relation to water-borne disease, 36-37
pollution of, 4, 26, 105, 107
results of examination for streptococci, 30-31
typhoid and Gärtner bacilli absent from, 102
Rockford (Illinois), description of typhoid epidemic in, 107-109

SALINE solution, composition of, 173
Sample collecting boxes, 138, 141
Samples, method of labelling, 138-140
Sand filtration, cost of, 59, 137
Sanitary value of water, 127
Secondary cultures, *B. Coli* test media for, 172
method of making, 158-159
Sedimentation, as factor in purification of water, 78
Sewage, search for typhoid bacillus in, 36, 115
Sources of water supply, arguments against use of rivers as, 4
Specific pollution in relation to storage, 106
Springs, purity of, 2
Standards, bacteriological, 191
chemical, 15, 192
Statistical information, Metropolitan Water Board, 190
Sterilisation methods, by excess lime, 65-77
dose by hypochlorites, 62, 64, 192
by other methods, 65
Storage, in relation to purification, 78 *et seq.*
pressure filters as an alternative to, 51
summarised advantages of, 96, 98
summarised disadvantages of, 100
Storage reservoirs, method to be adopted if inadequate, 50
remedy for algal development in, 100, 191
results of examination of water from Chelsea, 91-95
Stored water, *B. Coli* in, 91-92, 95
colour results of, compared with river water, 46
Storm water courses, as safeguards to purity of supply, 39

INDEX

Streptococci, classification of types of, 29
  method and results of examination of faeces for, 28-30
  ratio to number of bacteria in river water, 31
  results of examination of river water for, 30-31
  vitality of in water, 32
Streptococci test, composition of media used in, 28-29
  delicacy of test for, 31
  reasons for adoption of, 27
  value of, 32
Sub-cultural methods in *B. Coli* test, 160-164
Sugar-gelatine media for *B. Coli* test, composition of, 173-174
Sulphate of calcium, removal of, 76-77
Supply, sources of water, 1-2
  sources of London, 2
  source of other named towns, 1

Tabellaria, a cause of taste and smell in water, 100, 191
  microphotograph of, 196
Taste due to algal growths, remedy for, 100-101
Temperature of River Cherwell at Oxford, 87
  in relation to vitality, 86-88
Tests for pathogenic bacteria. *See* Pathogenic bacteria
Thames, results of bacteriological examination of river, 15, 16, 18
  results of chemical examination of river, 5-6
Treatment for algal growths, 100, 191
Turbidity, of Chelsea stored water, 94-95
  of River Lee water, 5, 7
  of River Thames water, 5-6, 93
Typhoid bacillus, characters of, 184-185
  definition of "cultivated" and "uncultivated," 103
  delicacy of method employed in isolation of, 35, 182
  media employed for isolation of 185-188
  method for isolation of, 33, 183
  results of examination of river water for, 34-35
  results of examination of sewage for, 36, 115
  vitality of in relation to temperature, 86-88
  vitality of in river water, 83-86

Typhoid carriers, danger from, 79
Typhoid death rates, comparison between American and European cities, 133
  England and Wales, and London, 4, 192
  reduction of, resulting from improved water supplies, 117-121
Typhoid fever epidemics: English of recent date, 192
  in American cities, 107, 110, 121
  at Rockford (Illinois), description of 107-109
  reason of immunity of towns from, 37
Typhoid fever, cause of diminution in death rate of, 103
  endemic, current views on, 109-117
  incubation period of, 192
  seasonal incidence of, 192
Typhoid-like microbe, isolation of from river water, 34
Typical *B. Coli* test, definition of, 103

Vibrio Choleræ. See Cholera Vibrio
Vitality, of cholera vibrios in river water, 80-82
  in relation to temperature, 86-88
  of streptococci, 32
  of typhoid bacilli, 83-86

WATER, amount of, required for bacteriological examination, 138
  from upland sources, *B. Coli* in, 1
  from wells, purity of, 1-2
  routine method for bacteriological examination of, 151 *et seq.*
Water bath, at constant temperature for agar tubes, 150-151
Water-borne disease, epidemics, 192
  immunity from risk of, 102
  method of gauging quality of river water in relation to, 37
Water supply and disease, 102 *et seq.*
  financial advantages of pure, 126 *et seq.*
  of American cities, 144-145
  sources of, 1-2
Wells, Kent, results of examination of, 2
  shallow and deep, as source of supply, 1-2
Wires for inoculation, description of, 149
Wool plugs, coloured. *See* Media.

RICHARD CLAY AND SONS, LIMITED,
BRUNSWICK STREET, STAMFORD STREET, S.E., AND
BUNGAY, SUFFOLK.

Macmillan's Science Monographs
8vo.

STUDIES IN WATER SUPPLY. By Dr. A. C. HOUSTON, D.Sc., M.B., C.M., Director of Water Examination, Metropolitan Water Board. 5s. net.

RESEARCHES IN MAGNETO - OPTICS. With Special Reference to the Magnetic Resolution of Spectrum Lines. By P. ZEEMAN, Sc.D., Ph.D., D.Sc., Nobel Laureate, Professor of Experimental Physics in the University of Amsterdam. 6s. net.

ELECTRICAL ENGINEERING.—"In general the material in the different chapters has been arranged historically, so that a connected narrative of the progress in this science, and embodying the important experimental and theoretical contributions of the author, is available to all."

THE COTTON PLANT IN EGYPT : STUDIES IN PHYSIOLOGY AND GENETICS. By W. LAWRENCE BALLS, M A., Botanist to the Egyptian Government Department of Agriculture. 5s. net.

NATURE.—"There can be no doubt of the freshness and originality of mind with which Mr. Balls has attacked a great diversity of problems in their application to the cotton plant. . . . Starting with the intention of improving the Egyptian cotton crop, the author found himself led on from one problem to another, and to the solution of each he makes a real contribution, often approaching to the dignity of discovery."

STUDIES IN RADIOACTIVITY. By Prof. W. H. BRAGG, M.A., F.R.S., Cavendish Professor of Physics in the University of Leeds. 5s. net.

NATURE.—"The book can be strongly recommended not only to the physicist, but to all those who are interested in the fascinating field of enquiry which has been opened up by the discovery of new types of penetrating radiation."

STUDIES IN TERRESTRIAL MAGNETISM. By C. CHREE, M.A., Sc.D., LL.D., F.R.S. 5s. net.

ATHENÆUM.—"These 'Studies' are not suited to the requirements of the beginner in the subject, but rather to those of the advanced student or the professional magnetician. Such readers will find a mass of interesting details in the book."

Macmillan's Science Monographs
8vo.

STABILITY IN AVIATION. By G. H. BRYAN, Sc.D., F.R.S., Professor of Mathematics in the University College of North Wales. 5s. net.

MATHEMATICAL GAZETTE.—"It is fortunate that the task of writing one of the first mathematical books on aviation has been undertaken by one who is not only a mathematician of first-rate eminence and a specialist in this particular line, but is also an experienced teacher. The reader will find the difficulties of the subject reduced to a minimum by the clearness of the exposition, and the ease with which every assumption is emphasised, the notation explained, and the results summarised."

CRYSTALLINE STRUCTURE AND CHEMICAL CONSTITUTION. By A. E. H. TUTTON, D.Sc., M.A., F.R.S., A.R.C.Sc.(Lond.). 5s. net.

NATURE.—"It is a goodly story that Dr. Tutton has to tell, and well is it told: without wearying the reader with an unwieldy mass of details, he presents in all essential completeness a vivid picture of an unusually coherent series of investigations. . . . The book is one that should be read and studied by all interested in crystals, their properties, and their formation."

VOLUMES IN ACTIVE PREPARATION.

STELLAR MOVEMENTS AND THE STRUCTURE OF THE UNIVERSE. By Professor A. S. EDDINGTON, M.A., M.Sc.

EARTHQUAKE ORIGINS. By R. D. OLDHAM F.R.S., F.G.S.

CONDENSATION NUCLEI. By C. T. R. WILSON, M.A., B.Sc., F.R.S.

MUTATION IN OENOTHERA. By Dr. R. R. GATES, Lecturer in Biology, St. Thomas's Hospital.

LONDON: MACMILLAN AND CO., LTD.

RETURN TO the circulation desk of any
University of California Library
or to the
NORTHERN REGIONAL LIBRARY FACILITY
Bldg. 400, Richmond Field Station
University of California
Richmond, CA 94804-4698

ALL BOOKS MAY BE RECALLED AFTER 7 DAYS
2-month loans may be renewed by calling
(510) 642-6753
1-year loans may be recharged by bringing books
to NRLF
Renewals and recharges may be made 4 days
prior to due date

DUE AS STAMPED BELOW

OCT 06 1994

20,000 (4/94)

TD34
H75   321775

Houston

UNIVERSITY OF CALIFORNIA LIBRARY

ImTheStory.com

Personalized Classic Books in many genre's

Unique gift for kids, partners, friends, colleagues

Customize:

- Character Names
- Upload your own front/back cover images (optional)
- Inscribe a personal message/dedication on the inside page (optional)

Customize many titles Including
- Alice in Wonderland
- Romeo and Juliet
- The Wizard of Oz
- A Christmas Carol
- Dracula
- Dr. Jekyll & Mr. Hyde
- And more...

CPSIA information can be obtained at www.ICGtesting.com
Printed in the USA
BVOW04s1724030314

346526BV00017B/879/P